THE POWER AND THE WISDOM

John L. McKenzie Reprint Series
(in order of original publishing)

The POWER and the WISDOM

An Interpretation of

THE NEW TESTAMENT

by John L. McKenzie, S.J.

WIPF & STOCK · Eugene, Oregon

IMPRIMI POTEST:
IOANNES R. CONNERY, S.I.
Praepositus Provincialis

NIHIL OBSTAT:
JOHN A. SCHULIEN, S.T.D.
Censor librorum

IMPRIMATUR:
✠ WILLIAM E. COUSINS
Archbishop of Milwaukee
March 8, 1965

Wipf and Stock Publishers
199 W 8th Ave, Suite 3
Eugene, OR 97401

The Power and the Wisdom
An Interpretation of the New Testament
By McKenzie, John L.
Copyright©1965 by The Estate of John L. McKenzie
ISBN 13: 978-1-60608-048-1
Publication date 12/11/2008
Previously published by The Bruce Publishing Company, 1965

Series Foreword

MARK TWAIN ONCE RUMINATED, "It ain't the parts of the Bible I can't understand that bother me; it's the parts I do." John L. McKenzie, commenting on the same subject from another perspective, wrote, "The simple see at once that the way of Jesus is very hard to do, but easy to understand. It takes real cleverness and sophisticated intelligence to find ways to evade and distort the clear meaning of what Jesus said."

But McKenzie, like Twain, was himself a person of exceedingly high intelligence, distinctively witty, with a double-edged sword's incisiveness. As the first Catholic elected President of the Society of Biblical Literature, President of the Catholic Biblical Association, fluent in ten languages, sole author of a 900,000-word Bible dictionary, of over a dozen books and hundreds of essays, John McKenzie attained worldwide recognition as the dean of Catholic biblical scholars.

But again like Twain, McKenzie possessed a cultivated reservoir of abiding empathy—cognitive and emotional—for ordinary people and what they endure, millennia-in and millennia-out. He insisted: "I am a human being before I am a theologian." Unlike many who become entrenched in a hermetic, scholarly world of ever-multiplying abstractions, McKenzie never permitted his God-given faculty of empathy to atrophy. To the contrary, he refused to leave his fellow human beings out in the cold on the doorstep of some empathically-defective theological house of cards. This refusal made all the difference. It also often cost him the support, or engendered the hostility, of his ecclesiastical and academic associates and institutional superiors—as so often happens in scholarly, commercial and governmental endeavors, when unwanted truth that is the fruit of unauthorized empathy is factored into the equation.

John McKenzie produced works of biblically "prophetic scholarship" unlike anything created in the twentieth century by any scholar of his stature. They validate, with fastidious erudition, what the "simple see at once" as the truth of Jesus—e.g., "No reader of the New Testament, simple or sophisticated, can retain any doubt of Jesus' position toward violence directed to persons, individual or collective; he rejected it totally"—but which pastors and professors entrenched in ecclesiastical nationalism and/or organizational survivalism have chronically obscured or disparaged.

In literate societies, power-elites know that to preemptively or remedially justify the evil and cruelty they execute, their think-tanks must include theologians as part of their mercenary army of academics. These well-endowed, but empathically underdeveloped, theological hired guns then proselytize bishops, clergy, and Christians in general by gilding the illogical with coats of scholarly circumlocutions so thick that the opposite of what Jesus said appears to be Gospel truth. The intent of this learned legerdemain is the manufacturing of a faux consensus fidei to justify, in Jesus' sacred name, everything necessary to protect and augment an odious—local, planetary and/or ecclesial—status quo.

John McKenzie is the antidote to such secular and ecclesial think-tank pseudo-evangelization. Truths Jesus taught—that the simple see at once and that Christian Churches and their leaders have long since abandoned, but must again come to see if they are to honestly proclaim and live the Gospel—are given superior scholarly exposition via McKenzie. This is what moved Dorothy Day to write in her diary on April 14, 1968, "Up at 5:00 and reading The Power and the Wisdom. I thank God for sending me men with such insights as Fr. McKenzie."

For those familiar with McKenzie this re-publication of his writings offers an opportunity to encounter again a consistent scholarly-empathic frame of consciousness about Genesis through Revelation, whose major crux interpretum is the Servant of Yahweh (Isaiah 42). Ultimately embodied in the person of Jesus, the Servant is the revealer of Abba almighty—who is "on our side," if our means each person and all humanity. For all Christians, John L. McKenzie's prophetic scholarship offers a wellspring of Jesus-sourced truth about the life they have been chosen to live, the world in which they live, and the Christ in whom they "live and move and have their being."

(Rev.) Emmanuel Charles McCarthy
September 2008
Brockton, Massachusetts

...CHRIST THE POWER OF GOD AND
THE WISDOM OF GOD
—1 Cor 1:24

PREFACE

The kind reception given by the public to a book on the Old Testament called *The Two-Edged Sword* has encouraged both the author and the publishers to attempt a similar book on the New Testament. This is the book. The preface of *The Two-Edged Sword* contained some explanation of the nature and purpose of that book, and even some apologies for its composition. So much literature on the Bible has appeared since 1956 that such explanations and apologies seem unnecessary here; apologies are in order, but they are of a different type.

The first apology no doubt must be an answer to the question why another book on the New Testament should be written. The excuse that no such popular work exists is not valid here; popular works are now abundant, both those written in English and those translated from other languages. The only answer an author has to this is that he thinks he has something to say which has not been said, or has not been said in this way. If this seems arrogant, the imputation must be borne gracefully. This claim to originality should not be exaggerated. I can say here with conviction what I said in *The Two-Edged Sword,* that scholars will recognize my indebtedness to my colleagues in every line of the book. As in *The Two-Edged Sword,* I have not documented this indebtedness; a policy which was there adopted with deep doubts about its risks has now been vindicated. I believe that the splendid results of recent scholarship can be communicated to a wider public.

The place of the New Testament in the Church is not entirely like the place of the Old Testament. Most Catholics think they are somewhat familiar with the New Testament; and while they find Paul obscure at times, they do not have the same uncertainty about the New Testament which they feel about the Old Testament. In the composition of this book I experienced a growing conviction that the thing with which we believe we are familiar is not the New Testament; it is a conventionalized popular understanding of the New Testament. The simplicity of the New Testament can be deceptive. We have lived with it so long that its explosive power has become sweet reasonableness. More than the Old Testament it has been rationalized into harmony with a way of life which is often a compromise between the world and the Gospel. I notice this not as a preacher but simply as a professional interpreter. It is our office to explain the text. The difference between the two Testaments is obvious here. The Old Testament interpreter tries to communicate the theological resources of the Old Testament to a public which is little aware of these resources. The New Testament interpreter finds that he has the unpleasant task of liberating the text from certain encumbrances. He does this with hesitation, and with the awareness that his writing may exhibit a militant tone which he would be happy to remove. But in this area any statement which has not been made before in just these terms is liable to be taken as militant.

Therefore it seems prudent to repeat in substance here what I said in the preface to *The Two-Edged Sword*. This book bears the subtitle "An Interpretation of the New Testament," and it is a personal interpretation. I am not a spokesman for the Church nor for the corps of biblical interpreters, although I do my best to see that my personal interpretation is not in direct opposition to the Church or to the consensus of scholars. But if a personal interpretation is personal, it will move in directions in which others have not moved. This personal interpretation is stated with as much persuasion as I could muster. It is subject to criticism, which should be uttered with the same freedom with which the interpretation is written.

Others beside the author have contributed to the production of this book. I gratefully acknowledge their contributions to whatever success the book may have, but they have no share in its defects. The Reverend John R. Connery, S.J., and the Reverend John Amberg, S.J., have provided substantial assistance which have made the writing much easier. My secretary, Mrs. Mildred Kearney, has typed the manuscript for publication. Mr. William E. May of the Bruce Publishing Company has given expert editorial assistance and has prepared the manuscript for the press. The Reverend Robert J. Fox, S.J., and Miss Anita E. Weisbrod have generously assisted the author in the composition and the revision of the text. These and many others have supported the work by their encouragement and their belief that this book can render a service to its readers. There is no conventional expression of gratitude which is adequate for these services; but it should be said that without such support this book would not have been written.

JOHN L. McKENZIE, S.J.

Loyola University
Easter Sunday
April 18, 1965

CONTENTS

xi

III

IV

V

VIII

IX

X

XI

XII

XIII

XIV

THE POWER AND THE WISDOM

I

THE WORLD OF
THE NEW TESTAMENT

Historical and Theological Reality

The Incarnation (in the faith of Christians) is a historical event; when Christians affirm that the event is historical, they mean to affirm its reality. The birth, life, and death of a Palestinian Jew named Jesus of Nazareth is also a historical event, for all who have any knowledge of the past. To accept the second of these statements as historical is not to accept the first. If one does not believe that the birth and career of Jesus of Nazareth is the Incarnation in which Christians believe, he does not thereby deny the historical reality of Jesus; he denies the theological reality. The Christian affirms both realities. When the Christian speaks of the Incarnation he has in mind not so much a historical incident as an enduring reality. But this enduring reality is rooted in the historical incident; were it not, the Incarnation would degenerate into a mythological form. To speak of the Incarnation as a mythological form would not remove the Incarnation from the realm of reality; but it would take away that peculiar reality of history which Christian faith has always affirmed of the Incarnation.

Our interest in this chapter falls on the historical reality of the Incarnation; the theological reality of the Incarnation will meet us later in the course of this exposition. The historical reality of this event has always needed emphasis and explanation; the history of Christian theology exhibits a steadily recurring tendency to dehistoricize the Christ event, to remove it from contact with the concrete situation of history and suspend it in a timeless and spaceless vacuum. Such an exaggeration all too easily follows from a one-sided consideration of the theological reality of the event; for the Incarnation, if it is an enduring event, is no less real in Christian faith now than it was at the time of its occurrence.

1

Christian artists who have painted the events of the life of Jesus have often unconsciously set the figure of Jesus into the landscape and the people of their own time. We have all seen and admired presentations of the Nativity, the Epiphany, the miracles, the Crucifixion in a Tuscan scene of the fifteenth century. By this technique artists have affirmed the enduring reality of the Incarnation. They may also have obscured its historical reality. Many who view their paintings think that it is offensive pedantry to point out that the historical reality of the scene was totally different. What interest has this pedantry, they may ask, for genuine simple faith and piety? At the risk of being an offensive pedant, I am compelled to say that a historical reality is known in its fullness only if it is known as historical; and that a theological understanding of a historical-theological reality, sufficient as it may be for simple faith and genuine piety, is open to distortion and misunderstanding and in any case fails to reach the fullness of insight which is possible.

The Historical Situation of the Incarnation

The Incarnation is a historical event; this means that it can be dated and placed. In Christian faith — and now, because of the world dominance of a Europe which was once Christendom in most of the world — the Incarnation is the point which divides world history into two eras: before Christ and since Christ. By a calculation reached in the sixth century of our era the birth of Jesus was placed in the 753rd year from the foundation of Rome, and in the 31st year of the principate of Octavius Caesar Augustus. The events and the writing of the New Testament can be said for practical purposes to fall within the hundred years following this date. We now know that the calculation on which our era is based is in error by a few years; exact dates for the birth and the death of Jesus cannot be given. It is estimated that his birth occurred a few years before the beginning of our era and that his death occurred very near the year A.D. 30. The events of the New Testament fall in the area of the eastern Mediterranean lands, mostly in Palestine, and the geography is bounded by the desert of Palestine, and by Rome, barely touched, to the west.

Asia Minor and continental Greece are almost as important as Palestine. The barbarian lands to the north are not touched, nor are Egypt and the coast of Africa.

When the Christ event is set in its chronological and geographical framework, certain connections are at once established. As a theological reality the Christ event transcends space and time; as a historical reality it is subject to historical determinations. The Incarnation is the kind of event it is because it occurred when and where it did; had it occurred elsewhere at another time, it would not be the same. To what extent is its theological reality determined by its historical reality? A precise answer to this question cannot be given; but that it is determined can be denied only if the Incarnation is removed from history. The Christ event occurred and is related in certain languages; wherever it is narrated elsewhere, it is narrated in translation. The persons and the events are located in a definite culture; the events presuppose elements of this culture which cannot be presupposed in other cultures. The words in which the events are narrated have meanings which are not given them by the persons who act in the events and who relate them; the meaning of the words is already given by the culture to which these persons belong. The hearers and readers of the New Testament traditions and documents determined what is to be said more than we realize, just as all readers do; for the speaker and the writer must first of all be intelligible before they can convince, persuade, move — or even excite hostility. The people who determined that the New Testament should be spoken and written in these terms rather than those, with one emphasis rather than another, are not the speakers and writers of the Gospel alone; they are the Jews and Greeks who were addressed, and who by their cultural affinities imposed their own patterns on those who would proclaim to them a gospel. We shall see how entirely novel the gospel was — at least we shall attempt to see it; but its novelty had to be revealed in the speech familiar to the audience.

A description of the world of the New Testament would and indeed does fill many books larger than this; and a mere thin summary of the material which has been published by so many excellent scholars would serve no purpose. It could even deceive the reader into thinking that he knows something of this world.

Nothing better can be achieved here than to leave the conviction that anyone who wishes to read the New Testament seriously must take the trouble to learn something of the world in which the events occurred and were written. But one may hope to achieve a little more. These modest objectives are: first, to communicate some sense of the importance of historical factors; and secondly, to select some elements which help us to see more clearly how the New Testament is a product of its times. These objectives will be in view for the whole course of this exposition; but some enumeration of factors which are vital is in place at the beginning.

The Roman Empire

The world of the New Testament is effectively the world of the eastern Roman Empire. And when we mention the Roman Empire, we must pause and take a long look. The Roman Empire was not just another state. It was a political society unique in world history. No state before or since has unified such a large number of people of such varied origins; the population of China or India is larger than the estimated population of the Roman Empire, but these nations are much more homogeneous than the Mediterranean basin ruled by Rome. The peoples of the Empire themselves called it the *oikoumenē*, the inhabited world. Beyond the frontiers of the Empire, for all they knew, there was nothing but a vast barren wilderness in which scattered tribes of barbarians wandered. With the snobbishness peculiar to the Greeks and to those who shared Greek culture inhabitants of this Empire simply annihilated these barbarians by an act of the mind; they were not active participants in the civilization of the Empire and therefore they were negligible. Some centuries elapsed before the inhabitants of the Empire were forcefully shown that they erred in treating the barbarians as non-existent; but in the first century the serenity of the Empire in its assurance that there were really no human beings outside it was undisturbed. The Empire was the world to those who lived in it. Rome was the world state, the first world state and so far the last. The Empire was almost as much a cosmic reality as it was a political reality. With rare exceptions – the Jews were one – the peoples of the Empire accepted the Empire as they accepted the course of nature. No other form of life was conceived or desired. Men needed the Empire for life and for the full exercise of the powers of life as they needed rain, sun, vegetation.

The Empire was accepted. Rome was an empire, and it is of record that it was often a cruel, oppressive, and predatory empire; but it was accepted. It was accepted because it fulfilled the functions of government better than any government in the memory of recent times. And it was accepted with the reverence due to a cosmic force; the Empire was worshiped as divine. The cult of the Caesar was an inheritance from Hellenistic kings, and its origins probably lie in the ancient Near East; ruler worship was not suited to the genius either of Greece or of Rome. But the power of the Empire was so far beyond the power of earlier political forms that men needed a new formula to express their devotion. In a world where classical religion had collapsed, as we shall see in more detail, the only truly active and benevolent force which men experienced was the Roman government. Its benefits were real and tangible; and Caesar deserved worship more than Zeus, whose operations had become quite cloudy. The Caesar cult implies nothing about the sincerity of the religious sentiment of those who worshiped the Caesar. What the cult implies is that Rome demanded and received that type of supreme allegiance which only a religious sanction can establish. Men believed in Rome whether they believed in anything else or not. The imposing reality of the Empire left no room for philosophical discussion about the existence and attributes of this god.

The Predecessors of Rome

That Rome was accepted was due to more than the force of its arms. A government which creates and maintains stability over the entire Mediterranean basin for three hundred years can scarcely be conceived to govern without the consent of the governed. I have said that Rome fulfilled the functions of government better than any government in the memory of recent times. One must survey the history of the two hundred years before Augustus to understand that Rome moved into a political power vacuum in the eastern Mediterranean lands. The states which were conquered by Rome or which surrendered to it were such eminent examples of mis-government that even the peoples of the Hellenistic age noticed it. To rapacity these states added incompetence. The history of the two hundred years is a history of almost uninterrupted war. These wars were not the total wars of modern times; but they were economic disasters in their own way. Studies show that Greece, one of the most thickly populated areas of the world in the fifth century B.C., was largely a burnt-out and depopulated wilderness in the first century B.C. Josephus, the historian of the Jews, often exaggerates. Discounting the exaggerations, it is diffi-cult to understand how any one was still living in Palestine after Jewish internecine feuding when the Roman legions under Pompey occupied the shattered country. Numerous other examples could be cited in which Rome moved into political chaos. This does not imply that the Romans moved in from noble motives as the bringers of peace and order. Too many Roman governors grew rich from their provinces to permit such a favorable judgment. Many stu-dents of ancient history, I know, will agree with my own impression that it is impossible to study the Romans closely and remain sympathetic to them. But it is quite easy to see why those who had been ruled by types like the Seleucids, the Ptolemies, the Antig-onids and such would look at the Roman legions somewhat as Andromeda in the Greek myth looked at Perseus. The Roman in the first century meant one thing above all else to the peoples of the Empire, and that was peace. They were thoroughly tired of what Homer, in a simpler heroic age, called man-ennobling war. One army in the country was far better than two or more.

Roman Administration

The Romans generally established not merely peace as the cessation of war, but peace as law and order. There were excep-tions to this. It is not remarkable that there were exceptions; it is remarkable that most of the exceptions are known to us from Roman sources. It is not remarkable that some Roman governors were thieves and murderers; it is most remarkable that many of these men were called to account. Tacitus, a Roman historian, put in the mouth of a British chieftain the celebrated description of

Roman policy: "They make a desert and call it peace." Many of the details of the worst of Roman provincial administration are known from the speeches in which Cicero prosecuted Verres for his rape of the province of Sicily. Verres was unspeakable; but he was prosecuted and escaped conviction by voluntary exile. A breakdown of Roman administration of the province of Syria under Nero brought to Judea a succession of procurators who ranged from merely incompetent and dishonest to men whose unfeeling cruelty suggests a psychopathic condition. These men hastened the outbreak of the tragic Jewish rebellion, if they were not entirely responsible for it. But these were, as far as we gather, exceptions. The Roman administration was not unconcerned with the good of those whom it governed.

It is of no small importance for the history of the early Church that the Roman peace made travel possible throughout the Mediterranean area. Before Roman control was established in the East, travel was extremely hazardous, not only because of incessant war, but also because the roads were infested with bandits and the seas with pirates. Julius Caesar, himself captured by pirates as a boy and held for ransom, was later able to execute by crucifixion eight hundred members of a pirate gang. Roman repression followed the approved methods of the ancient world; a little information on the tactics of ancient brigands does not excuse the barbarism of Caesar, but it makes it easier to understand. The effects of the Roman peace were felt in the world of commerce and the world of ideas. Goods were exchanged on a scale not previously known; the entire Mediterranean basin became a common market. A degree of prosperity was attained beyond anything known previously. People moved from one part of the world to another with ease. All this meant a cultural leveling, the completion of a process begun in the preceding centuries at which we must look more closely below. In most of the Empire, particularly in the East, there was a common language and a common culture. For the primitive Church this meant that its missionaries could travel anywhere with ease and speak to nearly anyone with no serious block to communication.

Hellenistic Culture

The common culture of the Empire was not Roman. The Roman genius is seen at its best in the administration of law, in military organization, and in the construction of roads, bridges, and monumental buildings. There are areas in the Near East where no road has been built since equal to the Roman paved roads. The man who said that he cared not who wrote the nation's laws if he could write its songs is directly contradicted by the Roman poet Virgil, who allowed others to cultivate the arts while Rome governed. By "others" he meant the Greeks. In New Testament times we are not dealing with classical Greek culture, but with that strange and fascinating cultural phenomenon called Hellenism. Here again we must stop for a longer look.

Hellenism is the name given to the cultural revolution which was initiated by the whirlwind conquests of Alexander from 334 to 323 B.C. Students of the Near East have little concern with the Greeks before Alexander. The flowering of classical Greek art and thought in Athens of the fifth century made no immediate impression on the old world of Mesopotamia, Syria, and Egypt, ruled at this period by the Persians. Before the fifth century the Greeks are scarcely known at all; compared to the older civilizations of the East the early Greeks were barbarians — the Greeks' own word for others than themselves. Alexander conceived of himself not only as the avenger of the Greeks against the Persians and as the agent who removed forever the constant threat of Persian power; he was also a cultural missionary bringing Greek civilization to the benighted lands of the East — where the alphabet borrowed by the Greeks had been created. But the dynamic and creative force of Greek culture cannot be denied; once the armies of Alexander opened a channel to release it, Greek culture took possession of the ancient Near East with a swiftness and a totality which is awesome.

Had Alexander not died prematurely the course of Hellenism would have run in another manner. He could, it seems, have maintained the vast territories which he conquered under a single government. But after his death his empire was divided among his generals, who fought each other for a generation until the successor kingdoms were stabilized at the end of the fourth century. Wars between the successor kingdoms continued for the next century and a half; by that time they had destroyed each other or were destroyed by the advance of Rome. Each of the successor kingdoms was Greek, but the Greek element was limited to a ruling class and was superimposed on the majority of the population. What emerged was not pure Greek culture but Greek culture modified by the peoples who adopted it. The sharp lines of classical Greek culture were blurred; the culture was leveled in its wide diffusion, and a uniformity emerged which was not broken by the local variations which did exist. The literature and art of Hellenism were produced in enormous quantities; but they are imitative rather than creative. Historians notice wryly that the age of Hellenism, like our own, was a period of scholarship and criticism rather than of original work. But the scholarship and criticism spread the knowledge of Greek art and thought over a wide area. We are concerned, of course, with the intellectuals when we deal with art, literature, and scholarship; but these activities affected others besides the intellectuals. Greek became the common language, the *Koinē* shared by all the peoples of the Near East. Native languages survived as local peasant dialects and were not the vehicles of literature. With the language came Greek patterns of thought; and with the art came the articles of daily use manufactured in the Greek style. The traveler in the Near East today sees products like Coca-Cola and Esso advertised in Arabic, sees the Arab gown and the European suit or frock brushing each other in the streets and the camel or the ass competing for the right of way with a Buick; and he knows that he is seeing a reenactment of the wonderful cultural conglomeration which was Hellenism.

The Hellenistic City

The focus of Greek life was the city, the *Polis*. One of the most remarkable traits of the Greeks was their ability to combine the finest political theory (which, like most theoretical thinking, they invented) with a nearly unsurpassed lack of capacity for self-government. The Greeks invented democracy, both the word and the idea; and their history is almost entirely a history of despotism interrupted by civil war. But the ideal of the *Polis* as the best way of life endured untarnished by the sordid political history of the *Polis*. Alexander and his successors established Greek cities throughout the Near East; and when they had done this, Greek culture was firmly imbedded.

What distinguished the *Polis* from the cities of the ancient Near East was the *agora*, translated not too accurately as marketplace. The *agora* was much more than a place to buy fruit and vegetables. It was a large open space in the center of the city, surrounded on at least two sides by porticoes, called the *stoa*. The Stoic philosophers drew their name from the *stoa*, and the name illustrates their use; the porticoes, shaded against the Mediterranean sun, were pleasant places in which to sit or stroll and carry on discussions. Around the *agora* were the public buildings which made the *Polis* a city and not a village: the Council House (a tribute to the Greek ideal of local autonomy), the theater (often supplemented by an odeon for choral performances), a place of public assembly for political and other speeches, the library, the gymnasium, and the temples. Here the Greek man could carry on all the activities which made him a gentleman (in Greek *kalos kagathos,* literally "beautiful and good"). He could hear prose and poetry read, he could hear philosophy discussed, he could view tragedy and comedy, he could discuss public affairs and engage in philosophical dialogue, and he could enjoy physical exercise. In Roman times he could also relax in the public baths. The ruins of such cities in the steppes and the deserts of Syria — one thinks of Jerash and Palmyra — strike the modern visitor as incongruous; one would as readily expect to find Tiffany's in the north woods of Ontario, and perhaps our new and luxurious communities in the western deserts are as incongruous as Palmyra. But these ruins are witnesses of the power of the Greek way of life. They were the centers from which Greek culture spread into the hinterlands.

Hellenistic Religions

For the student of the New Testament the religious picture of the Hellenistic-Roman world is of the first importance; and here one nearly despairs of putting some order into the confused religious phenomena one finds in the Empire. In the museums of Europe and the large cities of the Near East there are examples of art which aptly illustrate this confusion. The gods of classical Greek religion, Apollo and Aphrodite for instance, are represented not in the sensuous youthful beauty so familiar from reproductions of Greek art but in the exotic and sometimes harsh lines of Near Eastern art. In contrast to this there are representations of Near Eastern deities who have been rejuvenated by the artist in the beauty of Apollo and Aphrodite. The name which scholars give to this mixture of forms is syncretism; the men of the Hellenistic world experienced a religious as well as a cultural leveling, and generously accepted the gods of other peoples in addition to their own. But they often failed to distinguish gods from gods, or they gave the foreign gods the divine form which they knew. The result was strange conceptions and titles of Zeus in the Near East, and equally strange Eastern deities worshiped in Rome.

Actually the classical religion of Greece, widely adopted as some forms of it were, seems to have become mere formal cult by New Testament times. This was the public and official religion of the cities and the temples and the statuary, and for this reason its remains are more majestic. The literature indicates that it meant very little to the ordinary man. It is difficult likewise to define the extent to which the cult of the divine Caesar elicited any genuine religious sentiment. The cult of Caesar was primarily a civic act and a public pledge of allegiance; and the fact that a civic act could be a religious act itself witnesses how much the idea of religion as such had been weakened. Caesar could be a god because the difference between the divine and the human was not very clearly recognized. "Atheism" in the ancient world meant the refusal to worship the gods of the public official cult; there were very few men who felt any conviction which prevented them from taking part in this cult. Yet the philosophical literature leaves no question that many intellectuals did not believe in the reality of the Olympian deities at all. It is unlikely that this skepticism was limited to the intellectuals. There is no way to determine how many of the people of the Hellenistic world had no religion at all — no belief and no cult. They accepted the public and official cult as a superficial observance and made no search for anything deeper.

The Mystery Cults

When man rejects one religion he usually substitutes another religion or something which he thinks does the work of religion. The religious sentiment which the public cult lacked was furnished by the mystery cults. The name of "mystery" for these cults comes from the oath of secrecy taken by the initiates; and the members were so faithful to their oath that details of the mystery cults are not well known. The general outlines of the cults and the principle behind them, however, are known; and it is easy to see how the cults responded to the religious needs and demands of the Hellenistic world. They offered just what the public and official cults did not offer: personal communion with the divine and a rebirth to a new life. This is admission to "salvation," a theme which recurs in the mystery cults. Most of the cults are forms of the fertility rites of the Near East; and the communion with the divine has strong sexual aspects. The regeneration which the cults promised was a regeneration of nature and a closer integration with nature; it is not clear that most of the cults promised immortality. The initiation consisted in the ritual recital and reenactment of the myth of the cult hero or heroine; when the candidate symbolically experienced the action of the myth, he entered into communion with the divine life represented in the myth. Those who had passed through the various grades of initiation were often called the "perfect," which means that they were ritually complete. There was no moral emphasis in the mysteries which we can detect.

Their strange attraction was due to several factors, it seems. One was the exotic character of the gods and of the rites. Another was the fellowship of the mystery group, usually symbolized in a ritual banquet. A third was the democratic character of most of the cults; social differences were not recognized within the cult group. Here the mystery cults filled a vacuum created by the political developments of the Hellenistic world. The ancient Greek city-state, the *Polis,* was a religious as well as a political community. The *agora*, we noticed, was the seat of the temples and the point of assembly for political, cultural, and religious activities. The *Polis* broke down as a political society after the conquests of Alexander; the political unit was the Hellenistic monarchy, which in turn yielded to Rome. The relaxation of political loyalty to the city involved a relaxation also of the religious community. The Hellenistic man was locally detached; in the modern term, he was to some degree alienated. He was homeless and rootless. The mystery cults supplied the need both for community and for religious security.

Even from this brief sketch it is evident that there are some points of resemblance between the mystery cults and Christianity. A number of theories have been proposed based on these resemblances, and some points must be considered in more detail below (Chapter VIII). Here our interest is the place of the mystery cults in the religious life of the Hellenistic world; and it is not beside the point that Christianity could be presented as a response to the religious needs to which the mystery cults responded. Certain common terms and ritual similarities are easily explained by the eastern origin of both Christianity and the mysteries. As we shall see, both exhibit a cultic pattern which is so widely diffused in the ancient Near East that no dependence can be argued. In one way the mystery cults were competitors with Christianity; in another way, it seems, they opened the way for the penetration of Christianity into the sophisticated world of Hellenism.

Philosophy

One hesitates to introduce philosophical thought as an element of the New Testament world. Did philosophical thought have any more significance for the vast majority of the population of the Roman world than it has for the vast majority in the modern world? When we deal with Christianity, we shall see, we are not dealing with the little world of the intellectuals and the artists. In the period of the New Testament there was no contact between this world and the gospel. The gospel was proclaimed and believed by those social classes which the thinkers and artists of the Roman world ignored. Yet the writings of Paul show that he had at least heard some of the terms of Stoic philosophy; and it can be assumed that some of his listeners had also heard them. And since Stoicism was one of the most "popular" philosophies which has ever been devised, it deserves some attention here.

Stoicism

Stoicism was popular in two senses. In the first sense it was popular because it was accepted by more people than any other system. In the second sense it was popular because it was more easily grasped by a large number of people. Stoicism demanded no intensive education, no profound thought, no high degree of insight. It was beautifully simplified; and the Stoic ideal, it seems, was cherished by people who had no deep understanding of the system. In all fairness it must be said that the Stoic ideal has a certain fascination; it was one of the better products of the Hellenistic world, and for that reason it was a stronger obstacle to Christianity than the mystery cults. It is rather surprising how much Stoic morality has been incorporated into the writings of Christian moral teachers; more than a few elements of the system are now thought of as Christian rather than as Stoic by many Christians.

Stoicism was a splendid system for the Hellenistic man, rootless and homeless, as I have called him, who had lost the dignity of the citizen of the *Polis* and become the subject of an absolute monarch. The Stoic ideal, in the one word which the Stoics preferred, was self-sufficiency. The self-sufficient man was superior to any situation which he might meet; the world of the Stoic was a realistic world in which the scope of personal self-determination had been reduced. The Stoic could face life on his own resources because he had learned complete control of his emotions; apathy, lack of feeling, is a Stoic word turned into English. Lack of feeling meant that the Stoic was determined neither by pleasure nor by pain. He was the master of his destiny, even if he was a slave; only the wise man is king.

Man's primary duty is to do good; and in Stoicism the good is that which is conformed to nature. By a logic less than rigorous the Stoics based their morality on their cosmology. The universe is one, animated by one divine spirit. Man participates in this spirit, and carries within him a spark of the divine flame. This and this alone is of value; Stoicism is an antimaterialistic philosophy, despite a materialistic cosmology. The contempt of the material component imposes at once an asceticism which forbids the grosser vices. The Stoic is indifferent to wealth and poverty, honor and dignity, length of life, food, drink, and sex; there is a strange echo between this summary of Stoic principles and the ideal presented by St. Ignatius Loyola in the Principle and Foundation of the Spiritual Exercises. A more remarkable consequence of the Stoic conception of the unity of the world is the conception of the world as a cosmopolis, one great city. All men are therefore fellow citizens; and Stoicism alone in the ancient world thought of humanity as such, believing that the community of human nature is superior to any differences of race, nation, or class. The two greatest Roman exponents of Stoicism were contemporaries; one, Marcus Aurelius, was an emperor, the other, Epictetus, was a slave.

The defects of the system are obvious. Stoicism really had no belief in a personal god; its god was Nature. It was cold and self-centered; there was nothing in the system to keep self-sufficiency from becoming pride. The Stoic could not admit his spiritual need and seek other resources than those of his person. If life became so intolerable that self-sufficiency was endangered, Stoicism encouraged voluntary departure from an impossible situation by suicide. But the defects did not keep the Stoic from doing what he conceived to be his duty to other men; and we do not know how much the subjects of Roman proconsuls may have owed to the Stoicism of their rulers. For Stoicism was very popular among the ruling classes of the Roman Empire. In one sense it is a rich man's philosophy; it is easier for a man of wealth to be self-sufficient.

Stoicism, like the other philosophical systems of the Hellenistic world, was really a substitute for religion. The Stoics had no trouble taking part in the public cult, even the Caesar cult; for the objects of the cult were to them symbolic designations of the World-Soul, the Divine Fire. Other systems had similar rationalizations of mythological gods. But there could be no cult offered to a World-Soul. The Epicureans were candidly hostile to the deities of mythology; no writer has ever been so furiously antireligious as the Roman Lucretius. But the philosophers did not attack popular religion. They believed that religion was a restraint on the masses, who were not restrained by philosophical discipline; religion was not exactly an opiate of the people, but it helped to keep the people from total moral collapse. To us this rationalization appears feeble; classical religion has almost no moral bent at all, and one wonders whether the philosophers were finding a way out of following their thinking to its logical consequences. Stoicism gave moral direction to the life of its followers; it was a purely humanistic morality which effectively made the deity unnecessary, but it was moral. And as long as the cosmopolis was in a way incarnated in the stable Roman Empire, it was difficult for the gospel to reach men who pledged the meaning of human existence on their self-sufficiency, the one thing which the gospel denied them.

The Hellenistic Man

Can we sum up the Hellenistic man from the mass of data into which we have merely dipped? No more than we can sum up the modern man. We can describe the large outlines of the world in which he lived, its political structure, its interests and activities; but the world is made up of individual persons, and it was to the individual person that the apostles of the gospel appealed. We have some idea of what the apostles proclaimed and some idea of the response they received. We know more of their success than we do of their failures; the literature of the New Testament comes from people who accepted Christianity, not from those who heard the proclamation and who refused it. We have some idea from the epistles of Paul what the difficulties were which new Christians encountered. But we cannot really give a thumbnail sketch of the Hellenistic man; this abstraction never existed. But men existed in the Hellenistic world, and it is these men who, as we have noticed, defined the terms in which the gospel was proclaimed. It had to be attractive to men who had become anonymous members of a world state, who were largely detached from organized religion, who were open to an enormous variety of exotic cults and superstitions, and who accepted nothing more than a very loose moral code.

Judaism

The gospel did not arise in the Hellenistic world; it arose in Judaism, a little island which maintained its identity distinct from the Hellenistic world. Judaism was recognized both in Roman law and in popular opinion as an indigestible mass which had not been assimilated. The authors of the New Testament were Jews, mostly Palestinian; we are sure of only one Gentile author in the New Testament, Luke. Palestine was the place of origin of the gospel; and Palestinian Judaism was the antithesis of the Hellenistic world in every point which I have listed at the end of the preceding paragraph. The gospel was originated and proclaimed in a clash of cultures.

It is impossible here to trace the historical events by which the Israel of the Old Testament became the Judaism of the first century of our era. The very names Israel and Judaism suggest a difference between the two. In the first century the designation Israel was used only in religious literature. The name Jews was used both by Jews and by others to identify them. The word comes from the tribal and royal name of Judah; and it comes from the territory in which the Israelite religious community was reestablished under the Persians in the sixth century B.C. By the first century of our era Judaism had spread into Galilee; but outside of Judea and Galilee the ancient land of Israel had very few Jews.

What was a Jew? He was not as such a member of a political community. Jewish independence had disappeared when the Romans entered Palestine in 63 B.C. The satellite kingdom of Herod included much more land than the territory in which Jews lived. Herod himself was not regarded as a Jew by the Jewish community; his Judaism was limited to the external observances which he thought necessary to keep his Jewish subjects from open rebellion. After the death of Herod Judea itself was administered directly by a Roman procurator, and other parts of Palestine were divided among other Roman governors and various satellite kings like Herod Antipas, the ruler of Galilee. The Romans recognized that Judea presented unique problems of administration and the procurator enjoyed a discretion granted to no other officer of this

rank. The Romans respected the religious principles of the Jews
to the extent that they did not demand participation in the Caesar
cult nor military service, which would have involved participation
in the Caesar cult. Divine images were not erected in Jewish
communities. The Romans did not interfere in the administration
of the Jewish law, with an exception mentioned in the gospels;
capital punishment was reserved to the Roman government. Theoretically Roman administration should have been able to run the
territory smoothly; in practice, a combination of the incompetence
and dishonesty of Roman officials with the intransigence and
fanaticism of Jewish groups was enough to maintain a constant
state of friction.

In spite of a good deal of ancient and modern mythology on the
subject, the name Jew did not then and does not now designate a
race. It did designate membership in an ethnic group which had
a common ancestry, a common history and a common language.
But some reservations must be borne in mind. The ancestry of the
Jews in New Testament times was mixed, like the ancestry of other
Near Eastern ethnic groups. The fiction of pure blood cannot be
maintained. The common language was Aramaic, which the Jews
had adopted from other peoples; and Palestine, like other Near
Eastern countries, was bilingual, employing both Aramaic and
Greek.

The unitive force in Judaism was not politics nor race but religion. A Jew was first and foremost one who accepted the Law
of Moses as a way of life. Certain external observances had become
signs of fidelity to Judaism, and had thus received an importance
which they had not had in early Israel; these were circumcision, the
Sabbath, and the laws of levitical cleanliness. These three were
enough to make social communication between Jews and Gentiles
somewhat difficult; the Jews were a segregated group because they
wished to be segregated, and Gentiles recognized the segregation.
The center of Judaism was the temple of Jerusalem, at the beginning of the Christian era under reconstruction through the
munificence of Herod the Great — the same munificence which he
exhibited in the construction of temples of Greek gods at Sebaste
and Caesarea. The temple was the only legitimate place of animal
sacrifice of Judaism. Worship outside of Jerusalem was conducted

in the synagogues. This institution, peculiar to Judaism, was a bond which held Jews together and maintained the unity of Judaism as a religion. The worship consisted of prayer and hymns, the reading of Scripture, and homilies.

The Law

The restriction of the cult to the temple of Jerusalem meant that for Judaism the primary factor was not the cult but the Law. The Law will demand our attention more than once in the following exposition, and we shall have to look at it closely. For the present we can say that the Law meant the five books of Moses as explained by tradition. The addition of the element of tradition is highly important. The Pentateuch is a code of laws incorporated in a narrative of the origins of Israel. These laws were conceived to be a complete guide to a life perfectly submitted to the will of God. Actually the Law is not such a complete guide; and it could become such a guide only by a complex process of interpretation, expansion, and application to cases not explicitly covered. By the beginning of the New Testament period the Law had long been an object of study through techniques which had become professionalized and which were practiced by a professional class. These professional scholars were called scribes; the New Testament also refers to them as lawyers. They were addressed as rabbi (master) and enjoyed great esteem within the Jewish community. To describe them as religious and cultural dictators may exaggerate their influence; but there is no doubt that they were the most influential class within Judaism, and that they more than anyone else determined the character of Judaism.

The observance of the Law, particularly its prescriptions of levitical cleanliness, set the Jews apart from the Gentile world; but there were other and deeper effects which should not be ignored. The moral level of Judaism was far above the level of the Hellenistic world as a whole. We have noticed that Stoicism presented a superior moral ideal; but Stoicism did not form tight little communities culturally as well as religiously distinctive, and aware of it. The pressure on Jews to conform was tremendous; and all the information we have supports the thesis that the Jews did not fall into the grosser vices of Hellenism. The encounter of the gospel with Judaism is placed on a more subtle level of morality. The Law made the Jews a monotheistic bloc in a world of polytheism, superstition, and philosophical rationalism. The Jews themselves were well aware of this difference, and they were vain about it; they ridiculed the polytheism of the Gentiles, and many Gentiles were compelled to respect a creed which was so far superior to any species of Hellenistic religion. We have noticed that the Jews were not required to participate in the acts of the official cult; this excluded them not only from military service, but from any participation in public life. The Gentiles did not respond to Jewish polemic with humility; ever since Pompey had entered the Holy of Holies in 63 B.C. and found it empty, the exotic worship of an empty room had become an object of Gentile satire.

Judaism Outside Palestine

Judaism was not confined to Palestine. During the centuries before the Christian era Jews had migrated to other countries in large numbers. Very probably the movement westward did not begin before the conquests of Alexander. The motives of the migration are not clear, and no single factor explains it. No doubt large numbers of Jews were taken prisoner in war and enslaved. Others migrated of their own will to escape the poverty of Palestine. By the beginning of the Christian era the number of Jews living abroad (called the *Diaspora,* a Greek word meaning "dispersion") was large; exact figures are lacking. In Alexandria the Jews had an entire quarter of the city, governed by their own municipal officers. They had certainly reached Rome by the begining of the Christian era; and there was no city of any size in the eastern Mediterranean area which did not have a Jewish colony. The Jews of the Diaspora settled in cities; their employments seem to have been merchandising and the crafts. Nothing in the literature of the period suggests that they were regarded as wealthy. They worshiped in the synagogues and were in more or less constant contact with Jerusalem, the spiritual center of the Jewish world.

Judaism and Hellenism

A distinction must be made between Palestinian Judaism and Diaspora Judaism under more than one head, and particularly on the degree in which the Jews resisted Hellenism. The Jews of Palestine had had their encounter with Hellenism and had emerged still themselves. The history of Judaism between the fifth century and the third is extremely obscure; but it seems clear that the cultural impact of Hellenism in Palestine was severe, if we limit culture here to material culture. The spiritual elements became a point of combat. The books of the Maccabees speak of a group of Palestinian Jews who wished to assimilate Jews to Gentiles entirely; it is somewhat surprising to the modern reader to learn that the symbols of Hellenization were the wearing of the Greek hat and the erection of a gymnasium in Jerusalem. The gymnasium was a horror because it was the Greek custom to exercise in the nude; but the gymnasium would have been a more insidious danger because it was an intellectual as well as an athletic center. The hat remains somewhat mysterious, except that for reasons not quite clear it often becomes supremely important what one puts on one's head. The Hellenizing party was supported by Antiochus Epiphanes, the Seleucid king of Syria, who attempted enforced Hellenization of all his subjects for political reasons; it seemed the only way in which he could unify his sprawling and diversified territories. The imposition of the worship of Greek gods and of the divine king was too much for Jewish scruples; and only when Antiochus began his campaign, it seems, did the Jews realize that Hellenism was of one piece, and that one could not accept the material culture without ultimately surrendering to the religious and intellectual and ethical elements of Hellenism also. The Jews undertook a military resistance, successful after some thirty years only because the Seleucid monarchy was weakened by internal quarrels. At the end of the period the Jews had accepted more of Hellenism than they recognized, but they were more firmly united and more obstinately determined to remain themselves by preserving the life of the Law.

The Jews of the Diaspora could not have maintained the rigid position of Palestinian Judaism even if they had so desired. They formed smaller and isolated communities in the Hellenistic cities, and closer association with the Gentile world was imposed upon them. While they maintained the worship of the synagogues and the study of the Law, they did not maintain with equal fidelity the study of Hebrew. The Bible was translated into Greek for their benefit; and the characteristic beliefs of Israel were thus expressed for the first time in the common language. This was a step of great importance; for when the apostles of the gospel entered the Greek world, their religious vocabulary had already been created. Furthermore, there arose among the Jews of the Diaspora a number of writers who attempted an exposition of Judaism in Greek for the Gentiles. The most celebrated scholars and apologetes of Judaism were Philo of Alexandria and Flavius Josephus. Both of these writers show that Hellenistic thought had affected them deeply. Philo's works were an exposition of Judaism as a philosophy superior to any Greek philosophical system. Even the Greek Old Testament contains one book, the Wisdom of Solomon, which is written in an imprecise philosophical language. These writers were not the only Jews whose thinking was Hellenized.

Jewish Sects and Parties

Palestinian Judaism was not perfectly homogeneous. The Gospels and other ancient sources mention various groups or parties within Judaism; it is difficult to find the proper name for these divisions. The New Testament and Josephus use the word "sect" to designate them; the word is used in Hellenistic Greek of philosophical schools, and it is not the most apt word to designate the type of division which we find in Judaism. These groups should not be compared to the sectarian divisions of Christianity nor to the political parties in a modern nation, although the divisions exhibit some differences in belief and some differences in the attitude which Jews took toward the Roman government.

The Pharisees

The Pharisees stood for the strict observance of the Law and were themselves the models of this observance. More than the other groups they resisted the Hellenization of Palestine. The traditions by which the Law was interpreted were the product of Pharisaic groups, and the Pharisees gave these traditions scarcely less authority than they gave the text itself; the scribes in their view were the heirs of Moses, and they traced an artificial connection between the scribes and Moses, the founder of the scribal schools. Readers of the Gospels are familiar with the meticulous external observance of the Law which the Pharisees demanded. Their insistence on external observance was not always matched by an interior devotion; and the attitude which the Gospels describe has brought the word "pharisaic" into our language to mean self-righteous, sanctimonious, or hypocritical. The term no doubt oversimplifies, just as the term "jesuitical" does; it appears that a large number of the members of the primitive community of Jerusalem were Pharisees. But one wonders whether for the Pharisees the Law had not come to replace the deity. For them the Law was a complete revelation of the will of God and an absolute assurance of salvation. In Pharisaic theology there was little or no room for that development called messianic, which we shall consider in more detail below (Chapters III–IV), and which Christianity claimed to be. The Pharisees had effectively renounced any hope of a further exhibition of God's power (or "reign") in the history of the Jews, and were content to treat the Law as terminal, its observance to be rewarded by a blessed resurrection. When the absolute validity of the Law was threatened, they could and did become deadly.

The Sadducees

The Sadducees seem to deserve the title conservative (or reactionary) on all counts. Theologically they were in one way more dedicated to the Law than the Pharisees, for they admitted none of the other sacred books to an equal canonical position. They rejected, however, the scribal traditions; and this meant that the Law sat more lightly on them. They were conservatives socially; for their membership was drawn from the wealthy landowning aristocracy of the priestly families. They attached much more weight to the temple cult than the Pharisees did; the Pharisees were at home in the synagogue, the Sadducees in the temple.

They accepted Hellenistic culture more readily and were less exclusive in their attitude toward the Gentiles. Even less than the Pharisees did they envisage any revolutionary or messianic development within Judaism; everything urged them to maintain the existing status, for they had nothing to gain from a change — except spiritual growth.

The Zealots

The Zealots are a more difficult group to define; and they are a third group in the same line with the Pharisees and Sadducees. The Romans called them *Sicarii*, "knife men" or assassins; the name comes from their practice of assassinating their political enemies in crowded streets. They bear some resemblance to terrorist groups in modern times; but their terrorism had a distinctly Jewish theological basis. William Farmer has proposed a thesis which makes them the heirs of the Maccabees. Unlike the Pharisees and the Sadducees, they did not believe that the condition of Judaism in the Roman Empire was a permanent state. The alien domination of the holy land of the people of election was an offense against the majesty of God. They conceived it to be the duty of the Jews to restore the Reign of God in Israel and to achieve that freedom which would allow the people of God to live in their own manner according to the revealed Law. But they were not content to wait for the apocalytic revelation of the wrath; the Reign of God would not come unless the Jews did what they could to hasten its coming. If the Jews mustered their forces, they could trust in the divine assistance which their fathers had experienced, and which aided the Maccabees to free the country from the Seleucid Empire. But Rome was not the Seleucid Empire. The Zealots, at first a small but dedicated minority, succeeded with the aid of Roman misgovernment in exciting a rebellion of the Jews in A.D. 66. The rebellion ended in the shattering disaster of A.D. 70 in which Jerusalem was destroyed, thousands of Jews were killed, and Palestinian Judaism and Palestinian Christianity were both annihilated.

The Qumran Group

The recent discoveries at Khirbet Qumran have disclosed the existence of a small group whose attitude is best described as withdrawal. This group is now identified by scholars with the Essenes mentioned by Philo and Josephus. They too exhibited the devotion to the Law which is the common element of Judaism; but it appears that they were satisfied neither with the Pharisees nor with the Sadducees. The Qumran literature exhibits genuine hostility to the priestly class. Their dissatisfaction with the Pharisees is less easy to document and less easy to explain; it is possible that they found lacking in Pharisaic Judaism the apocalyptic faith which is exhibited in the Qumran documents and in other Jewish literature of the period. This apocalyptic faith the Qumran group shared with the Zealots, although we do not know that they accepted the Zealot tactics. Archaeology shows that the monastery of Qumran was destroyed and abandoned in the Jewish rebellion. That the Qumran group were the defenders of the site in this last struggle is not clear; but they could have thrown their lot in with the Zealots partly from compulsion and partly from their own principles. The literature of the group, as most students of the Bible now know, shows remarkable affinities with the New Testament; but no conclusion has yet been drawn from this except that primitive Palestinian Christianity included some who had been associated with the Qumran group. Theologically the Qumran group was no closer to the primitive Church than were the Pharisees.

Summary

What can we say in summary after this fleeting glance at the world in which the Christian event occurred? The world which we view is so complex and so multiform that it seems to defy synthesis. Can one grasp the spirit and the ethos of this world any more easily than one can grasp the spirit and the ethos of our own world? And we have the insights into our own world which come only from membership. We Americans are often impatient with European observers who visit us for a few months and write analyses of what we are and what we wish to be. We do not know whether to be amused at their misunderstanding or irritated at their arrogance. Yet they are in a better position to analyze us than the modern scholar is to analyze Hellenistic civilization from its literature, its art, and the remains of its buildings. The scholar can read and he can explore; but the Hellenistic world is silent. We cannot engage in personal conversation with these people. We must try to understand them as well as we can; we must know that we shall never understand them.

Our glance at this world should, I think, leave us with one impression. When the New Testament speaks of "the fullness of time," its writers do not mean that the Incarnation occurred at the most apt moment. Any moment for the incarnational intrusion of God into the world is the right moment; any moment is also the wrong moment. The intervention of God makes history; it is not conditioned by history. I see nothing in the Hellenistic world which makes me say that this world was ready for the proclamation of the gospel; I see nothing which makes me say the world was ever better prepared. At any moment the incarnational event initiates a revolution. And if this be true, the incarnational event is both historical and timeless. The revolution which it initiates is permanent, for it is never at home in the world of history. The revolution never ceases to be an irrational factor in historical calculation. It has no historical cause; and who is to measure its effects in historical terms? And if they are measured in these terms, how much is learned about them by these measurements?

I do not here reverse what I said at the beginning of this chapter. There the Incarnation was presented as a historical and a theological reality. I conclude by saying that the two aspects cannot be sharply distinguished. The paradox of the Incarnation compels us to look at it — if the metaphor will be pardoned — from all sides at once. We never see all sides at once, of course; and the realization of this is perhaps the best insight one gains from a study of the world in which the Christian event began.

II

THE GOSPEL

The Oral and the Written Gospel

The New Testament begins with the Gospel according to Matthew, Mark, Luke, and John. If we look at the traditional titles of these works, we see that one Gospel is indicated rather than four. We now use the word "Gospel" to designate each one of these four works, the only four of their kind; but in its original use the term "gospel" did not designate a literary form. There is only one gospel as there is only one Christ and one Church; and it is this one gospel which lies behind the four works. More than that, it authenticates the four works. We must, when we study the Gospels, ask what the gospel was in the primitive Church; for the gospel was in the Church before the Gospels were written.

The English *gospel* renders the Greek *euangelion* through an Anglo-Saxon link, *godspel;* the word means "good news," and several modern translators, wishing to break away from conventional terms which have become meaningless, have substituted "Good News" for *gospel.* It does surprise the reader of these new translations when he meets the Good News according to Matthew; but the surprise has one salutary effect at least, that it makes the reader wonder what Matthew thought he was doing. That is the question which we shall treat in this chapter.

The Proclamation

It is extremely difficult to date any of the four Gospels earlier than the 60's of the first century. Before the gospel was written it existed only in oral form; at the moment we are not concerned with literary materials which may have been used by the writers of the Gospels. The gospel as such was spoken, not written; and the almost technical term which the New Testament uses for the speaking of the gospel is proclamation, *kerygma*. Proclamation is more than simple utterance; it is the utterance of a herald who proclaims official news in public. The proclamation of the herald is not open to discussion, and the herald does not intend to convince or persuade. The message is a message of authority, and one can do nothing but accept or reject it. We shall return below to what the apostles thought their mission was; but the idea of proclamation shows how they conceived it. We shall also return to the kind of acceptance which they thought the message demanded; the technical term for this acceptance is faith.

Following the lead of C. H. Dodd, scholars believe they have reconstructed the content of the proclamation from the discourses related in the Acts of the Apostles. These discourses as they stand are the work of Luke rather than of the apostles, but scholars are agreed that Luke has faithfully reported both the content and the style. Behind the discourses in Acts is the proclamation of Jesus himself. This proclamation is summed up thus: Repent, for the Reign of God is at hand. We must consider in Chapter III more fully what is meant by repentance and the Reign of God; what we notice now is that the proclamation of the apostles was not identical with the proclamation of Jesus. We shall find that the lack of identity is merely verbal; but this verbal difference reveals the basic element of the gospel. Jesus proclaimed the coming of the Reign, and the apostles proclaimed the coming of Jesus; and they did not think they were altering his gospel when they proclaimed their own. The proclamation of the apostles makes explicit something which the proclamation of Jesus as the Gospels present it did not make explicit: that the Reign of God is initiated in the person of Jesus.

Hence what the apostles proclaimed was a brief declaration of the life, death, and resurrection of Jesus and a statement of the demands which the Christ event imposes. God has made him Lord and Messiah (Acts 2:36). He is the Author of life (Acts 3:15), and by his death repentance is possible which prepares men for his Second Coming (Acts 3:19–21). In him alone is salvation

(Acts 4:12). He is ordained to be judge of the living and the dead, and all who believe in him receive forgiveness of sins through his name (Acts 10:42–43). Forgiveness of sins is proclaimed through him, and everyone who believes is freed from things from which the Law of Moses cannot free (Acts 13:38–39). The simplicity of this proclamation is evident. The saving event is presented and a call to action is issued. The answer should be immediate: faith and baptism. Certainly this simple proclamation developed in complexity with the passage of time, and the New Testament itself is the witness of the first stage of this development; but it was not the intention of the apostolic Church that the growing complexity of the proclamation and of the response should alter the nature either of the gospel or of faith. In the course of this exposition we shall have to look more closely at the growth of the gospel.

The Proclamation in Hellenism

The proclamation in the passages I have cited is addressed to Jewish audiences and is couched in the terms of Judaism. In Acts 17 there is an account of a discourse of Paul given at Athens in which the language of Judaism is not used. Instead of alluding to Jesus as Messiah and Lord and to repentance and judgment Paul quotes Greek poets and uses terms which reflect if anything the vulgar type of Stoicism. The narrative hints that this discourse was not well received; and commentators think that Paul had this failure in mind when he wrote to the Corinthians that he did not proclaim the gospel to them in lofty words or wisdom, and recognized nothing except Jesus Christ and him crucified (1 Cor 2:1–2). We have no record of the proclamation of this gospel of Christ crucified to a Gentile audience unfamiliar with the religious ideas of Judaism; but if we are to take Paul at his word, he did not attempt again to clothe the gospel in the philosophy and rhetoric of Hellenism. In this Paul's method corresponds to what was said in our first chapter. The Christ event was historical, occurring in a definite point in time and space. Paul did not attempt to detach it from history, even though this might appear to be an additional obstacle to those who did not know this history. The gospel was not another philosophy; it was the proclamation of an event, and the event should be related as it happened.

That the gospel did become clothed in the language of Hellenism is an obvious fact; but this did not occur in the apostolic generation. No attempt to synthesize the proclamation of the event with Greek thought appears before the second century of the Christian era. The motives of this development are complex and interesting, but they do not belong to a discussion of the New Testament. It is sufficient here to note that among these motives was the intellectual curiosity of men educated in the Hellenistic tradition. The apostolic Church, as far as we know it, was innocent of intellectualism. This implies no value judgment on intellectualism. When the intellectual accepts faith, it is not the same psychological process as the faith of the simple and unlettered. He must believe in his own way, and he has always insisted on formulating what he believes is his own way. Our interest here lies in the historical fact that the first form of the gospel ignored the needs of the intellectual; it sticks to the account of the event and refuses to philosophize about it.

The Proclamation in Summary

It is impossible to summarize the Good News any more succinctly than it is summarized in the apostolic preaching; but let us get clearly in our minds what is proclaimed. Liberation from sin is proclaimed, a liberation which will enable man to endure in the judgment which is to come. This liberation is effected in the person of Jesus Christ, who was crucified, died, was buried, and rose from the dead. Through the resurrection God has proclaimed him Lord, and his dominion is supreme over every power. The proclamation calls to belief that God's saving power is manifest and operative in Jesus Christ and in no other. The believer must renounce sin and accept the existence of God's power over sin communicated to him through Jesus Christ. This is the basic gospel which is the theme of all the New Testament writings, and which is not obscured in any elaboration of the apostolic preaching.

The Synoptic Gospels

The first of these elaborations which we have to consider is the written Gospels. The Gospel of John demands an explanation of its own (See Additional Note). Matthew, Mark, and Luke are grouped under the designation of Synoptic Gospels. The name "Synoptic" was coined by J. J. Griesbach in 1774. It signifies that these Gospels can be printed in parallel columns, a synopsis, as Griesbach published them. We can sum up in a few statements what it has taken hundreds of scholars several generations of work to formulate. This community of content and arrangement comes from the use of common sources. Mark, the earliest of the three, is a source for both Matthew and Luke. In addition Matthew and Luke both knew another source which Mark did not know; it has been called Q (from the German *Quelle* or "source") and several other names, but its content was principally a collection of the sayings of Jesus. Besides these, Matthew and Luke each had sources not available to the other; and it is highly probable that Matthew and Luke did not know each other's work. Each of the above statements needs qualification and expansion, and the serious student of the New Testament will look for this in the works where these questions are treated formally.

Behind the three Synoptic Gospels is the oral tradition, what we have called the proclamation of the gospel. The outline of Mark, which can still be seen in Matthew and Luke despite their expansions, is the outline of the proclamation. Or rather it is a much fuller statement of what is outlined in the discourses of Acts. It is highly important to notice that only half of Mark contains the sayings of Jesus, while the sayings comprise the major portions of both Matthew and Luke; we shall return to this point. Mark often refers to the teaching of Jesus but rarely quotes it. In him can be seen the apostolic emphasis on the Christ event as event and not as a body of doctrine. By the time the Gospels were written the preaching had spread over a wide area and had become diversified in its presentation.

The Multiple Written Gospel

Matthew, Mark, and Luke were evidently written for different circles of readers, and scholars can identify the circles. This, however, does not explain most of the differences between the three Synoptic Gospels. There is no reason we can give why the parables of Luke were not as apt for the readers of Mark and Matthew as they were for the readers of Luke. The most obvious answer is that these parables were unknown to Mark and Matthew. If this be granted, then some interesting questions arise about the variations in the content of the apostolic preaching.

The Proclamation and the Teaching

Or should we say apostolic teaching? It seems we should. The missionary methods of the apostolic Church differed from our own methods in many ways; and the most striking difference is that faith and baptism came first, and then instruction. The eunuch of the queen of Ethiopia was ready for baptism after a single proclamation (Acts 8:26–39). The Church insists on much more than this before the catechumen is ready for baptism now. I have no intention of raising an issue on disciplinary practice; but the difference in practice is not due merely to the fact that the material of catechetical instruction is more extensive now. We know that the apostolic Church very early had what it called "the teaching"; but knowledge of the teaching was not required for baptism. The apostolic Church considered that faith in the proclamation was required and sufficient for baptism; once a person had believed, he could then be taught the full content of what he had believed in principle.

In what did the teaching consist? It is certain that it included an explanation of the person and mission of Jesus in terms of the Old Testament. This is so important an element in primitive Christianity that we shall have to return to it in more detail (Chapters III–IV). One can see this element in all the Synoptic Gospels, particularly according to Matthew. But it is already in Mark, and it is as early as the proclamation; the grounding of the gospel in the Old Testament is seen in the discourses of Acts. A second element of the teaching was the sayings of Jesus. This also is seen in Mark; but the growth of the sayings in Matthew and Luke is notable. The sayings also will demand closer attention subsequently. We can observe now that the Synoptic Gospels represent not only different circles of readers and writers, but different stages of development of the teaching.

The Gospel as Encounter

The question is not well put if we ask why three Synoptic Gospels were written. The authors did not think they were writing three Gospels — or would not have thought it had they known each other's work. It was the one gospel written three times, and the threefold writing needed no more explanation than the manifold preaching of the gospel by Peter, Paul, and others in different cities. The question is not why the threefold gospel was written, but why it was written at all. For the gospel is seen as a personal encounter with God in Jesus Christ. The apostle incorporated his preaching in his person; and without such an encounter a personal response could not be demanded. It is evident from the nature of the proclamation that the Gospels were not written as a substitute for the oral proclamation. In this sense they are not the gospel but the teaching, or rather the expanded proclamation of the gospel with elements of the teaching added.

The Authors of the Gospels

The question who wrote the three Synoptic Gospels is not as simple as it appears. The traditional attribution of them to Matthew, Mark, and Luke includes only one of the Twelve among the authors. Modern criticism has had little trouble with the claims of Mark and Luke; but it has had more than a little trouble with the claim of Matthew, and in the present climate of criticism the authorship of this Gospel must be left open. If the traditional attribution of the first Gospel is not well founded, then we have the threefold record of the apostolic witness without any apostle included among the authors. The attribution of the other two

Gospels to Mark and Luke shows that the primitive Church did not consider apostolic authorship of the written Gospels a factor of importance. The authors of the Gospels were in possession of the apostolic witness. The witness endured in the living word in the Church whether it was written or not. The authors of the written Gospels were the agents of the Church when they wrote the Gospels. It was not their personal authority which authenticated the Gospels; it was the authority of the Church which accepted them, and perhaps commissioned them to write. This acceptance and commission is not what makes them inspired writings; this is another question which we need not enter here. Our concern here is with the position of the authors of the Gospels in the Church and with the position of the Gospels in the Church. The Church accepted the Gospels because they were the written record of her own proclamation and teaching. In a not improper sense the Church herself is the author of the Gospels; the authors wrote what the Church proclaimed and taught. This does not deny that they were authors; they were not mere scribes or recorders, and a comparison of the three Synoptic Gospels makes this abundantly clear. But they were not independent authors proposing their personal witness and authority; they were the spokesmen of the Church. Their personal identity had nothing to do with their commission to write. The Church wrote through Mark, Luke, and the unknown scribes who produced Matthew. She could as easily have written through Barnabas, Silas, or Apollo.

The Apostolic Witness

I have spoken of the apostolic witness; and this term introduces us to the question what the Church thought it was doing when it wrote the Gospels. Behind the Gospels, we have noticed, is the gospel, the word of the proclamation, which does not cease to exist with the writing of the Gospels. The proclamation in the concrete arose from the memory of a group of men who had known Jesus personally and who were commissioned by him to continue the proclamation which he had begun. Their attestation of what he was and what he had said and done is the only way in which the primitive Church knew Jesus at all. The witness could be communicated to others, of course; but the unique authority of the personal witness of the apostles could not be communicated. The men who had known Jesus personally died after the first generation of the Church.

Early tradition explained the composition of the Gospels as done in response to the requests of Christians that the personal memories of the apostles be preserved in writing. This seems altogether natural; it seems so natural that we wonder why we have only four written records of these apostolic memories. And then we wonder whether the desire to preserve the apostolic memories is the real reason for the composition of the Gospels. The question becomes more annoying when we observe that the Gospels are really not collections of the apostolic memories. Whatever the authors thought they were doing, it was more than this. And here we meet a question to which the early Church left us no answer, and it is difficult to conjecture an answer. We must suppose that local needs, not necessarily the same in each instance, moved the Church where the Gospel was written to have the writing done. Luke at least was aware that others had written before him. The fact that the Gospel of Luke shows no acquaintance with the Gospel of Matthew does not mean that Luke was unaware of the existence of that Gospel. And it is interesting to note that while Luke's introduction does not necessarily refer implicitly to either Mark or Matthew, no scholar thinks that Luke refers to any other attempt to write a Gospel than these two. He may be referring to written sources, which would be collections of the material used in the Gospels, but the four Gospels were and are the only representatives of the type of literature called a gospel.

The Literary Form of the Gospels

If we define that literary form, we shall have answered the question which the authors of the Gospels thought they were doing. The negative approach is not the most satisfactory approach, but here it can be useful. The Gospels are not biographies of Jesus. Two of the four begin with the beginning of the public life of Jesus. None of them pretends to be a complete account of even the public life of Jesus. Modern writers compose books under the title "The

Life of Jesus Christ" with the assurance that they are not writing a Gospel. The Gospels lack a satisfactory geographical and chronological arrangement. Most of the incidents are imprecisely located. The authors have evidently arranged the incidents in an order which they thought suited their purpose; they were not bound by any chronology given in tradition. No portion of the life of Jesus is narrated so circumstantially as the passion. Mark, the shortest of the Gospels, is as full on this event as any other, and his Gospel has been called a Passion narrative with an introduction. One cannot establish from the Gospels with certainty even the length of time which elapsed between the baptism and the death of Jesus. Still less can one establish the date of the death of Jesus without a margin of error of a few years. A biography in even the minimum sense of the word should contain such information as this.

There is a deeper reason why the Gospels are not and cannot be biographies. The biography is the history of a personal life with a beginning, middle, and end. The biographer can study the enduring influence of his hero; but the Gospels do not think of Jesus as having enduring influence. They think of him as living, indeed as living with that fullness of life which is proper to him and which was hidden in his incarnate existence. His life merges into the life of that reality which continues his life on earth, the Church. This theme is expressed in the twofold work of Luke, the Gospel and the Acts. The Gospel is more than the life of a single human person; it is a recital of the act of God.

The Gospels and Apologetics

The Gospels are not apologetic treatises. We have observed that they were written in the Church for the Church. The proclamation, it is true, was addressed to those who had not yet believed; but the recital of the saving event was not limited to unbelievers. The Gospels were written from faith for faith. The writers accept Jesus as Messiah and Lord and describe him as such. They did not take the position of detached investigators who examine and weigh the evidence. Indeed, the modern apologetic approach to Christianity has no corresponding element in the New Testament. The apologetic approach is a rationalist system of demonstration and conviction, devised in answer to a rationalist doubt. Such a system can arrive at nothing except a reasoned conclusion; and the proclamation of the gospel was not intended to issue in a reasoned conclusion. The proclamation was not addressed to the intellect but to the whole man, and the response was elicited from the whole man. That the apostles and those who heard them were both incapable of rationalizing about their proclamation does not mean that all Christians should reject rationalizing in all ages; I suppose this book, like most modern books on the Bible, exhibits a degree of rationalization which we modern men cannot escape entirely. It is a part of our cultural heritage. But we are dealing with the New Testament, and it is important that we try to understand the New Testament in its own terms.

The Gospels and Theology

Similarly the Gospels are not theological treatises; and this is true even of the fourth Gospel, which approaches theology more closely than do the Synoptic Gospels. Theology in the modern sense means a systematization of belief; and systematic exposition of belief can be done only in philosophical terms. No philosophy has the sole and exclusive rights to Christian belief. The privileged position of Thomism in the modern Church is of recent origin in terms of the history of the Church; and the privileged position of Thomism can be said to be less fixed, I think, than the primacy of the bishop of Rome or the monarchical episcopate. Since Thomism itself is a historical development, one may assume that it has not in a kind of apocalyptic fashion ended further historical development. The first theological thinking in the Church was done in the terms of Platonic philosophy; and this philosophy as modified and adapted by most of the Fathers was dominant in theology until the Middle Ages.

One has merely to read the Gospels to see that they can be called theological writing only in an abusive sense. It would be difficult to find any literature of the Hellenistic period which is more innocent of philosophical ideas than the Gospels. They are not written systematically. They are centered about a person;

and they are recital, not exposition. They are the proclamation of an event; and the event is not submitted to analysis. It is not the basis of speculative conclusions. The proclamation is directed to elicit another event; and this other event is the response of the believer. As we shall see, this response is a communication of the event through faith and ritual reenactment. The believer reexperiences the event which is proclaimed; Christ is born in him, and he dies and rises with Christ. These patterns of thought, if they are compared to the patterns which we find in the Hellenistic world, resemble the mystery cults much more than they resemble Stoicism. Christianity was taken by some to be another mystery cult; it was never taken to be a new philosophy. The New Testament furnishes the materials of a theological synthesis; it is important that the theological synthesis should not be called a restatement of the New Testament. The synthesis says more; the additional elements may be true, but they are not the gospel.

The Gospels and History

The writers of the Gospels did not think they were writing history. It seems that this proposition may just as well be stated bluntly and then explained; for it needs explanation, particularly in the context of modern discussions of the Gospels. Much confusion has arisen because so many assume that the historical reality of events depends on the historical character of the literature in which they are recorded. A little reflection should make it clear that historical events are preserved in many other ways than historical writing. Historical writing is a well-defined form of literature which was known in the Hellenistic world. The form was not the same in the Hellenistic world as it is in our own world; it should be evident beyond dispute that the Gospels do not fit the definition of modern historical writing, and it can be maintained that they do only if one is unacquainted both with the Gospels and with modern historical writing. But they do not fit the definition of Hellenistic historical writing either. When the Gospels are compared with the works of writers like Polybius, Livy, and Flavius Josephus the differences are immediately apparent. If the Gospels are historical writing, we shall have to find some other name for the works of Polybius, Livy, and Flavius Josephus.

That the authors of the Gospels were not writing history does not imply that they were writing fiction or mythology or any other type of entirely imaginative narrative. They wrote the gospel; the altogether unique nature of the event which they narrated elicited an entirely new and unique form of literature. The gospel, as we shall have occasion to notice more than once, was revolutionary in character; and one of the first effects of the revolution occurred in literature. Conventional historical narrative might seem to place the event in the chain of historical sequence. We have observed that the Christ event is seen as historical, but not as merely historical. I do not imply that the writers of the Gospels consciously and deliberately planned and executed a new literary form; they were too artless for that. I do mean that the novelty of the event forced itself upon their expression; and in their desire to represent it as singular they found a form of expression which is also singular.

The Materials of the Gospels

Let us reconstruct if we can the materials with which the authors of the Synoptic Gospels worked and the methods by which they handled this material. Here we are fortunate in having a threefold Gospel. The Synoptic problem or question is the major critical problem of the New Testament; this is the problem of the relations of the Gospels to each other. The extensive community of material in the Synoptic Gospels — only 30 verses of Mark do not occur either in Matthew or in Luke or in both — allows us to see in parallel columns the astonishing liberties which the authors took, and allows us also to see the plan and purpose behind these liberties. What they had available was a body of oral tradition from which was formed the proclamation, the apostolic witness to Jesus Christ. That the proclamation early took a standardized form is suggested by all we know of the oral gospel and by the form of the Synoptic Gospels. The same cannot be assumed of the other material in the oral tradition about Jesus. This was the personal and group memories of the Twelve, and presumably of other close witnesses. The Gospels leave us no other conclusion than that these memories, outside of the proclamation itself, were anecdotal. This is to say that they were not structured. They were isolated memories of incidents and sayings. It is highly probable that some arrangement existed for some of this material before the written Gospels; but these arrangements hardly deserve the name of structures. Anecdotes were connected in the loosest possible manner. The catchword, in which the final key word of one anecdote appears in the first sentence of the next, is a common arrangement. This appears to be a purely mnemonic device; such an arrangement does not pretend to be either chronological or topical. But there appear to be also topical arrangements of sayings; the parables of the Reign are an obvious example of this. Matthew is particularly fond of topical groupings; but they are purely topical. Luke has put most of the material peculiar to himself in the journey of Jesus to Jerusalem, which runs from 9:51 to 19:28; the same journey runs through Matthew 19–20 and Mark 10. It appears that Luke had to adhere to an existing structure in which there was no other place for the material peculiar to him; but Luke is the third of the Synoptic Gospels. Critics are usually unwilling to admit very many preexisting arrangements of the material; the presumption, they think, is that any arrangement comes from the author of the Gospel unless it is clear that it came from some other source. And this emphasizes the anecdotal character of the apostolic memories.

Form Criticism

A word should be said about form criticism, which has been the object of numerous censures uttered by people who have not read the writings of critics. And I note parenthetically that "form critic," like "higher critic," is a barbarism which betrays nearly total ignorance of critical literature. Form criticism assumes on the basis of nearly universal experience that oral tradition tends to follow set patterns of expression. A little reflection on the popular tradition familiar to all of us will remove any doubt about the legitimacy of this assumption. The dialogue and suspense in any humorous story must lead to the "punch line," at which point the story must end. The fairy story follows a rigorous structure; and anyone who has dealt with children, or who remembers his own childhood, knows that children will not suffer deviations from the form. Each repetition of a refrain must be uttered; shortcuts are forbidden in this literary form. Form criticism adds to this the principle that one can isolate the oral form and recover it from the written form, which sometimes obscures the oral form. It is possible from the form to reconstruct the origin and purpose of the story. For example, a saying of Jesus was not repeated in a vacuum. Many of the sayings were remembered and repeated in answer to a definite question in the primitive Church, and usually a question unconnected with the original saying. But when the saying is further repeated, it is repeated with the question to which it had become an answer. A miracle story is sometimes told for itself; at other times it is merely an introduction to the saying with which the story ends. Did miracle and saying originally belong together, or were they associated in the apostolic memory? The same saying, or sayings which are very similar, appear in different contexts; which of these represents the original context, and which the different form — or do any of them? The difference is explained in form criticism not from the repetition of the same saying by Jesus himself or from variations in his own phrasing, but from the adaptation made by the primitive churches of the sayings of Jesus to their own particular needs and questions.

In a sense the work of form criticism is more a study of the primitive Church than it is a study of Jesus, and its best work has perhaps been done in this area. But many of those who practice form criticism regard it as "the quest of the historical Jesus." To this idea we shall have to return. But form criticism has shown in a new way what is meant by living tradition. Jesus in the primitive Church was not a plaster figure. He was a vital memory, indeed he lived in the Church; and the members of the Church dealt with the traditions of Jesus as they would deal with Jesus himself, asking him questions and finding answers. The Church was convinced that it had not exhausted and could not exhaust the meaning of the Christ event; and as its understanding of the Christ event was deepened, the traditions about Jesus were enriched.

The Sayings of Jesus

To us it seems that the very words of Jesus would be the supreme treasure to be preserved above all else. We think this because of a cultural background which leads us to emphasize doctrine more than event, to prize clear and precise formulation, and to recover the exact account of the past. The primitive Church did not share this background. In one passage where the formula seems to us to be of the highest importance, the institution of the Eucharist, the four formulas in the New Testament make it impossible to recover the exact words of Jesus even here. Shall we recite the Lord's Prayer in the shorter version of Luke instead of the longer version of Matthew, which we use? Do the eight beatitudes of Matthew or the four beatitudes and four woes of Luke represent the very words of Jesus? Or do either of them? There can be no doubt that not all of the words placed in the mouth of Jesus in the Gospels were spoken by him. When the primitive Church sought an answer to its problems in its memory of Jesus, it did not hesitate to form sayings which it believed reflected his teaching. The Church did this with the assurance that it knew him well enough to declare his mind where he had not explicitly spoken. And it can be noted here that while we have excluded the Gospels from the literary form of historical writing, it was an accepted convention of Hellenistic historical writing that the author should create speeches and dialogue which he thought suitable to the situation. If the authors of the Gospels had done this, they would have done nothing contrary to the accepted conventions of historical writing.

We think they did not do this because they were not writing history, and because they did not possess the art of writing creatively. But we know that they felt more freedom in constructing the words and the narratives than we should allow them — or rather than we should allow ourselves. Let us accept them with their way of doing it and not compel them to be understood in our way. It is rather pitiful to hear devout Christians say that their faith is rooted in the historical character of the Gospels. The apostles and evangelists would not understand this proposition, and if they could be brought to understand it they would be scandalized. Their own faith, I think they would say, was rooted in an experience of God in Jesus Christ, an experience which the witnesses communicated to the Church through the word of the gospel.

The Gospels and Faith

For this is what the gospel presents, and what the Gospels present: Jesus Christ as an object of faith. The apostles believed in him whom they preached; and they were convinced that the presentation of that unique reality which they had experienced ought to be enough to generate the same faith which they had. I say an object of faith because it is evident from the Gospels that the faith of the apostles matured slowly. It did not reach maturity until after Jesus had risen; and their experience of his words and deeds occurred when their faith was dim and inchoative. The Gospels are not witnesses of a dim and inchoative faith but of an adult and sturdy faith. They proclaim the full reality of Jesus Messiah and Lord. This means that their faith transfigures the account. In the maturity of faith they understood things which they had not understood when they experienced them, and they related these things with a fuller understanding. Jesus is proclaimed Messiah in the Gospels with a clarity which his own proclamation lacked; this we shall examine in more detail in Chapter IV. The element of power which appears in the miracle narratives is manifest in the Gospels; but the witnesses realized the existence and meaning of the power only when their faith had become adult. Were this history, the development should be traced, but it is not history; it is the proclamation of the act of God, and the act of God must be revealed for what it is. The apostles did not conceive it their duty to drag their converts through the same painful process which they had gone through themselves.

The Quest of the Historical Jesus

I have already mentioned "the quest of the historical Jesus" in passing. This celebrated phrase was used as the title of the English translation of a book written by Albert Schweitzer in the early twentieth century; the German title was, more prosaically, *From Reimarus to Wrede*. The book was a review of nearly one hundred years of critical investigation of the life of Jesus done on the presupposition that the historical Jesus is not presented in the Gospels, but that he can be recovered by critical analysis. In another celebrated phrase the investigation accepted the antithesis between the Jesus of history and the Christ of faith. The investigation finally broke down, and many scholars renounced any attempt to recover the Jesus of history. Rudolf Bultmann, for instance, wrote that we know next to nothing about the Jesus of history; and what is more significant, he treats the historical Jesus as of not much importance in the origins of Christianity.

"The Jesus of history" and "the Christ of faith" represent what I called in our first chapter the historical reality and the theological reality. There I said that these are not two realities but one; and if one does not maintain their unity, one is hopelessly involved in the problem of the Jesus of history and the Christ of faith. In the New Testament and in the primitive Church the Jesus of history is the Christ of faith. He whom they had known and heard was Messiah and Lord. It is quite true that they did not recognize him as Messiah and Lord by historical experience alone. The confession of these titles is an act of faith. The disjunction between the Jesus of history and the Christ of faith rests on an assumption that the historical Jesus, if he could be recovered, was not Messiah and Lord, and that these titles were created by the primitive Church. The primitive Church believed that the theological reality was revealed and slowly discovered.

Ultimately we know Jesus only in the testimony of the primitive Church, which is the written record of the apostolic witness. We must accept this witness as a witness both of experience and of faith. The primitive Church was less concerned with an exact report of the words and deeds of Jesus than we should be; it was very deeply concerned that its witness should present the reality of Jesus Messiah and Lord with all possible fidelity. The Church was satisfied that popular anecdotal memory could present this reality. If the presentation failed to retain his exact words, if the memory of the incidents of his life varied in details, if the anecdotes were enriched by a symbolism which made explicit the object of faith — all these things were not a distortion of the reality.

Another and perhaps a deeper problem lies beneath "the quest of the historical Jesus." Much of modern apologetics has responded to the quest and its assumptions by stoutly affirming the historical character of the Gospels. I have attempted to show that this thesis is an oversimplification which complicates the problem. The quest is the fruit of a scholarly movement originally unconnected with biblical studies called "Historicism"; since the attitude of historicism is nearly dead, I venture to sum it up as the belief that there is no reality except that which is contained in historical documents. Both the hypercriticism of the quest and the response of apologetics tacitly agreed that the records of Jesus were not trustworthy unless they met the canons of historical criticism. More than this, they tacitly agreed that a witness of faith was *ipso facto* suspect unless it could be reduced somehow to the testimony of a disinterested witness. One senses a feeling that the primitive Church and its writers have made things very difficult for us, and that we would prefer that they wrote straight history instead of Gospels and confessions of faith. But the difficulty is not irremediable; we think we can rewrite the Gospels. And if we do, is it impossible that faith in Jesus Christ will be replaced by faith in the Gospels considered as purely historical documents?

Summary

We have, I think, come some of the way toward an answer to the question what the Gospels are, and what their authors thought they were doing. Perhaps we can take the answer no further. The authors of the gospel found an entirely new way to write the experience of an entirely new reality. Certain limitations were imposed upon them by the fact that their source was ultimately collective and personal anecdotal memory. Other limitations arose from the absence of conscious literary art and technique in the writers. The most severe limitation of all is imposed by the subject about which they wrote. The person of Jesus was and remained mysterious. The gospel respected this mystery and reflected it faithfully in the proclamation and the teaching. Not all questions could be answered, and some should not even be asked.

If the reader of the Gospels believes that he can study their hero as easily as he can study Julius Caesar or St. Augustine, he has not even grasped the fundamental truth of the proclamation. Unless he is willing to accept the faith of the Gospels that the Christian event escapes rationalization, he remains outside the experience which the Gospels are intended to communicate. He will have to surrender to the fact that the Christian event will upset him, that neither he nor his life will ever be the same once he has felt its impact; and he will never know clearly why. For the acts of God are not subject to review by human judgment.

An Additional Note: The Gospel of John

The discussion carried on in this chapter has centered around the Synoptic Gospels — Matthew, Mark, and Luke. I should be evasive if I did not add a note on the fourth Gospel. That it differs from the Synoptics is apparent. It does not differ from them in its intention to be a faithful presentation of the reality of Jesus. Scholars have sometimes said that the Jesus of John is not the Jesus of the Synoptics. Despite the differences, this position cannot be sustained. It can be more easily sustained that the teaching of Jesus contained in the fourth Gospel is not the same teaching as that found in the Synoptics. But the difference is not such that the two presentations are opposed.

Whether Jesus himself was or could be the common origin of two presentations so different is a question which admits no certain answer. The weight of scholarly opinion regards the fourth Gospel as written with a much larger element of personal interpretation; I say much larger, for the Synoptics also are written with personal interpretation. One may put the statement in the usual terms: the fourth Gospel contains less of the exact words of Jesus than the Synoptics. The long debates and discourses of the fourth Gospel are in striking contrast to the sayings of the Synoptics. This does not imply that anecdotal memory does not preserve such pieces. The arrangement of the fourth Gospel is evidently more artificial than the arrangement of the Synoptics, and both discourses and incidents contain a more generous use of symbolism.

The fourth Gospel is traditionally called the most recent, and this tradition is still accepted. It is more easily understood how John could have been written after the other three; and John must almost of necessity presuppose the other three. It was usually maintained up to recent times that the restatement of the Gospel in John was created in a Hellenistic situation for the needs of Hellenistic Christians. Since the discovery of the Qumran documents this can scarcely be maintained. There are more literary contacts with Qumran in John than there are in the Synoptic Gospels; and these contacts must be earlier than A.D. 68. John is as Palestinian as any other Gospel, and in some ways the most Palestinian of all.

Did the themes peculiar to John, not found in the Synoptics, appear in the teaching of Jesus himself? If they did, then we must suppose that the proclamation recorded in the Synoptics excluded these themes; and this assumption is not easily defended. If the themes appeared in the teaching of Jesus, they must have been less prominent than they are in John, where they have occupied the entire foreground. The simplest explanation is that John represents the gospel as it was taught in a Palestinian group distinct from the Palestinian communities known from the Acts of the Apostles. This assumption does not affect the accepted view that John is the latest of the Gospels; it affects substantially the view that the teaching of John is a more recent development. Everything points to the conclusion that the teaching of John is as primitive as the teaching found in the Synoptics; and the Church recognized that John's account of the Christian event was equally valid with the account of the Synoptics.

The literary attribution of the fourth Gospel rests on a tradition as well supported as the tradition for the Synoptics. So little is known of John personally that there is no reason to question the attribution. There is ample reason to question the tradition that the Gospel was written at Ephesus; and if this part of the tradition is doubtful, the whole tradition is not strengthened. Here, as for the Synoptics, the literary attribution to this or that individual is less important than the attribution of the Gospel to the Church.

III

THE REIGN OF GOD

God as King

In the New Testament translations in common use, Jesus proclaims the coming of the Kingdom of God. The Greek word which is translated "kingdom" and the Aramaic word which lies behind it signify something other than kingdom or realm; modern scholars prefer to translate the word by "reign." Behind this term there lies a long Old Testament tradition; and this must be reviewed if we are to grasp the meaning and the implications of the proclamation of Jesus.

The belief that Yahweh, the God of Israel, was king does not certainly appear in the primitive stages of Israelite belief. The absence of the belief implies no limitation of the power of Yahweh; the title of king reflects a social and political structure which we do not find in early Israel. When the idea of a monarchy was first proposed in Israel, it was rejected by some on the ground that Yahweh was king; and a human kingship was thought incompatible with the Reign of Yahweh.

The kingship of the gods was professed in the religions of other peoples of the ancient Near East; and Israel needed no departure from known patterns to venerate Yahweh as king. But its patterns are not the same, and this is due to the unique character of Yahweh. Yahweh can be conceived as king of Israel, as king of all nations, and as lord of nature. He can be conceived as warrior-king and as judge; for these were the two functions of kingship in the ancient Near East. All these conceptions appear in the Old Testament; their mutual relationship and development create interesting problems which need not concern us here.

The Reign of Yahweh

The Old Testament looks to a coming Reign of Yahweh; for it is evident that the fullness of his Reign is not manifest in the historical world. Most men do not acknowledge his sovereignty; foreign nations have their own kings and their own lords. His dominion over nature, based on creation, is beyond question; but this likewise is not acknowledged by all men. The idea was further complicated in the course of Israelite history by the disappearance of Israel as a political society. That Yahweh was king of Israel meant little when there was no Israel. The coming of his Reign then demanded an act of deliverance and the reestablishment of Israel as a people. This deliverance could be accomplished only if the powers which had usurped Yahweh's Reign over his own people were subdued.

Therefore Yahweh's Reign was not fully effective. That it was inhibited by equal or superior powers was inadmissible; the limitations of Yahweh's effective sovereignty could be explained only as the work of Yahweh himself, who for his own reasons permitted hostile powers to work. In Israelite thinking this would afford an occasion for Yahweh to manifest his power in a more spectacular manner. To appear as warrior and judge he needed enemies to conquer and to judge. The voices in Israel who questioned why the wicked prosper (Jer 12:1) or how long Israel must cry for help (Habk 1:2) were few; these questions raised deeper issues of the problem of evil and of history which Israel usually did not raise. If Yahweh had his own time in which to impose his Reign, that was soon enough.

Yahweh the Conqueror

This time lay in the future; and when it came, Yahweh would assert his Reign in a kingly manner — that is, by conquest and judgment. The prophetic books often contain passages in which the downfall of the Gentile nations is predicted; and Yahweh is the conquering warrior who brings them down. He is the judge both in the sense that he vindicates Israel and that he condemns the enemies of Israel. His Reign is established by a tremendous display of power which shatters all mere earthly power. Submission is gained as the Assyrian conquerors gained the submission of those they conquered: by terror. But the terror of Yahweh is the terror inspired by righteousness and holiness; it is, however, terror, and it is important to remember that this is the dominant way in which the coming of the Reign of God is conceived in the Old Testament.

Israel in the Reign of Yahweh

In this victory and judgment the position of Israel is unique. It is to be an object neither of conquest nor of judgment. Its election as the people of Yahweh will find fulfillment; the people of Yahweh will share in the victory and will participate in the judgment, and they will rule the nations of the Gentiles. The elect Israel is eternal, like Yahweh who chose Israel. Israel cannot fail because the promises of Yahweh cannot fail.

This is the biblical background of the idea of the Reign of God; and this biblical background was expanded in the literature of Judaism written shortly before the beginning of the Christian era. At a time when the fortunes of Judaism had never been lower, there was a revival of the expectation of the Reign of Yahweh. The expansion of the idea was more exclusive, more intolerant of the Gentiles, more grandiose in the conception of the victory of Yahweh over the nations than the Old Testament texts. As we have noticed, the party of the Zealots was motivated by an expectation that the Day of the Lord could not be far off.

The Eschatological Reign in the Old Testament

To what extent the coming of the Reign should be called eschatological is a question which does not admit a simple answer. The term "eschatological" itself needs careful definition. The term by its etymology indicates a final phase; the Greek *eschaton* means "the last." The eschatological Reign ends history. More than this, it is not a product of historical forces. It is an inbreak of the saving and judging power of God which cannot be produced or hastened by the actions of men. It lies outside history. But this finality of the Reign does not of itself imply an end of the world; this feature is called "apocalyptic." If the coming of the Reign is conceived as occurring on the scene of history, if nature is the weapon of Yahweh's wrath but is not itself dissolved, if the nations of men remain and the condition of man is not changed, then the conception is not apocalyptic; and one may ask whether it is eschatological. Such a conception would seem to freeze history rather then end it.

The victory and judgment of Yahweh in the Old Testament are not clearly eschatological before the most recent books. The prophets see the saving and judging acts of God in the movements of contemporary history, like the fall of Assyria or Babylon. Nothing of apocalyptic imagery seems to be lacking in the passages where these reversals of history are described. Yet they are not genuinely eschatological because they are not represented as terminal. And they certainly do not imply a change in the human condition. The Old Testament in its preexilic portions lends support to the interpretation that eschatology is merely imagery, that the turns of history are always in a sense final; fallen, fallen is Babylon not to rise again. No such doubt can be expressed about the later biblical books and Jewish apocalyptic literature. When the Reign comes, it will be more than a new assertion of Yahweh's power to save and to judge; it will be the last and perfect exhibition of that power, and after this exhibition there will be no other objects on which it can be exercised.

Jesus and the Reign of God

When Jesus proclaimed that the Reign of God was approaching, he spoke in an atmosphere which was heavily charged. The degree of tension can be seen in the board which was affixed to his cross; the charge on which condemnation was legally possible was claiming the kingship of the Jews. There are several allusions in the Gospels to expectations aroused by his proclamation; the most pathetic of these, surely, is the question asked by his own disciples (Acts 1:6). When one considers the overtones of the Reign, one is tempted to wonder why Jesus chose this phrase as a keyword and did not choose a more neutral term. The answer, it seems, is that the mission of Jesus was more intelligible as a proclamation of the Reign than it would have been in a more neutral term. He spoke in the language and in the traditions of Israelite and Jewish belief. By proclaiming the Reign he said that the promises were near fulfillment, that the Day of the Lord was near, that what the Jews expected and hoped for was approaching. No other fulfillment could be expected. The Reign which he proclaimed was terminal for Judaism. By the use of the term Reign he made it clear to the Jews that the event which he proclaimed was decisive.

The New Idea of the Reign

But could a Jew recognize in the Reign proclaimed by Jesus the Reign which he expected? Almost every one of the elements we have noticed in the Israelite-Jewish eschatological Reign is omitted from the proclamation of Jesus. This is more than startling. The omission is not aggressively proposed; Jesus does not brusquely tell his listeners that they are all wrong and that they must correct their ideas. Nor does he mask the novelty of his proclamation; there are no soft phrases which reassure his listeners that no really great change is demanded of them. He simply proposes the Reign as something which is new, but which is really the true Reign promised by the prophets. Yet where is the new transfigured Israel? Where is the conquest of the Gentile nations? Where is the judgment of the enemies of Israel?

Jesus assumes with authority the function of interpreter of the prophets. He does not overturn the traditions of Israel, but he gives them direction. We deal here with more than a collection of texts; the words of Jesus were uttered in a complex of ideas in which the Old Testament, the fantastic imagery of apocalyptic writers, and various superstitions had become hopelessly tangled with each other. This complex of ideas he overturned; his action on the popular belief in the messianic Reign was revolutionary. In the popular belief the symbolism of much Old Testament writing about the Reign had been interpreted with exaggerated realism. It scarcely seems too much to say that for many Jews God had become a means for Israel's purposes. The dominant theme in the Reign as seen by the prophets is the sovereign will of God; and it is this which Jesus proclaimed.

The Call to Repentance

In the first chapter I alluded to the fact that the religious and moral level of Judaism was notably higher than the religious and moral level of the Hellenistic world; we noted also the spiritual security which the Jews felt in their knowledge of this. Jesus attacked this security directly. The Gospels report his proclamation as beginning with a call to repentance. The Jews might very well ask, repent of what? The Law and the temple cult and the synagogue worship had established the Jews in firm and good relations with God. The attitude of Jesus to the Law demands full attention, and we shall give it later in this work (Chapter X); we may notice now that Jesus taught clearly that the law was not a sure and sufficient guide of conduct, and that it was not a complete compendium of the revealed will of God. His war on Pharisaic observance and on the pride of those who practiced it is a recurrent theme in the Gospels. The temple cult he treats as a mere transitory episode. In neither of these essential institutions of Judaism is the will of God certainly found. More is demanded, and Jesus has come to tell what it is.

Jesus and Judaism

We can notice first that Jesus makes it clear that it is not enough to be a Jew. John the Baptist had said that God could raise up children of Abraham from stones. The security which comes from membership in a group is shattered. Membership in a group is not a substitute for personal decision, and group responsibility does not absolve the individual from his own responsibility. Jesus proclaimed the Reign not to Judaism as a group but to individual persons. It was very probably not until the full consequences of the decision were realized that the apostles could say of themselves that they left all things and followed Jesus. The community of those who make the decision was formed anew of people who had heard the proclamation and chosen to obey it; it was not a transfer of a group from one leadership to another.

Jesus attacks here not only the collective security of Judaism but a universal human tendency to run with the herd, to hide within the attitudes and decisions of the crowd. It is so easy to do what is right as long as enough people have done it before us — or to believe that what so many people have done before us must be right. It is doubtful that Christians have very often generalized this part of the teaching of Jesus and applied it to their own case. They are willing to allow the Church or particular organizations within the Church to fill the place in their own lives which the Law and the traditions occupied in Judaism. The proclamation of Jesus contains no indication that he intended to retain the structure of Judaism.

We can notice next that the proclamation attacks a religion of routine. This again is related to the place of the Law in Judaism and the response of Jesus to the Law, which we have postponed; but we must observe here that the proclamation of the Reign was not a call to the Jews to keep right on doing what they were doing. We do not find in the proclamation of Jesus the polemic against empty ritual which we find so often in the prophets of Israel. But we find that he rejects the related idea that the fulfillment of the will of God can be reduced to a routine. There is no one decision one can make which makes further decisions unnecessary. Still less does the proclamation leave room for a theory of prefabricated decisions and solutions of problems. The will of God cannot be reduced to a rule. It is a living and a constant reality; it is spirit and not letter. One may indeed have rules and codes, for they serve the useful purpose of reducing to routine things which are not very important; but if one thinks that one has captured the will of God in rules and codes, one has not risen above the ethics of the Pharisees.

The Reign as the Will of God

The Reign is the fulfillment of the will of God. Jesus proclaims that this fulfillment is to be accomplished by God and by man. God enables man to fulfill his will in a new way. Judaism demanded that the Jew fulfill God's will by the observance of the Law. Jesus announces that man must fulfill God's will by submitting to a regeneration of himself. There is a combat in the achievement of the Reign, but it is not an apocalyptic combat against the powers of this world. The enemy which opposes the Reign is sin; and sin in the concrete is every man. The Reign does not deliver man from secular power but from his own sin. Here Jesus revitalizes parts of the prophetic teaching which had been obscured both by emphasis on the Law and by overenthusiastic eschatology. The prophets, in particular the preexilic prophets, preach the guilt of Israel with a consistency which becomes nearly monotonous. They see no hope for Israel except in a moral regeneration. The new Israel must have a new heart and a new soul; in the new Israel everyone will know the Lord.

Self-Righteousness

The theology of Judaism exhibits a profound consciousness of guilt. The terrible experience of the fall of Israel and Judah and the dispersion of the people of Israel and Judah had impressed Judaism with the reality of God's judgments. The Psalms, for example, are full of confessions of guilt and petitions for forgiveness. What had happened to this awareness of sin? For one thing, the restoration of a Jewish community had become a token of forgiveness. For another, the Jews of the postexilic period were aware that they did not exhibit the faults which were denounced by the prophets; in particular, they were innocent of the cult of false gods. In addition, the Law became the assurance that they lived in submission to the will of God. These factors helped to form a community which Jesus candidly addresses as self--righteous; and it is impossible for the self-righteous to accept the will of God.

The Meaning of Repentance

The Greek word which is translated "repent" (or even less felicitously "do penance") is *metanoein*. The fault with the translation is not that the word does not mean repentance, but that it means so much more. One repents of one's sins; Jesus demands that one repent of what one is. The ritual of Judaism included, as we have noticed, confession of sin and ritual offerings for sin and guilt. What did Jesus ask beyond this? The Greek word means literally "a change of mind"; and one is reminded of Paul's exhortation to the Philippians to put on the mind of Christ Jesus. What Jesus demands is a personal moral revolution. One repents of one's sins; more that this, one becomes something else — not the same man struggling against sin, but a man who thinks differently, whose desires have a different direction, whose motivation is different. One begins a new life, one is reborn. And the childhood of this new life is the sonship of God.

The Moral Revolution

Adolf Harnack once summed up the teaching of Jesus as the fatherhood of God and the brotherhood of man. This was "Liberal Christianity." It omitted so much of the New Testament that it could not be sustained; but Harnack did, of course, seize on two central themes — which, we may add, he did not discover. The importance of these themes is such that we shall have to give them more extended consideration. They illustrate the point which we are considering here; for they are the basis of the new attitude, the personal moral revolution which Jesus introduces. Both stand in direct antithesis to the spirit and practice of Judaism of the first century. It is not without interest that the antithesis is less striking if we compare these two beliefs with the Gentile world. Stoicism, as we have noticed, approached an ideal of the brotherhood of man; but the fatherhood of God, in the sense in which Jesus proclaimed it, has its only points of contact in some passages of the Old Testament. The two beliefs establish a new relationship with God and a new relationship with one's fellow man; and the direction of the moral revolution is set by these cardinal truths.

Total Repentance

How deep is the change which Jesus demands? And how extensive is the submission to the will of God which establishes the Reign? The answer to both is total. The Pauline metaphor of the old man which is put off and the new man which is put on is not to be minimized into conventional morality. The Gospels contain several passages in which Jesus is so merciless when he is asked what submission to the Reign demands that we are somewhat surprised. His pedagogy is admirable, and we are impressed by the way in which he leads people from the easy to the difficult — one is tempted to say, from the possible to the impossible. But he could be short and sharp when compromise was in the air. His words about leaving father and mother, wife and home, about letting the dead bury their dead, about looking back after one has put one's hand to the plow, about the rich and the camel passing through the needle's eye, are memorable; and they have caused Christians more than a little anguish. The history of our theological and ascetical thought is full of recurring efforts to rationalize some of this unyielding firmness out of the gospel and make it possible for the Christian to eat his cake and have pie in the sky as well. One could be faithful to Judaism by observing a certain number of known and definite rules. The demands of Judaism were severe compared to the demands made by Hellenistic religion and morality, but it had a comfortable ceiling which could be seen. The proclamation of Jesus shook this entire structure. One's trust in the Father could have no reservations. No one could tell what total submission to the will of God might demand; Jesus was very clear on what would follow a submission which was less than total.

The Reign of God as Jesus proclaimed it emerges as a religious and moral revolution in the life of the individual man. It initiates a new relation with God and a new interpersonal relationship among men, as we have noticed. It establishes a new principle of action, a new standard, and new motives. The extent to which it overturns existing conventional ideas and values will occupy us during most of this book. When I call it a personal revolution, I lead to the questions: Is it a social revolution? Is it a political revolution? The answer to these questions will be taken up at the length they deserve (Chapters XI–XII). Here, however, we must meet a question which follows from our survey of the Jewish conception of the Reign: Is the Reign proclaimed by Jesus eschatological?

The Eschatological Reign in the New Testament

The reader of the Bible who is unacquainted with the academic discussions of theologians is usually surprised to learn that eschatology is and has long been one of the most hotly disputed theological and exegetical problems. A mere review of the discussion would make a book of ample proportions. I abstain from such a review here; I think it is possible to treat the problem in a general way without tracing the complicated pattern of theological arguments. But candor demands that I state that the exposition which follows is a personal synthesis which is subject to revision — if not to rejection.

Let us recall the extremely basic definition of eschatology given above: the belief that history issues in a divine act which terminates history and inaugurates a new age, a new dimension of reality. The problem of New Testament eschatology lies very simply in the fact that some texts appear to be clearly eschatological and other texts appear with equal clarity to exclude eschatology. These latter texts include those in which the final act seems to be the appearance of Jesus himself; if this is final, then we are living in a posteschatological era, which is a contradiction in terms — or the definition of eschatology must be broadened so much that it seems to lose meaning.

A Problem of Definition

There are two problems of language which touch on the central problem. One is the problem of the definition of eschatology. The definition which I offer is given as merely descriptive; it is intended to summarize a large number of passages and to state the central idea of these passages. Most scholars have defined eschatology in similar terms. The central idea as I have defined it is finality; history ends in a divine act which may be called metahistorical. Details are irrelevant to this central theme; and the almost endless variations in detail found in eschatological passages can be ignored, as long as these passages conceive of such a term of history. Difficulty arises when too many elements are introduced into the definition of eschatology. We logical and discursive thinkers are always in danger of schematizing the flexible conceptions of ancient literature and measuring them according to an abstract idea which the ancient writers never formed. We may not say, "This is what eschatology ought to be," and then include or exclude ideas according to what we have defined; we may only say, "This is what eschatology is in the literature where it is found," and be ready to accept inconsistencies.

Popular Eschatology

The second problem of language is created by popular traditional Christian eschatology. In the catechism eschatology has long been the doctrine of the four last things; Death, Judgment, Heaven, and Hell. It will be observed that one of these four, death, does not fit into the summary description I have given. Death does not end history; the individual person is not history. Death is not a meta-historical divine act; it is the common and universal end of the individual person. It has led to a division between individual eschatology and collective eschatology which is nonsense in terms of New Testament eschatology. New Testament eschatology is concerned with the world and man.

Popular traditional eschatology creates a problem because it has incorporated so much of what can only be called mythology. I observe in parenthesis that in calling it mythological I do not imply that it is thereby untrue; many things can be conceived only in mythological terms, and eschatology is one of them. I may say in the plainest prose, "God is judge." I may draw a picture or write an imaginative narrative in which God sits on the throne of the judge, hears pleas, and delivers a solemn verdict. I have added nothing to the content of the prose sentence; I may have made it more vivid and therefore more meaningful. But if I give my picture the authority of a photograph or my narrative the value of an eyewitness, I have given my mythology a reality which it does not possess. There can be a thousand pictures and a thousand narratives in which God is described as judge, and they can all be equally true if they communicate the truth that God is judge.

But mythology, like philosophy, can be true or false. Mythology is always false when the images are conceived as absolute realities — when heaven, for instance, is conceived as absolutely up and hell as absolutely down. It is false when it distorts the reality — if God as judge, for example, were to be presented as an unjust judge. In popular traditional eschatology there is a bewildering admixture of true and false elements which one can scarcely hope to sift through. The Last Judgment as it is usually imagined depends far more on the ingenuity of Christian artists than it does on biblical sources. The vivid imagery of Dante's *Divina Commedia* has contributed much more to the common understanding of eschatology than theological and exegetical thinking. Much of the popular imagery is derived from the apocalyptic literature of Judaism, on which the New Testament Apocalypse also drew.

Mythology is not equally well adapted to all ages; and many modern people have found apocalyptic mythology distasteful. Unable to distinguish the myth from the reality signified thereby, they have rejected the entire scheme of eschatology as a remnant of barbaric superstition. If one does this, then much of both Old and New Testaments becomes meaningless; and one is forced into such restatements as liberal Christianity. The fundamentalist defender of the Bible, on the other hand, is impelled by the liberal doubts to affirm even more stoutly that the myth itself is the reality — that the fire of hell really burns, for example, in spite of some rather obvious speculative difficulties involved. Both parties have reached an implicit agreement that mythology is not a valid process of thought. Here we are assuming that it is.

New Testament Eschatology

The problem, we noticed, is that there are eschatological and noneschatological passages in the New Testament. No one doubts the presence of eschatological passages. The "Synoptic Apocalypse" (Mk 13:5–37 = Mt 24:4–36 = Lk 21:8–36) is thoroughly eschatological. It speaks of the universal tribulations which precede the end of days, of the appearance of the Son of Man in the clouds of heaven and the ingathering of the elect. Matthew (25:31–46) adds the great picture of the Last and General Judgment of all mankind.

A comparison of these passages with the apocalyptic writings of Judaism shows that much of the imagery is derived from these writings. The coming of the Son of Man, the coming wrath, and the coming judgment are themes found frequently enough in the Synoptic Gospels. There is a reward of heavenly bliss for the righteous; and no document of Judaism speaks more plainly of the damnation of Gehenna than do the Gospels. The appearance of the Son of Man is the beginning of the end of history and of this age; the concepts of "this age" and "the age to come" are found in Jewish literature.

The eschatological ideas of the Gospels are found in the Epistles as well. Paul usually speaks of the second coming of Christ as something which can be expected by his contemporaries. In 2 Thessalonians Paul refers to details of the eschatological belief which are not paralleled elsewhere; and we can deduce from this that elaboration of eschatology was a large part of the teaching of the primitive communities. Similarly in 1 Corinthians 15 Paul has the most extended consideration of the resurrection of the dead in the New Testament. The Apocalypse is the most eschatological book of the New Testament, and its imagery is luxuriant. One would think that the mythological character of the end process in the Apocalypse would be so obvious as to need no explanation; yet its quaint myth of the binding of Satan for a thousand years and the reign of the saints for this period (Apocalypse 20) has been taken very literally by some distinguished names in the history of Christian thought.

I have given here a mere sampling of the eschatological themes in the New Testament, because a complete listing seems unnecessary; the presence of these themes is not and cannot be disputed. But the meaning of the themes has been disputed. Even the Synoptic Apocalypse is not as obvious as it seems. It is possible to interpret the entire passage, particularly if one takes Mark, the earliest form of the discourse, as referring to a historical event: the destruction of Jerusalem by the Romans in A.D. 70. The representation of historical events in eschatological images is found in the Old Testament, as we have noticed; and such an interpretation of the Synoptic Apocalypse does no violence to biblical patterns of thought and expression. The other allusions to the end process can be rationalized into the end process of the individual person; for each person death is the final act. A study of the writings of Paul shows that the eschatological theme is much less evident in the later epistles than it is in his early writings; and this has been interpreted to mean that Paul outgrew the primitive eschatology of his early years. The expectation of the Second Coming (the Parousia) grew faint with the passage of time; and it is thought that Paul, with the rest of the primitive Church, gradually came to realize that the Church was to endure for a long time.

The Eschatological Church

The character of the Christian and the Church in the New Testament can be viewed in two ways. Many scholars have argued that the primitive Church thought of itself as an eschatological community. By this they mean that the primitive Church had no consciousness of an enduring destiny. It never thought of itself as more than a small community of the elect which would withdraw from the world and await the Parousia of its Lord. Within the community the way of life taught by Jesus was to be practiced; in the words of Paul, they would proclaim the death of the Lord until he came (1 Cor 11:26). This world was passing away, and the Christian should not take the business of this world seriously (1 Cor 7:29–31).

It must be admitted that this view of the Church can be supported by texts; it must also be admitted that if these texts are made the controlling factor, most of the New Testament cannot be fitted into this view. The ambiguity of the New Testament reflects the ambiguity in the mind of the primitive Church itself; the Church did not immediately reach a full understanding of what it was. When the New Testament is viewed as whole, the understanding of the Church as a tight little unworldly eschatological group huddled in expectation of the coming of its Lord on the clouds seems a vast distortion. I do not personally believe that this represents the mind of any New Testament writer at any time; but I am ready to concede that the fullness of the Christian mission was not seen in its clarity by all early Christians all the time. We shall have occasion to refer to other uncertainties in the minds of early Christians; and we should not be surprised that they were uncertain.

The Eschatology of Jesus

Does this ambiguity reflect any ambiguity in the mind of Jesus himself? The instinctive answer of the believing Christian is a firm negative; and the negative is better supported by the text of the Gospels than the affirmative. Jesus is never represented as being uncertain. If he did not know what his mission was, then no one has ever known. But if the Church felt uncertainty in the understanding of his mission and the mission of the Church, then we must say that his teaching was not so clear that further exploration of his meaning was unnecessary. And there is no reason why we should not think that his teaching was often pitched to the level of understanding of those to whom he spoke. We know that they did not at once realize what he was. Until they realized what he was, they could not understand what the Church was; and the ambiguity concerning the eschatological character of the Church is a counterpart of the ambiguity of their imperfect understanding of the person and mission of Jesus Christ.

John and Eschatology

The Gospel of John presents another complicating factor. John's statements about the resurrection of the body are as numerous and as clear as those of any New Testament writer; but outside of these, the Gospel approaches the noneschatological. Judgment is a frequent theme in John; but the judgment is usually seen as present or even as past. The coming of Jesus is itself a judgment, possibly the judgment. Eschatological imagery is missing; there is no convulsion of nature and of history, no Parousia, no ingathering of the elect. If John, as we have noticed, is the most Palestinian rather than the least Palestinian of the Gospels, these omissions are significant. The Gospel of John was not written as a supplement to the Synoptic Gospels. The background of eschatological mythology is Palestinian; and a Palestinian writer who does not employ it knew what he was doing.

A Problem of Synthesis

Our problem, then, is to make a synthesis which the New Testament itself does not contain; and we should be aware that in synthesizing we may lose some of the elements. If the primitive Church taught in its eschatology beliefs which did not come from the teaching of Jesus himself, then we must say that his teaching has been so distorted that we have no reliable source of it at all. And if, on the other hand, he conceived his community as a purely eschatological community, he was so far out of touch with the realities of history that his teaching becomes irrelevant. Both of these consequences are intolerable; and a synthesis of New Testament eschatology must avoid either of them. If we arrive at either, then this book on the New Testament could be ended here; for there would be no profit in a study of the New Testament.

Eschatological Tension

Let us admit that in the New Testament there is what has often been called a tension between history and eschatology. This tension corresponds to two other terms which have become common in recent theological literature, the eschatological character of the Church and the incarnational character of the Church. In the first of these terms the Church is conceived as tending to a fulfillment which will be reached only in the eschatological process; in the second term it is conceived as having a function and mission in the world. Despite the apparent paradox, both characters must be retained; for both are solidly founded in the New Testament idea of the Church. The emphasis at times falls on one rather than another; in critical moments of history theology turns to the eschatological idea as the only solution of the crises of history. In more tranquil times the Church can be more aware of her mission in the world. The tension in the New Testament is reflected in the life of the Church, which has a fulfillment in the world yet at the same time knows that its fulfillment in the world is not complete and final.

I have observed above that if New Testament eschatological terms are taken too rigidly we find ourselves in a posteschatological era. Yet the theme recurs in the New Testament that the Reign is initiated by the coming of Jesus. We must understand that the Reign has a dimension after him which it did not have before him. He is an eschatological figure in the sense that he is final; and he is final in the sense that he will not happen again. He is not only the word of God, he is God's last word. The New Testament speaks with conviction of the fullness of revelation in Jesus Christ; and the Church has always understood that there cannot be another gospel. He begins the last age; and when this is understood, one feels that the tension between history and eschatology has become more acute.

The Term of Eschatology

The entire course of biblical thinking, in both Old and New Testaments, demands an eschatological term at least in the minimum sense in which I have defined it. In ancient Near Eastern mythology and in Greek philosophical and historical thinking the course of events is an endless chain, a treadmill, or a revolving circle. Ultimately the course of events becomes meaningless as a whole, for it leads to nothing and accomplishes nothing. In this view the individual person becomes if possible even more meaningless. Man lives in history and makes it; and if the story of the race as a whole is a pursuit of nothing, how can the individual person achieve anything? The tone of despair which is heard so often in the literature of Greece and Rome is deep; and if the gospel had nothing to say to this despair, it could not rise above the level of philosophy or the mystery cults. For the men of the Hellenistic age human life was ruled by Fate or Fortune; human life did not make sense and was not supposed to, for Fate and Fortune are personifications of the irrational.

In biblical faith, if God did not rule history, then history is greater than God — which is to say that man is greater than God, and this is to say that there really is no God. God can rule history only if he rules it purposefully; otherwise his rule would not differ from the caprice of the gods of ancient religion or from the irrationality of Fate. His purpose in both Old Testament and New Testament is salvation and judgment. This purpose is executed in each turn of history; in the Bible God is always savior and always judge. But the Reign of God must mean more than the exercise of the will to save and to judge in particular cases; if it does not, then God is engaged in a perpetual struggle with hostile forces which he never wins and never loses. History relapses into the mythological pattern of the cyclic struggle between good and evil, light and darkness, order and chaos. It is a very reasonable view of history, but it is not the biblical view.

The biblical view of God's power and righteousness demands that the powers which resist him must be finally overcome. We observe that the Bible does not attend to the problem implicit in the temporary conflict between God and hostile powers; the assurance of a final victory made further consideration of this problem unnecessary for them. We may be driven to further examination of the problem by our speculative curiosity; but we are here engaged with the New Testament, and we can see that the New Testament faith in God is not satisfied with a partial victory of God. Eschatology is the answer of the Bible to dualism; and it is impossible to conceive an answer to dualism which does not accept some kind of eschatology.

The New Testament idea of man leads with a like necessity to eschatology. No ancient religious or philosophical system arrived at the ideal of human unity which is seen in the New Testament. Modern individualism is not a part of its thought. The New Testament does indeed reveal in an entirely new fashion the dignity and importance of the individual person, and, as we have noticed, it calls for a personal decision; but the individual person does not live in solitary grandeur. He is one of the company of mankind, one of the children of one Father, a member of one body. The New Testament is well aware of the actions of man in society — which is one definition of history. Man must proceed to his destiny as a society; history must reach its fulfillment as history. The New Testament does not view mankind as a stream of isolated atoms falling through a void; and without eschatology, does not human destiny issue in such an atomic stream? The system of Teilhard de Chardin is a new statement of eschatology, although not all of his readers have recognized it. Teilhard sees not only mankind but all of nature converging toward a single eschatological fulfillment. And he means a fulfillment; the process of evolution in his thinking is not an endless process. An endless evolution which never reaches a term is a purposeless evolution; and a purposeless process cannot be incorporated into a theistic view of the world. What I point to here is his vision of nature and of man as one great unity whose fulfillment is found in the perfection of unity. This is exactly the element in biblical thinking which I wish to emphasize here.

The Eschatology of Nature

For biblical eschatology is not only concerned with man. In a striking passage Paul sees the whole creation longing for its liberation; for it too has been in bondage because of man's sin (Rom 8:19–23). The Apocalypse sees a new heaven and a new earth; the author echoes Isaiah 66:22. The eschatological process is more than once described, explicitly or implicitly, as a new creation. For God is Lord of nature as well as of history. He must reassert his dominion over nature, which man has attempted to usurp. The conception is indeed mythological, but it expresses a profound truth. Teilhard has expressed this truth in scientific language which is itself mythological in character. A regeneration of God's creation must include the scene of history as well as the actors. Nature, like man, has not reached its potential fulfillment in the present age; and it remains frustrated unless it shares in man's destiny, as it has shared in his history.

The Incarnation in Eschatology

We turn to the problem posed by the New Testament that the last age begins with the coming of Jesus. Here we do well to recall a biblical conception of history which, as I expressed it in an earlier work, sees the present both as recapitulating the entire past and as implicitly containing the entire future. One may call this way of thinking mythological rather than historical or philosophical, and I have no quarrel with the word. With the coming of Jesus the power which will establish the Reign has made itself known, and its activity has begun. The Reign of God is effectively present. With Jesus fulfillment begins, and history will never be the same. It is at this point that we realize that our categories of eschatology are too rigid for the flexibility of New Testament thought; and we should loosen the categories rather than harden New Testament thought.

We have observed that the purely eschatological Church is not a faithful summary of New Testament teaching. The Church is in the world and for the world, as Jesus himself was in the world and for the world. Its concern, like his, cannot be with the eschatological solely. Jesus proclaimed how men ought to live; and he had no intention that this proclamation should have no effect in the world of men. He was conscious of the dynamism of his person and message. A Church which would live withdrawn in eschatological expectation is hardly a continuation of the life and work of Jesus of Nazareth, who was in the world and of the world as much as a man could be. He illustrated perfectly the principle that one does not win people by refusing to associate with them; and the Gospels relate that in the opinion of the Pharisees he was not selective enough in his associations — in fact, they charged, he liked low company. I remarked above that the primitive Church could understand what it was only when it understood what he was. Possibly it took the community some time to realize that its life was too withdrawn for the followers of Jesus of Nazareth. Whether the Parousia was near or far, they had to do what he did, which was to go to people and proclaim the coming of the Reign. The tension between history and eschatology could not be speculatively resolved. Practically it was resolved by doing what Jesus did, and that was to engage oneself in history. The hour of the Parousia, Jesus had said, was unknown even to the Son — by whom he meant himself. He certainly meant at least that the hour of the Parousia was of no concern and no importance to the Church; and this left the Church no alternative but engagement in history.

The Reign and the Church

And this leads us to the final question I propose here: Is the Reign identical with the Church? Alfred Loisy after his departure from the Church wrote that Jesus proclaimed the kingdom but what came out was the Catholic Church. Plainly Loisy did not think the Reign is the Church; and I trust that it is possible to deny their perfect identity without being associated with the thought of Loisy. In the New Testament the identification is never made. If we understand the two realities at all, it cannot be made. The Reign is larger than the Church. The Church herself is subject to the Reign; and the establishment of the Church is not the eschatological consummation of the Reign.

Yet if the two are not perfectly identical, neither are they perfectly distinct. Jesus came to inaugurate the Reign; the immediate effect of his work was the foundation of the Church. The Church in any hypothesis must have a unique position in the Reign; and I suggest that this position was so entirely unique that the primitive Church did not understand it at once, nor has it always been understood by the later Church. In the hypothesis of an eschatological community the Church was to await the inbreak of God. This the Church found was not its function. The Church was to continue the life and work of Jesus. It must continue the proclamation of the Reign which he initiated, and carry on his teaching. The Church is the eschatological reality in the sense that it is the means by which God has chosen to effect the Reign. Probably it was a shock to the members of the primitive Church to realize that this was their function; it is easier to be the passive recipients of God's acts than to be the agents through whom he acts. It was still more of a shock when the Church realized that the work of Jesus was a sheer work of personal endeavor and personal influence. It believed that he would appear in power and majesty in the Parousia; when he appeared in history he had come as a Palestinian peasant who became a rabbi and who disposed of no other resources than his own toil. More than that, the supreme act by which he established the Reign was his death. Once the Church realized this she could carry on the mission of Jesus. As long as she continues to realize it, she is still able to carry on his mission. She has never been without those who understand the function of the Church.

IV

What Was Jesus?

The titles of Messiah and Lord have been applied to Jesus several times in the preceding chapters. These titles, we noted, were used in the primitive Church; and these titles with a few others closely related express the Church's conception of the person and mission of Jesus. This conception we must study; for — and I apologize for the repetition — we know Jesus only in the proclamation and traditions of the primitive Church. We know what he said of himself only as the Church reported it. If the Church did not tell us what he was, then there is no way in which his true identity can be ascertained.

What single word can we use to describe what Jesus was in the Palestinian Jewish community? He himself once asked his disciples who men said he was, and they adduced various answers (Mt 16:13–14; Mk 8:27–28; Lk 9:18–19). It is somewhat puzzling that all of the answers identified him as a *revenant;* he was John the Baptist or Elijah or one of the prophets. Clearly the Jews could not fit him into the categories of their own religious leaders. Usually he was addressed as *rabbi,* "master," the title of respect given to the scribes; and he was asked questions about the Law and its interpretation which should be directed only to a scribe. Yet he was clearly more than a scribe; he was not a pupil of a scribal school, nor did he own allegiance to any of the scribal traditions. He did not fit the popular idea of the prophet as well as did John the Baptist. The traditional prophetic formulae such as "Hear the word of the Lord," "Thus says the Lord," "The Lord has spoken" were not uttered by him. He spoke with authority, not like the scribes (Mt 7:29; Mk 1:22). We know that the scribes spoke with a certain authority, yet Jesus was considered to speak with even more; and it was probably the tone of authority in his words which led people to think of him as one of the prophets returned. But, unlike the prophets, Jesus did not appeal to the authority of God to vindicate his words.

The New and Unique Position of Jesus

It is not surprising that we also fail to find a word to describe the position of Jesus; for no one had ever appeared in Israel or in Judaism who occupied a similar position. In him all the religious figures and all the religious gifts of Israel merge. In the merging they are transformed from what they were in the Old Testament. Jesus conceived and spoke of his mission in Old Testament terms, but the terms describe a new reality. The novelty contributes to the mystery of Jesus. He remained mysterious to his personal associates, and he still remains mysterious; we have not yet fully understood who and what he was. Who do we say he is?

Jesus pursued the interrogation. Did the disciples share the uncertainty of other Jews? Had their close association with him given them an insight not gained by others? Peter alone answered the question; he addressed Jesus as the Messiah, to which Matthew adds "the son of the living God," a good example of the expansion of a tradition. Peter may have spoken in the name of the group, at least in the sense that he voiced an idea which they all had but which they had not expressed. The version of Matthew seems to single out Peter for this perception, since the blessing of Jesus is spoken to Peter alone. Here Peter applies to Jesus a purely Jewish term. Jesus indeed corresponds to no known religious figure in Judaism; he is the one and incomparable religious figure which has no predecessor and no successor, the person whose coming is the decisive event in the history of Israel. Jesus accepts the title; and he goes on to announce his coming violent death. To understand why Peter was so scandalized we shall have to look at the Jewish title which Peter applied to Jesus.

Messiah-Christ

The titles Messiah and Christ represent one and the same Hebrew word, the meaning of which is *anointed; messiah* is a rough transliteration of the Hebrew word, and *christ* an English form of its Greek translation. In ancient Israel sacred objects were anointed; the rite symbolized their holiness and the presence of God. The anointed person in early Israel was the king; in Judaism the rite was also employed for priests. The symbolism for persons is the same as for objects; it designates them as holy and as persons in whom God is present. The anointing of the king signified his charismatic leadership; through the anointing he received the spirit, the mysterious divine power which enabled him to see more clearly and to act more vigorously. The Messiah is a Hebrew way of saying "the king"; as a technical term it meant the king who would fulfill kingship, and who would bring Israel to its destiny.

The Messianic Idea in the Old Testament

The messianic belief of Judaism in New Testament times is an extremely complex collection of ideas partly drawn from the Old Testament and partly from other sources, the whole appearing in a fluid form which makes it difficult to define. The Old Testament idea itself is complex enough, but we are not dealing with a pure Old Testament idea when we deal with Jewish messianism. The Old Testament basis is fundamentally a belief in the eternity of the dynasty of David, and therefore in a restoration of the dynasty. It is further elaborated by themes of the empire of David and Solomon. The dynasty of David reigned by divine election, and the Davidic king was an adopted son of Yahweh; in these two features the dynasty of David has assumed traits which originally belonged to Israel. Hence the dynasty begins to partake of the eternity of Israel; a restored ideal Israel demands a restored and ideal David. The ideal king does not appear in every literary expression of Jewish messianism; the disappearance of the monarchy had taken away some of the life and color of the image. But it was still a vigorous hope in Judaism of New Testament times.

The King Savior

For a full study of the idea of kingship and its messianic development we must refer readers to books where this Old Testament theme is set forth in detail. The king was a charismatic leader, by which is meant one on whom the spirit reposed. The spirit is seen in the Book of Judges; it is a divine impulse, mysterious in origin and unpredictable in its effects, which moves men to heroism in war. It seizes an ordinary man and endows him with the qualities of leadership. In the ancient world this meant the qualities of the warrior: strength, boldness, and perseverance. It meant less the qualities of intelligence than the qualities of heart and of physique. The leader should be able to overcome in personal combat any man whom he led as well as any adversary. In the charismatic military hero daring and prowess were more desirable than careful planning; the kind of war in which he was engaged could be ended by one bold stroke.

The judge was a temporary emergency leader; when the Israelites chose a king they committed themselves to a permanent leader who ruled in peace as well as in war. Here the qualities of intelligence become important. The king was the administrator and the defender of law. He still needed boldness in execution, but he also needed a discerning heart to decide cases. This and his righteousness equipped him to vindicate the law — for he vindicates rather than administers it — and to establish judgment and righteousness in the land. The establishment of judgment and righteousness is a favorite theme in the descriptions of the ideal king and kingdom. Saul and David were both warriors; when Solomon acceded to the throne, the legends of Solomon told how he asked not for long life or riches or the life of his enemies, but for an understanding heart (1 Kgs 3:5–14).

The Ideal King

From these elements the picture of the ideal king in Isaiah 9:6–7 and related passages is formed. This solidly moral conception of kingship is not always retained in Jewish apocalyptic literature; the warrior king who annihilates the enemies of Israel is often more prominent than the shepherd of righteousness and judgment. This element was strengthened, as we have seen, by the long submission of the Jews to the rule of foreign empires. The true and free Israel could not exist unless it was liberated from these powers; and the liberation would demand a military operation greater than any victory which Yahweh had given his people in the exodus from Egypt and the settlement of Palestine. No one less than another and greater David could lead such an operation.

The position of David as the founder of the eternal dynasty and the ancestor of the messianic king is assured by his place in Israelite tradition. The literary form of these traditions is largely the work of the palace scribes of Jerusalem or of scribes influenced by their work; and the historical David has been transfigured. The transfiguration does not affect the solid historical memory that he liberated Israel from the most serious external threat which Israel had faced up to his time, the Philistines; that he established the first organized government which Israel had known; that by conquest he extended the boundaries of Israel to a point which they reached only during his reign. Of all the kings in Israelite history he most perfectly approached the ideal. One title of the messianic king was "Son of David."

The King and World Empire

It is very probable that the hope of the ideal king grew with the deterioration of the Israelite monarchy. The rise of such a hope is not to be expected as an ordinary development from political events; Israel's unique religious faith was responsible for this as for many other things. The faith of Israel in its own election and in the saving power and will of Yahweh would not permit it to fall into political cynicism with the decay of its institutions. But the hope does not appear immediately. The schism of the monarchy under Rehoboam and the gradual decline of the fortunes of Israel under the two kingdoms did not elicit any messianic response which we can trace in the Old Testament. The decline was not steady enough nor rapid enough to produce the conviction that the monarchy was moribund. Here another historical factor very probably affected Israelite belief; this was the rise of Assyria. The creation of the Assyrian world empire in the eighth and seventh centuries B.C. revealed possibilities which had not been seen in the reign of David. If Yahweh were to establish his king on Zion, he could scarcely be inferior to the great king, the king of kings, the king of Assyria. The messianic oracles of Isaiah display a breadth and magnificence which is not seen in such earlier utterances as the oracle of Nathan (2 Sm 7; Ps 89).

If we believe that the Assyrian conquests affected the idea of the messianic king, what must we think of the creation of the empire of Rome and the peace of Augustus? This was even vaster than the empire of Assyria, and much better administered. The life of the subject of Rome, as we have seen, was in general a better life than the peoples of the empire had known before the end of the civil wars and the accession of Augustus to the principate. The Caesar had become a god; and we do not read in the literature of Judaism the polemic against idolatry which we read in such passages as Isaiah 10 and 14 against the king who arrogates divinity to himself. We rarely find such polemic even in the New Testament; only the author of the Apocalypse is hostile to the Caesar. One may ask what more a messianic king could do than take possession of the Roman principate. In its own way Rome had realized a messianic kingdom; certainly the *Fourth Eclogue* of Virgil is strangely similar to some biblical messianic passages. The men of the first century did not know the weaknesses of the empire as we know them; it had become a cosmic principle, an essential constituent of reality. Probably a less apt historical situation for an announcement of the messianic kingdom never existed.

The Messianic Secret

This is the background against which the words Messiah and Christ in the New Testament must be read. The title Messiah-Christ meant kingship before it meant anything else; and everything suggests that to most Jews it meant nothing else. If Jesus applied this title to himself or allowed others to apply it, he at that moment accepted an identity which it would be difficult to deny or to explain. And the Gospels present him as showing the greatest reserve toward this title. On a basis of proof texts it would be easier from the Gospels to show that Jesus did not claim to be the Messiah than it is to show that he did make this claim. The background of the title makes his reserve quite easy to understand — if, that is, he was not the ideal king which the term in common use designated. Christians have never believed that he was the ideal king in this sense. The problem was to show that in him messiahship was fulfilled and that no other Messiah could be expected.

Over sixty years ago a German scholar, Wilhelm Wrede, wrote an exciting book on what he called "the messianic secret." In Mark (and in the other Synoptic Gospels as far as they depend on Mark) there is a puzzling chain of sayings in which Jesus refuses to allow any announcement of his messiahship to be made. Wrede solved this problem by the neat hypothesis that Jesus never claimed to be the Messiah. The entire idea of Messiah in Christian terms was the creation of the primitive Christian Church. The Church applied this idea to Jesus and explained the absence of such claims in the traditions of Jesus by creating the legend that he suppressed publication of his messiahship, committing its publication to the disciples.

The hypothesis is neat; it solves the problems of the reserve of Jesus. Like most hypotheses in "the quest for the historical Jesus" it solves one problem in a way which makes it impossible to solve all other problems. In particular, it makes it impossible to recover anything about Jesus; it destroys the sources. But Wrede dealt with a genuine problem, and this problem is bigger than the problem of the reserve of Jesus. The primitive Church did proclaim Jesus Messiah in a way in which he had not proclaimed himself. We have said that we know Jesus only through the witness of the primitive Church; to question that witness is to make it impossible to share the faith of the primitive Church. But it is legitimate to trace the interpretation which the primitive Church gave to the person and the words of Jesus.

This author feels a certain repugnance to quoting his own

publications; but I cannot say what follows any better now than I said it when I wrote it, and I beg indulgence for repeating it here (*Myths and Realities*, Bruce, 1963, pp. 239–240):

". . . let us take the theme of kingship. There can scarcely be any doubt, although we have no time to argue the point, that Jesus himself did not emphasize this feature of his mission; if anything, he dismissed it. There are too many Gospel passages which indicate this, in spite of the fact that the early Church did not hesitate to give him the titles of royalty. We have all heard the traditional explanation that it was politically dangerous to claim royalty, and I am sure we have all felt that there is something wrong with this explanation; Jesus as we know him made no decisions on the basis of political prudence. If he had a claim to kingship he would have asserted it. Let us ask whether his dismissal of royal messianism did not come from the inner character of his mission. Kingship, we noticed, indicated an ordered and peaceful society, and Jesus certainly intended to move toward such a society. But he had to deny that such a society is possible by political means; it comes from the inner regeneration of each man. Jesus is the initiator and agent of this process of regeneration; he is the king-savior by offering a principle of salvation more certain and effective than the warmaking and the lawmaking of a king."

The Kingship of Jesus

John alone (18:33–37) has the only explicit claim of kingship recorded of Jesus; and the claim is a disclaimer of kingship of this world. Whether John reports the very words of Jesus here is unimportant; the entire content of the Gospels shows that he reports the very mind of Jesus. Jesus disclaims absolutely any relationship with political power. Political power has nothing to do with the reign which he initiates. The implications of this disclaimer will be treated in more detail elsewhere in this work (Chapter XII); for it seems that Christians have rarely taken these words of Jesus seriously in their full meaning. The kingship of Jesus, like the Reign of God, is not a power of this world. Yet it is a power.

Kingship in the Infancy Narratives

This saying found in John is very probably a particularly good example of the way in which the primitive Church framed its record of Jesus so as to answer questions explicitly which he had answered implicitly either in his person itself or in sayings which did not treat the question directly. There are other passages which are also examples of the interpretation of the Church; and these are less evidently spiritual in their presentation of the kingship of Jesus. The reader of the Gospels can scarcely miss the fact that allusions to Jesus as Messiah-King are more common in the infancy narratives of Matthew and Luke than they are elsewhere in the Gospels. The infancy narratives create a number of critical and exegetical problems which are too many and too complex to be treated fully here; but we may notice that if these narratives are taken as rigorously historical they raise a problem of "the messianic secret" compared to which Wrede's formulation of the problem is nearly trivial. That which was sensationally proclaimed before a larger public in the infancy narratives is concealed during the public life. Even the uncritical reader feels vaguely that there is something wrong here; but he dismisses it, because the Bible is expected to have its own universe of discourse.

The purpose of the infancy narratives was less to satisfy the curiosity of the primitive Christians about the early life of Jesus than it was to proclaim his kingship; and here we must put these narratives into a larger theological background. How much of a living memory was there of the early years of Jesus? This question cannot be answered. The picture of Luke sitting at the knees of Mary with his notebook in his hand is long established in popular tradition; it should be noticed that this picture has no justification in history. And one who reads the narrative of Matthew and Luke and compares them closely will have to ask himself where Matthew drew his information, if Luke drew his from Mary. Superficial harmonization here is more difficult than it is elsewhere in the Gospels. In addition, there are other historical problems which are not yet solved; and the student who wishes to go into this question deeply must acquaint himself with these problems. We have as yet no census which can be identified with the census mentioned by Luke; and a census is not to be postulated out of thin air. We have no way of combining the census with the datum of Matthew that Jesus was born before the death of Herod the Great in 4 B.C. It is hard to explain why Josephus, so deeply hostile to Herod, should not have the story of the massacre of Bethlehem; Josephus was not so dedicated to pure fact that he could not have repeated the story without implying anything favorable to the Christians. It is also hard to explain why Matthew says nothing of a residence at Nazareth before the birth of Jesus. I mention these problems rather than solve them; but a historical analysis of the infancy narratives is impossible unless they be met.

For our purpose here we can view the theological purpose of the infancy narratives, which is much easier to apprehend. In every one of the infancy anecdotes Jesus is proclaimed Messiah and King. He is revealed as the one promised in the Old Testament; in him the promise of the eternal dynasty is fulfilled. Whatever may have been the memories upon which these narratives were composed — memories not used by Mark — they have been unified into a single theological statement. Under the statement of messiahship and kingship is included the statement of the virgin birth and of the absence of human paternity; Jesus is a man, but not a purely human figure. He is the natural son of the Father.

Eschatological Kingship

We ought to look for some reason in the life of the early Church why this statement was thought necessary and useful; and we have the background which gives us the reason. The Church proclaimed that Jesus was King Messiah in a way in which he did not proclaim himself; his kingship was eschatological. Faithful to his own teaching, the Church disclaimed any political involvement. But it affirmed that the Reign of God would be fulfilled under the kingship of Jesus. Indeed, the Church found the title of king too narrow for the power of Jesus; it preferred the title "Lord." This was a part of the titulary of the Caesar, and a title of several gods of Hellenistic religion. St. Paul could write that although there are many gods and many lords, for us there is one God, the Father, and one Lord, Jesus Christ (1 Cor 8:5–6). The title of lord conveyed an idea of absolute and unlimited sovereignty which "king" no longer conveyed in the Hellenistic world. In addition, the Greek word *kyrios* is the usual translation in the Septuagint of *Yahweh*, the personal name of the God of Israel; the popularity of the title in the early Church can scarcely have been unrelated to this. Where the Old Testament speaks of the day of the Lord, the New Testament speaks of the day of the Lord Jesus Christ.

We have observed that this kingship is eschatological, by which we mean that the fullness of power is revealed and exercised not in history but in the eschatological process which terminates history. To confess that Jesus is Lord is an act of faith for the Christian; when Jesus appears in power the confession will be compelled. The power is not yet manifested; for it is better that men should confess his lordship by faith than that they should be overwhelmed by majesty. The lordship of Jesus illustrates the tension between history and eschatology of which we have spoken. Jesus is fully Lord in history; the eschatological manifestation of his lordship adds nothing to his power. But his power operates in history in a more subtle way; it is revealed in his coming in the flesh, and it is experienced by those who believe in him. That history restrains the exercise of his power is not conceived by the primitive Church; and thus the Church escaped certain theological problems. The one passage where the point is almost raised is 2 Thessalonians 2:6–8, and there it is clear that the writer, however he conceives the process which he so obscurely describes, does not conceive it as a limitation of the power of God manifested in Jesus Christ.

Lordship and Resurrection

The Church, we have said, proclaimed Jesus Lord in a way in which he had not proclaimed himself; and it was aware of what it was doing. It conceived his lordship as being actualized in his resurrection and glorification. I say "actualized" rather than "revealed," for the language of the New Testament here does not readily fit the categories of recent theology. St. Paul wrote that Jesus was "designated" or "constituted" Son of God in power by his resurrection from the dead (Rom 1:5). No one can seriously think that Paul believed that Jesus "became" Son of God by his resurrection, and this is not what he wrote. But he did not write "revealed" either; it is clear, although he uses an obscure term, that he thought of Jesus as receiving something by his resurrection. What he received was the exercise of lordship in a way in which he had not exercised it before. He has overcome death, the ultimate restraint of all human power; his power is more than human. But the exercise of power is not yet entirely fulfilled, and will not be until he delivers the kingdom to God the Father after destroying every rule and authority and power; then all things are subject to him, and he to the Father (1 Cor 15:24–28).

Transformation of Gospel Narratives

It is unnecessary to heap up texts to show that Jesus is confessed as Lord in the New Testament; I have cited these texts of Paul because they show the historical-eschatological tension, and because they exhibit the idea of growth in the lordship of Jesus. Now the Church did not think that Jesus was ever any less than the reality which was fully revealed in his death and resurrection; and it is in affirming the identity of Jesus of Nazareth and Jesus, Christ and Lord, that the transformation of the Gospel narratives is most evident and most frequent. Jesus is confessed as Lord in the anecdotes of his words and deeds, although the lordship was not recognized at the time the incidents occurred. In this transformation the infancy narratives find their situation in life. It is almost as if the primitive Church anticipated modern discussions about Jesus' "discovery" of his messiahship; the infancy narratives affirm that he never discovered that he was King Messiah, that he had never been anything else but King Messiah. He had not merited his position; it was his by eternal nativity. There was never a time when his lordship was not visible to the eyes of faith; but his appearance in the flesh was an obstacle to faith, in particular to those who looked for the conquering King Messiah of popular belief. It was a tragic fact by the time the infancy narratives were written that Israel had not recognized its King Messiah.

The Lowly King

One may adduce one action of Jesus himself which was related to his kingship; this was his entrance into Jerusalem for his final visit to the city. His disciples and others acclaimed him as son of David and spread palm branches on the road which he traveled mounted on an ass. The acting out of Zechariah 9:9 was evident:

"Rejoice greatly, daughter of Zion! Raise a cry, daughter of Jerusalem!

"See, your king comes to you; righteous and victorious is he,

"Lowly and riding upon an ass, upon a colt the foal of an ass."

The key word in the text is *lowly;* in postexilic Judaism this had become a technical name for the devout. But it signified primarily a social state or class, the class of the impoverished masses. The king of Zechariah is one of these, not a great lord. Jesus could act out this text, because it described a feature of his kingship which he need not treat with reserve. He was no less King Messiah when he appeared as lowly; and he would not appear as King Messiah in any other traits.

Lordship in History

When we say that the Church viewed the lordship of Jesus as eschatological, we must not forget the tension so frequently mentioned. That would be no very effective lordship which was not exercised and manifested; and the Church intended to affirm that Jesus is Lord in reality, not merely in the confession of the Church. How, then, did the Church conceive his lordship in history? The complete answer to this question cannot be given at once; and much of what follows in this book will be expositions of the effective lordship of Jesus in history. Here we can sketch the outline into which details will fall.

Jesus Savior

The king in the ancient Near East, which includes Israel, was a savior. This was conceived in a twofold manner: by victory in war he delivered his people from external enemies; and by the administration of law he delivered his subjects from oppression by the powerful within his realm. By both activities he established righteousness; for the righteous man is not only the man with a righteous cause, he is a man whose cause is vindicated. The ancient Near Eastern ideal of the deliverer persisted in the title Savior (Greek *sōtēr*) applied to Hellenistic kings and to the Caesar, and to some of the gods of Hellenistic religion.

Savior as a divine title has an implication which is not seen in the Old Testament use of the word as a royal title. The savior god is in the first place a healing god; and the title is given most frequently to Asklepios, whose shrine at Epidaurus was a place of pilgrimage for the infirm in a way which suggests modern shrines like Lourdes. This aspect of salvation is not unrelated to the salvation effected by the king; but kings were not credited with healing power. There is no doubt that Jesus is called savior with reference to healing; but this is not the only sense in which he was believed to save. His healing, as we shall see in more detail, was only one work of the power which was manifest in him.

A constant theme of the Old Testament is the power and will of Yahweh to save. The nature of the salvation is rarely specified; it can be summed up as deliverance from the external and internal evils which menace life in an ordered society. In the ancient world the monarchy was the only ordered society known; and thus Yahweh is often called king of Israel. The Israelite king is an instrument through whom Yahweh saves. When Jesus is called Savior, the power and will of Yahweh to save are revealed in him. In him also is revealed the nature of the salvation which Yahweh achieves. In a single phrase, it is salvation from sin and death. It is not merely the preservation of life, it is the beginning of a new life. The evils from which the ancient king saved his people were rooted in something too deep to be reached by the royal power. When Jesus delivers man from the radical evils which afflict him, he renders all other evils impotent to harm. Salvation is not merely the removal of evil; it is solidly founded on the creation of a new reality.

This is the basis of the title of savior which the Church gives

Jesus. It is an entirely new and original conception of a word which is extremely common both in the Old Testament and in other ancient sources. Jesus Savior simply ignores the things to which men cling as ideals of salvation. He neither promises nor delivers political independence, good government, external and internal peace, prosperity, and security. The salvation worked by Jesus is, indeed, not indifferent to these things; he does not deny that they are good and that man suffers when they are absent. He never implies that they should be sought or even that they can be attained. If man reaches all of them, he is still not saved. If he is saved from sin and death, all these other things will be added; if he is not saved from sin and death, he is saved from nothing.

Jesus is Savior from sin and death both by a single act and by an enduring activity. The saving act, as we shall see, was his death and resurrection; the enduring reality is his presence in the Church. For the salvation which Jesus works is not received passively by those who are saved; it is entirely the work of God and not of man, but those whom Jesus saves are not carried helpless. The salvation of Jesus is reached by each individual person in a personal act. The individual must accept salvation; and he must deny that there is any other name under heaven by which man is saved (Acts 4:12). When one accepts the salvation of Jesus he rejects all secular saviors and all secular ideas of salvation; he puts all his trust and all his security in one savior. The saving act of Jesus is communicated each time one believes and is baptized; the Christian is not saved merely by recalling the memory of a past event, but by sharing in the living experience of the event.

Saving Power

The essential note of lordship is power; if Jesus is Lord, he must have power which is effective. The Gospels mention his power frequently; he speaks with power and he performs acts of power. We would indeed like to recapture in imagination the power with which the Gospels have invested his words; but even if we do we may not catch their meaning. The power of the words of

Jesus was not the psychological power of a compelling personality and persuasive speech, although we can easily imagine these things as present. It was the power which in the Old Testament is attributed to the word of God and to the word of the prophet, the power to effect that which it signifies. It was the kind of power which the Jews believed that the Law had, the power of God communicated through human speech. When Jesus spoke with power, it meant that his words were imposed upon his listeners. One who had heard Jesus speak had come to a moment of decision, and he could never be the same again. To the power of Jesus even nature yielded; and the agents of evil — disease, sin, and death — retreated before his speech and before his presence. We shall see in more detail what this power meant in the thinking of the primitive Church (Chapter VI). Despite its roots in the Old Testament, the power which is revealed in Jesus is new; neither its magnitude nor its direction were known until it appeared in him.

This power, we have said, is new; it is entirely unlike the popular idea of power. It is not political or military; and in the ancient world scarcely any other power was recognized. It was not a power which showed itself in cosmic disturbances. Jesus is represented as a wonder-worker; but the Gospel narratives do not create the impression that he was a fearful figure in this respect. One should compare the miracles of the canonical Gospels with those of the apocryphal Gospels in order to appreciate both the restraint of the former and the pathetic efforts of the latter to surround Jesus with an atmosphere of terror. This atmosphere he never created. His power was a power to save, not to terrify. Against the powers of this world he could appear helpless, as he did in his passion; Paul wrote that power is perfected in weakness. That the passion was an exhibition of power is a truth which the primitive Church did not perceive immediately; until it did, it could not grasp the true nature of the power of Jesus. Power in the vulgar sense is recognized only in a clash; power proves itself by winning a fight. The power of Jesus does not engage in fights; he is himself the supreme example of his own precept not to resist evil. He is also the supreme demonstration that evil is overcome by not resisting it; nothing he said or did implies that the application of power against evil has any effect.

King Judge

There is one more function of kingship which the Church attributed to Jesus; this is judgment. In the Old Testament judgment means something different from what it means in our culture. To us judgment is primarily a legal function. The Old Testament knows judgment as a legal decision; but it sees it primarily as the vindication of the righteous cause. The prayer "Judge me" is a petition for vindication, not for judicial review. In the Christian faith Jesus is the judge of the living and the dead, and this article of faith is explicit in the New Testament.

Matthew (25:31–46) alone has a scene which can be called a general judgment. The scene is symbolic to a high degree; and the passage is less a description of a judgment than a statement that the decisive factor in man's life is his treatment of his fellow men. It is a parable, much like the other parables in the same chapter. Yet this chapter has been responsible for a considerable amount of Christian art and literature on the last judgment which can only be called mythological, and that not in the good sense of the word. The judgment of God should not be likened to the riot after a football game; and this is what some Last Judgment scenes resemble. I trust the judgments of God are dignified as well as righteous. A similar mythology exists concerning the Particular Judgment, in which each man is summoned before the bar immediately after death.

The judgments of God are not legal processes, whatever they are. God is not subject to law, and he needs no examination of the evidence. His judgment is a vindication of the righteous and a condemnation of the unrighteous. Christian imagination has fastened on the aspects of reward and punishment with a delight which is sometimes morbid. A serious discussion of how the blessed can enjoy the torments of the damned leaves one speechless; we had thought that the kingdom of heaven would at least exclude barbarism, and would not be likened to a celestial Colosseum where it is the infidels and not the Christians who are thrown to the lions.

The judgment of God through Christ is a final establishment of righteousness. We do not know what this means because nothing in our experience corresponds to it. Nor do we know what participation in this dispensation means to the individual person. It means, in the words of St. Paul, that all things are subject to Christ, and Christ to God. More than this God has not revealed to us. The judgments of God in the Bible are indeed terrifying at times; in the Old Testament his judgments include things like the deluge, the fall of Sodom and Gomorrah, the sack of Jerusalem and Nineveh. Are these complete and full expositions of God's judgment? In the New Testament Jesus Christ is King Savior and King Judge. The novelty of the New Testament conception is that these two roles become one; he does not cease to be savior when he becomes judge. For the final establishment of righteousness is salvation, the only salvation for which man can hope. The Christian does not wish to escape judgment, he ardently desires to experience it. No man can hope for anything better. Judgment is vindication.

Judgment in John

The tension between history and eschatology appears in the Gospel of John and its treatment of judgment. For in this Gospel judgment is a present reality. The world and the unbelieving Jews are already judged, and they are not judged by a process ending in the pronouncement of a sentence. Jesus himself is judgment and judge merely by his appearance. When men encounter him they face a decision which cannot be evaded; and their own decision is the judgment. John is strangely free of eschatological imagery, as we have noticed (Chapter III); and it is particularly evident in his conception of the judgment. To refuse faith is to choose sin and death, and in John's language scarcely anything more seems necessary for the judgment.

God and Man in Judgment

This Johannine idea of the judgment allows us to draw some of the elements of the judgment together. Judgment is an act of God, an act by which he ends the conflict between good and evil. The judgment may operate in a particular moment of history; the eschatological judgment is demanded because the conflict cannot be endless. But judgment is also an act of man. Judgment affirms man's power to make a decision which is permanent and irrevocable. It affirms his power to act as a kind of pseudo creator, forming a world which is built according to his plans and specifications. If he builds such a world, it is his own work and not the work of another; and he must accept the responsibility for it. Man's cooperative effort to erect the city of this world is a matter of record; when he does it, he has made a judgment — the judgment of himself. Judgment can indeed be terrifying; but it is the power of man to destroy which is the most terrifying aspect of judgment.

V THE SERVANT OF THE LORD AND THE SON OF MAN

Jesus the New Israel

In the preceding chapter we have looked at the titles of King, Messiah, and Savior; and we have seen that these titles do not fully answer the basic question: What did Jesus proclaim himself to be? The title of Messiah was so deeply transformed that it needs much closer definition before it can be applied to him. Jesus himself did not leave what he was in obscurity; it is known in the witness of the Gospels and in the witness of the primitive Church. But what he proclaimed himself to be was obscure in the sense that it was paradoxical, difficult to apprehend and to believe. The transformation of the idea of King Messiah is only a part of his proclamation of himself; we must look at the new idea which emerged. This idea was not so new that it had no roots in Old Testament belief at all; but it is not the most prominent theme of the Old Testament, and it was a theme which received little attention in the thinking of Judaism.

As an introduction to our theme we may consider a feature of the mission of Jesus which is not exactly proclaimed either by him or by the primitive Church, yet is fundamental to the understanding of what he was. The Gospels show deliberate and careful efforts to present him as the new Israel, who in his own person brings to fullness the religious gifts and the destiny of Israel. By fullness we mean that in him Israel accomplishes all that it can do and all that God commissioned it to do. Israel endures in him and in him only. No doubt many interpreters are right when they see in this presentation an effect of the Christian proclamation to the Jews and of the polemic which ensued, some of which is recorded in the Acts of the Apostles; the relation of Judaism to Christianity, as we shall see more fully (Chapter X), was a central theme of the proclamation of the Gospel. But these interpreters are less surely right when they say that this counterposition to Judaism is entirely the work of the Church and does not arise from the words of Jesus himself. If Jesus did not think of himself as the fullness of Israel, then his memory has been so distorted that it is idle to wonder what he really was.

Jesus as the new Israel is presented in some arrangements common to all the Synoptic Gospels. The most striking parallel between Jesus and Israel is seen in the narratives of the baptism and the temptation. Like Israel, Jesus passes through the water and sojourns in the desert; the forty days correspond to the forty years. Like Israel, he is tempted; unlike Israel, he resists the tempter, and in each encounter the tempter is foiled by a quotation from the Pentateuch, the book of Israel's law and the history of its beginnings. Matthew has an emphasis on this theme peculiar to himself. Jesus begins his teaching upon a mountain, an echo of the proclamation of the Law on Mount Sinai. His Gospel is arranged in five divisions which suggest the five books of the Pentateuch. Jesus, like Israel, goes to Egypt and returns. John also has a peculiar emphasis in the account of the multiplication of the loaves; this miracle is the miracle of the manna of the New Testament, the bread of eternal life.

Jesus, then, reveals to Israel what it is; in him it recognized its true self. The entire Old Testament is the account of the striving of Israel toward a future fulfillment which is never more than dimly discerned. Jesus announces that the Reign of God has come, and this is the fulfillment. To Israel is put once again and finally the question which had been addressed to it by Moses and Joshua and by the prophets: will it submit itself to Yahweh or will it go after other gods? The other gods were not, in this decisive hour, the gods of Hellenistic or Oriental paganism; they were the more specious gods of the law and the traditions, the temple and the cult. Jesus challenges Israel to become itself.

Corporate Personality

What happens when Israel becomes itself? Here we turn to a theme which is of the highest importance in the interpretation of both Old and New Testaments, and which we shall meet several times again in the course of our exposition. The theme, set forth with clarity and persuasion by H. Wheeler Robinson thirty years ago, is the idea of "corporate personality." This is not a uniquely Israelite idea; it can be discerned in other ancient Near Eastern peoples and particularly in the ancient idea of kingship. Jesus retained this one element of the idea of kingship. Corporate personality means that a group is incorporated in the personality of its leader. The ancient king was the state and the nation. In him the people acted and suffered. His will was their will, his achievements their achievements, his failures their failures. His power was absolute, not in opposition to lesser powers within his kingdom but simply because there was no opposing power within the kingdom. Practice may not always follow theory, especially when the theory is not articulated; but everything suggests that ancient Near Eastern peoples accepted absolute monarchy because they identified the king with themselves. If the identity was relaxed, then the monarchy was in danger.

In the Old Testament the idea of corporate personality can be seen in the stories of the patriarchs. Abraham and Jacob each embody in his personality and character and even in the episodes of his life the ideals and the history of Israel. The people who sprang from them were foreshadowed in their persons; what Israel was to be was determined in outline in them. For the plan of God was harmonious and uniform, and he moves history in such a way that his purpose can be recognized, even if it cannot be comprehended. "Israel" was a definite reality from the moment of God's election of Abraham, and it was a reality which could be perceived as such in those who bore the election and the promises. For the author of the epistle to the Hebrews Levi paid tithes to Melchizedek through Abraham, for Levi was in the loins of Abraham when the encounter occurred (Hebrews 7:9–10); and so was all of Israel in the loins of its ancestors. The patriarchs and Israel form a community; and the community already exists in the patriarchs.

The idea of corporate personality can be seen in David also. David is first of all the person in whom his dynasty is incorporated; each of his successors is a continuation of David as the king elected by Yahweh, adopted as the son of Yahweh, and the heir of an eternal dynasty promised to David. The ideal king who will consummate the line of David, the King Messiah, is described in terms which echo the reign of David. David is the incorporation of Israel also. Yahweh establishes a covenant with David and his dynasty as he established a covenant with Israel; and in the literature of the kingdom of Judah the covenant with David tends to replace the covenant with Israel. If the people is covenanted through its king, it needs no covenant of its own. David represents Israel before Yahweh as he represents Israel in battle.

Hence when Jesus appears as the personal incorporation of Israel, he calls Israel to that peculiar union with himself which is seen in the ancestor and the king. Israel must become Jesus; his will must become the will of Israel, his character the character of Israel. Israel must identify itself with him and his mission. It must accept and follow his dedication. This is the supreme decision of Israel, for if it refuses this vocation it has no other vocation to which it can turn. This decision is not a decision to continue being what it was. We have observed that Jesus falls into no category of religious figure which can readily be recognized. His coming is something new in the history of Israel; it changes the course of Israel's history as the appearance of Moses changed it. Moses was the man through whom God created a people for himself; Jesus creates the people anew.

If Israel had to identify itself with Jesus in order to survive, then it had to see who it was with whom it must identify. If Jesus was a new religious figure, he nevertheless had to be described in terms which Israel could understand. These could not be the terms of Hellenistic or Oriental religion; had he presented himself in such terms, Israel would have been faithful to its traditions in rejecting him. The terms in which Jesus presented himself were Old Testament terms; and the first of these we may consider is the title of Son of Man.

The Son of Man

That this title had a peculiar force for the Jews is clear from the frequency with which it appears in the Gospels. That it was intended to have a peculiar force is clear from the fact that it is used in the Gospels exclusively by Jesus himself. It is absent from the epistles; the title was so definitely Jewish that it could not be used for Christians of a Hellenistic background. Here, it seems, the apostles of the primitive Church had a problem which is related to the problem which modern scholars have; for we have not yet fully understood this title, and the apostles did not know how to translate it. But we feel obliged to seek an understanding of the title; for if there was any title which Jesus used as characteristic of himself, it was the title of Son of Man.

There is a linguistic problem which we must mention, although we cannot solve it. In Aramaic, the language which Jesus spoke, the phrase "son of man" is the only phrase which designates an individual human being. In English the noun *man* can be used both of the race and of the individual. Hence the Aramaic phrase could mean "the man" or "this man" as a polite circumlocution for the first person. If this were the only use of the title, there would be no sense in seeking out the background of the phrase in biblical and extrabiblical literature. But when one tabulates the use of the phrase in the Gospels, one finds that the phrase is more than a circumlocution for the personal pronoun; for it is used in quite definite patterns.

Son of Man: Old Testament

The Old Testament background of the phrase is sparse; the passage which attracts attention is Daniel 7:13–14, translated thus in the Revised Standard Version:

"And behold, with the clouds of heaven
there came one like a son of man,
and he came to the Ancient of Days
and was presented before him.
And to him was given dominion
and glory and kingdom,
that all peoples, nations and languages
should serve him;
his dominion is an everlasting dominion,
which shall not pass away.
and his kingdom one
that shall not be destroyed."

The most commonly accepted interpretation of this passage sees in the son of man a personification of the people of Israel; the reign which is given Israel is identical with the Reign of God. The passage thus falls into the pattern of which we have spoken in the preceding chapter. If the son of man is thus understood, then the title indicates that Jesus here also presents himself as the new Israel. The dominion of the passage is clearly eschatological, not political; and the passage is in harmony with the eschatological kingship which, as we have seen, is the only kingship associated with Jesus in the New Testament (Chapter IV). Were this all, the passage would offer no more difficulty than other messianic passages of the Old Testament. It seems unnecessary to illustrate the term by the appearance of the title "son of man" in the Book of Ezekiel as an appellative by which the prophet is addressed; in Ezekiel certainly the term indicates the humanity of the prophet, but there is no other connotation which is echoed in the New Testament.

Son of Man: Enoch

But this is not all. The title is used in the apocryphal Books of Enoch of a superhuman savior figure not personally identified with Israel, "the Elect One, whose name is at present concealed, but who is destined to be revealed as the Judge of men and the Messianic Ruler in the Kingdom of God" (Vincent Taylor). The popular eschatological messianism of the Books of Enoch is in opposition to the eschatology of the New Testament in almost every point. If Jesus intended to present himself as the Son of Man described in these books, he would have obscured his mission by elements which could not be assimilated. We do not know how widely the ideas of the Books of Enoch were circulated; we have no reason to think they were so commonly known that the term would suggest the Messiah of Enoch rather than anything else.

Son of Man: New Testament

The New Testament uses of the title fall into three groups. The largest group speaks of the Son of Man coming on the clouds of heaven; this element of the Parousia comes from Daniel. The

smallest group uses the title in connection with the power of
Jesus to forgive sins and his authority over the Sabbath. The third
group uses the title in connection with the human condition of
Jesus: his homelessness, his ordinary manner of life, his associations with the common people. The most striking use of the title
is its recurrence in allusions to the passion and death. In John's use
of the title the passion and death are merged with the glorification
of the Son of Man in a way peculiar to John.

At first glance these three groups do not appear to be entirely
homogeneous. Interpreters have often asked themselves whether
the glorified Son of Man coming on the clouds represents the
words of Jesus himself or the interpretation which the primitive
Church placed on his words. If they are taken in the latter sense,
they fall into a pattern which we have discussed in the preceding
chapter. The second and third groups are more easily assimilated;
the proclamation of power which Jesus uttered demands treatment by itself, which it will receive later in this exposition
(Chapter VI), but the power to forgive and authority over the
Sabbath are not unrelated to the power which is seen in the third
group of texts. For it is in his passion and death that Jesus exercises
his power to save, and it is through his passion and death that he
acquires the fullness of his eschatological lordship. Jesus identifies
himself through this title as a man among men, and it is as such
that he must be accepted. The title excludes all secular and
political messianism, as it excludes any display of power except
the power of the Spirit. Whatever Jesus achieves, he achieves by
actions which do not issue from any human resources other than
the basic resources of human nature. To identify oneself with
Jesus one need be no more than a human being.

The title implies that there are no privileged persons in the
group which identifies itself with Jesus. He reduces all existing
differences to nothing, and in this sense truly creates a new humanity. He places the full potentialities of identity with himself
within the reach of every person. To realize these potentialities
one needs neither wealth nor status, not even the freedom of the
citizen as opposed to slavery. The possession of power or its lack
mean nothing. I spoke above not only of the humanity of Jesus,
but also of his human condition; for this is reflected in the title of

Son of Man. Jesus was a Palestinian villager of undistinguished family; efforts to make him an aristocrat of Davidic descent are pathetic. He was an aristocrat in the same way in which every Irishman is a scion of kings. He belonged to the overwhelming mass of the poor who formed over 90 percent of the population of the Hellenistic world. The universe of his parables is the universe of the lowly toilers. If one identified oneself with Jesus, this is what one was invited to be; and this is the genuine meaning of his words, "Learn of me, because I am meek and humble of heart" (Mt 11:29). This meekness and humility is the attitude of those who because of their lowly station and their lack of wealth and power cannot afford the luxuries of pride and aggressiveness; they are always at the mercy of those who are more powerful than themselves.

The Suffering Son of God

These implications are worked out in much greater detail in the New Testament, and we shall have to return to them; but they are suggested by the title of Son of Man. The title, combined with Jesus' manner of life, was sufficient to identify him. When we turn to the third group of passages, we see that his mission and destiny were the only mission and destiny within the reach of a "son of man." When Jesus used the title in connection with his passion and death, he merged the title of Son of Man with another Old Testament theme found in Isaiah 53. This is the theme of the Suffering Servant of Yahweh, as it is usually called; "slave" renders the Hebrew word more accurately. There is scarcely any passage of the Old Testament about which so much interpretative literature has been written in recent years; this interest is in contrast with the nearly total neglect of the passage in the rabbinical interpretations of Judaism of the New Testament period.

The Servant of the Lord

The passage describes a person of unknown identity who suffers on behalf of others, although he himself is innocent; and by his sufferings those for whom he suffers are relieved from affliction. The discussions of this passage have ranged about the identity of the person in the mind of the author; and here no satisfactory unanimity has been reached. I share the opinion that the writer intended no historical figure, but an ideal figure who would realize the destiny of Israel through his suffering and death. To call such a figure the Messiah is a slightly inaccurate use of the term; Judaism knew no Messiah except the King Messiah. More to the point here is the question whether the prophet intended an individual or a personification of collective Israel, for there are clear indications of both. This question is resolved by the view that the prophet intended the corporate personality, the individual in whom the people are recapitulated; and I believe that this is the only correct interpretation of the passage.

The number of allusions to this passage in the New Testament is difficult to count; many of the allusions are fleeting. But they are enough to establish the thesis that this passage had a central position in the proclamation of Jesus. No other passage can be intended in such lines as Luke 24:26, where it is stated that the Messiah had to suffer and so to enter into his glory. A mission of achievement through suffering and death was as obscure and distasteful to Jews and Greeks as it has been to men since the primitive Church; and the primitive Church found it necessary to base this proclamation on a clear biblical source, which showed that the mission of Jesus was planned and willed by God. Both for Jews and Greeks the proclamation of the Suffering Servant was a negation of some of their highest values. To Jews it was an annihilation of the King Messiah and the messianic Reign of God; and to Greeks it was a denial of the values of mind and courage on which Greek ethics reposed.

The early Church attributed the proclamation of this theme to Jesus himself; and no convincing reason has been urged to show that it should be attributed to another. It is as deeply imbedded in the Gospels as anything else; to repeat what we have said in other connections, if this theme is not the work of Jesus himself then we know nothing about his words or his person. Those who think that it was a rationalization by the early Christian community of the disaster which had overtaken their master have scarcely reflected that whatever the Suffering Servant theme is, it is not a rationalization of anything. It is the peak of faith in the Old Testament, the supreme affirmation of the power of God and the weakness of man. If this rationalizes, then the term "rationalize" needs a new definition. When we meet the theme of the Suffering Servant as proclaimed in the New Testament, we are at the very center of the Christian revolution.

The Saving Death

That suffering and death could be saving was not unknown in Greek philosophy and poetry. Both Greek legend and Greek history exhibit stories of men who died on behalf of their city and their people. The poems of Homer have a mystique of death and battle which reflects the temper of the heroic age; one senses the same mystique at the Arc de Triomphe or the War Memorial of Edinburgh or the cemetery of Gettysburg. The Romans too had their legends of heroes who died defending Rome. The Old Testament is less in touch with the heroic age; one may see something of the heroic attitude in the stories of Samson. But when Saul and Ahab die in battle, they are already men doomed by their rebellion against Yahweh. The nobility which men attach to death in these circumstances comes from the exhibition of courage in combat. The most touching death in Greek literature is the death of Socrates as related by Plato; but this is not seen in the same way as the death of the three hundred at Thermopylae. The death of Socrates was a monumental injustice and it is not seen as anything else. Not even of Socrates could it be said that he opened not his mouth like a lamb that is led to the slaughter (Is 53:7). It was not a part of a divine plan of salvation. The death of Socrates proved that a philosopher could preserve his serenity of mind even when he was faced with death inflicted unjustly; it was an example and nothing more, and it was not even an example except for the small intellectual minority who were capable of philosophical thinking.

By all the standards of the ancient world, Hellenistic or Jewish, the death of Jesus was miserable. Compared with the death of Socrates it is neither dramatic nor dignified. Plato represents his hero as engaged in sublime flights of philosophical speculation until the moment when he takes the hemlock — surely a quiet and decorous manner of execution, thoroughly as Athenian in its classic simplicity as the Parthenon or the Zeus of Phidias. Except for the affirmation of his innocence and of the genuine messianic quality of his mission, Jesus goes through his passion and death in nearly total silence. There is no heroic combat against great odds; Jesus dies with the passivity of the condemned criminal. By no stretch of the imagination can the passion episodes be called dignified; and the authors of the Gospels make no attempt to conceal the spectacle. Rather they appear to have tried to show that, as far as it is possible, the scene is devoid of any elements of human dignity and decency. Perhaps if we say this we credit them with more subtlety than they possessed. The simple and totally objective tone of the narratives shows that, whether by plan or by circumstance, everything conspired to make the death of Jesus an episode in which the dignity of man was reduced to its lowest possible level.

One can scarcely find fault with Christian art for casting about the death of Jesus a fine hazy glow of romantic beauty. Efforts to present the scene realistically have not been well received by Christians; and realism may fail to portray the truth of the scene as much as romanticism. The Gospels are realistic, but they are scanty in details; and painting is made up of details. The essential truth of the death of Jesus was not perceptible to the eyewitnesses; and a photographic reproduction would show us some naked men crucified and nothing more. Art has attempted in its own way to show that realism misses the point of the scene entirely; whether in trying to penetrate into the meaning it does not misrepresent the scene in its own way is another question. Whether Paul would have said of art what he said of rhetoric (1 Cor 2:1–2) I cannot tell; but the analogy is persuasive. The death of Jesus was not romantic; but we understand it no better if we fasten our gaze on its cruel realism. The death of Jesus was not morbid, although the external scene approached the morbid more nearly than it approached the romantic. It is recognized as true, good, and beautiful only by an act of faith.

The Saving Act

We are not considering here the fullness of the redeeming death; this will demand our attention later (Chapters VI–VII). We are trying to see the theme of the Suffering Servant in something like the way in which the disciples and the primitive community saw it; and they saw it as the theme which revealed the true identity of Jesus. By his suffering and death he accomplished the mission of deliverance which in Jewish faith was the work of the King Messiah — more properly, of God through the King Messiah. As the Suffering Servant Jesus is not the conquering king, not the prophet or sage, not the lawmaker; he is the Son of Man confronted with the realities of the human condition. He does not achieve his deliverance through war and conquest, through preaching and teaching to large numbers or to small, through the establishment of great and lasting organized institutions; he achieves his work through sharing deeply in the common experience of man. When Jesus suffered and died, he experienced nothing which millions did not experience before and after him. He achieved unique success not by being different from other men, but by being entirely like them.

What, then, gave his suffering and death its unique merit and value? We think, of course, of the merit and value of his person; we think of him as the Son of God. But this truth seems to obscure the value of his death rather than illuminate it. For if suffering and death are irrational in the human condition, which they are, they are even more irrational in the Son of God. St. Paul called the passion an emptying of self (Phil 2:7). When we think of the death of the Son of God, we deepen the mystery more than we explain it. Nor should we be so foolish as to attempt to explain it; but we ought to understand as well as we can its meaning for our own human existence. And there is no inner connection between the divine sonship of Jesus and his passion and death; there is, on the contrary, a baffling antinomy which invites us to seek more light on the meaning of the event.

The Necessity of Suffering

The Son of God was not subject to suffering as the Son of God; he was subject to suffering only as the Son of Man, the title which Jesus himself associated with his suffering. The Gospels show that Jesus spared no effort to prepare the disciples for the shock of his passion and death, so contrary to all their messianic beliefs. But how did he prepare them? He did not propose a philosophy or theology of suffering which would make it rational and intelligible, or even more tolerable. He simply affirmed its necessity. His coming death was not presented as an escape from suffering; and he taught the disciples that he offered them no escape from suffering through their association with him. To become identified with Jesus was to become identified with the Suffering Servant; and he who could not deny himself and take up his cross was not worthy to be a disciple. The secular and political messianism envisaged by so many Jews, including the disciples themselves, was obliterated by these instructions. Perhaps obliteration is too strong a term; the New Testament itself is evidence that the disciples were slow learners of this lesson. But Jesus certainly left no room for false messianism in the new Israel of which he was the corporate personality.

The Human Condition

As the Suffering Servant Jesus experienced nothing, we have noticed, which is not a part of the human condition. And he thus placed his achievement within the reach of all men. Those who identify themselves with him cannot share his divine sonship except by adoption; but they can share his human condition. Suffering and death are the normal human condition. Jesus does not ennoble them, but he makes them the means by which man is liberated from sin and death. Those who accept the human condition with him share in the redemptive act, the saving act of God. He demands nothing which is not within the reach of every man of every age. The ultimate futility in the life of unbelieving and hopeless man becomes the means of the ultimate fulfillment of the human potential. The deliverance of man is not to be accomplished by an act which can be shared by only a few. It is accomplished by perfect identity between Jesus and the race which he incorporates in himself. He meets man in the common destiny of all men.

The Cult of Suffering

There has long been a tradition in Christianity which has cultivated a mystique of suffering for its own sake; or so it appears to those outside the mystique, and they include most men. Many Christian ascetics have sought fuller identification with Jesus as the Suffering Servant by the deliberate refusal of pleasure and the deliberate infliction of pain on themselves. A morbid form of this asceticism keeps pleasure from others and inflicts pain on others. The number of venerable names associated with this tradition is alarming; and one questions it at the risk of appearing to be a lover of the good life. Nevertheless, it is open to misunderstanding, to say the least; and it can leave those who are unable or unwilling to engage in asceticism with the fear that they are underdeveloped Christians. The extreme forms of this asceticism, such as the Flagellantes and the Penitentes, have been rejected by the Church. But the people who hear of these sects and of their condemnation sometimes feel uneasy; they wonder where the difference lies between these sects and the saints who scourged themselves to blood, rolled in thorns, fasted to near starvation, and performed other such excesses. The difference, of course, is not in what the penitential sects did but in what they did not do. They make it clear that the mere cultivation of pain does not assure identity with Jesus the Suffering Son of Man. We speak of suffering and death because they are the concrete manifestation of the mystery and power of evil, and because no one lives who does not face them. We see that Jesus has made these irrational elements of life the means by which man realizes his destiny and shares in the saving act of God. We must also point out that mere animal pain does not save. Identity with Jesus suffering is first of all identity with Jesus loving, to put it in a single word.

For this reason I have preferred the term "human condition" to designate the suffering of Jesus. Writers have sometimes attempted to show that Jesus suffered more than any man who ever lived; they appeal to his delicate sensibilities, which they assume he had. It is difficult for us to realize how ordinary the life of this extraordinary person was; and I believe that until we do realize it we shall not fully realize his identity with us. But to the subject of his sufferings: he seems to have enjoyed excellent health and a reserve of physical strength equal to the ordinary, if not notably above it. He exhibited a finer emotional balance than any person known to history. He had enemies; but he also

had friends and enjoyed their company. He had an eye and an
appreciation for natural beauty and for the homely comforts of the
quiet life. He had no family problems of the dimensions which so
many must face. The pains of his passion, which we dramatize,
were routine in the harsh world of the first century. The Gospels
do not present us with a man whose every breath was painful; they
show us a sturdy peasant who recognized and used his wit and
eloquence, who enjoyed usually good human relations. Jesus did
not cultivate pain and did not need to cultivate it; he accepted
the human condition, and with it the inevitable pains which man
encounters. There is nothing exquisite about his life or his sufferings. It disturbs us that he could live so normally and so sublimely
all at once. The weakness of exaggerated asceticism is that it
implies that the life of Jesus is not quite good enough for the
Christian who wishes to identify himself with Jesus. This writer
confesses to a nearly immoderate admiration of Teresa of Avila,
who united holiness and good sense to a degree which is as
precious as it is rare. It is this happy blend which has always made
it difficult for me to understand how she could think that the
motto "To suffer or to die" was a faithful echo of the prayer,
"Father, let this chalice pass from me." Jesus suffered; but there
is nothing in the Gospels which indicates that he liked it.

Pain and Love

For it is a manifestation of the demonic in man that he can
make even of the passion a substitute for the basic and far more
demanding obligation of love. That a mystique of pain is possible
needs no demonstration; that it has nothing to do with the presence or absence of love likewise needs no demonstration. It is not
a legitimate deduction from the Gospels that pain is simply better
than pleasure. For many people pain is a greater spiritual danger
than pleasure. The passion is a share of the saving act only if the
entire saving act is shared. The mystique of pain is particularly
obnoxious when the law which makes the cultivation of pain the
supreme Christian heroism is erected into a law in which the
spiritual man governs the choice of others, denying them pleasure

and inflicting pain on the sheer plea that it is good for them. This attitude is without any support in the New Testament.

The cultivation of pain as a positive spiritual good is an exaggeration of the Gospel; but it remains true that Jesus demands that his disciples identify themselves with him as the Suffering Servant. If we reject the cultivation of pain for itself, we do not thereby adopt the cultivation of pleasure for itself. We shall see that the renunciation which Jesus imposes cannot be combined with the cultivation of pleasure. The saving act is accomplished through suffering, not through pleasure. The point I make here is that suffering is not incorporated into the saving act on its own sheer merits. The attitude of Jesus is ultimately simple and easy to apprehend; one is associated with the saving act through the suffering and death which are one's portion of life. One need seek neither pain nor pleasure; life affords enough of both. If one identifies oneself with Jesus, one need only follow the course which this engagement sets.

Salvation Through Suffering

Salvation through suffering has become such a conventional theme in Christian theological and ascetical teaching that it seems impossible to add anything to it. But we must make the effort; for each generation and each Christian must experience this truth for themselves. And it is worth remark that the practical faith of Christians in salvation through suffering is rarely equal to their speculative agreement to the principle. The habitual search of the Christian is directed to salvation through something else than suffering. We have noticed that Jesus lived an ordinary life, and that he made no effort to alter the conditions of that life. There were more social and political abuses in the Hellenistic world than we believe there are in our own country and our own times; about these Jesus said not a word. He was not silent because he was indifferent to the suffering which such abuses entail; his mission was not directed to save man from political and social abuses, but from something deeper which is the root of these abuses. Man need not await the removal of such disorders to achieve salvation;

he can achieve it within a disordered system. The proclamation of
the Suffering Servant, we have noticed perhaps too often, negated
political and social messianism. Has this negative been always
accepted by Christians?

Political Messianism

There have been and there are Christian species of social and
political messianism, and we can assume that there always will
be. Once Christians attain control of social and political means,
they feel that these means ought to be Christianized, that they
ought to be directed to the purpose of the Church. One cannot
decently quarrel with the effort to replace the unbelieving state
with the Christian state, the unbelieving social and economic
order with the Christian social order. But one ought to look closely
at such institutions; neither the state nor the social order is Christian just because most of the people engaged in them are Christians. And one can ask seriously that we reflect on what we have
achieved if we achieve a Christian state or a Christian social
order; this question is so important that we must return to it
later (Chapter XII). This much is clear; if we do these things, we
have not achieved salvation through suffering, we have not identified ourselves with Jesus the Suffering Servant, and we may possibly be attempting to escape this fulfillment of the saving act.
We may be attempting to establish the Reign of God by means
other than those which God has revealed to us. We may commit
our personal responsibilities to institutions and organizations. Assuming that a Christian state and a Christian social order are
possible — an assumption which has not yet been validated —
what force would they add to the Spirit dwelling in the Church
which is the Body of Christ? Would they exorcise the demonic
in man which makes salvation through suffering the awful necessity
under which man lives? Would they help him to bear his suffering
by identifying himself with Jesus the Suffering Servant?

The Scandal of Jesus

The quite ordinary life of Jesus remains the great stumbling
block, a part of the scandal of the cross. All the possible deviations

which I have mentioned come from one source, the Christian suspicion that what Jesus himself was and did is not enough for the Christian. We feel that we must attempt something more, and something more here must be something different; and quite often this something different will be something other than suffering. Or if it is not something different, it must be something exquisite, even exotic. I realize, of course, that such devices are beyond the reach of most Christians; but, as we have noticed, the idea of a spiritual elite can leave those outside it with the feeling that they are mediocre Christians by definition. As long as these misunderstandings persist, we have not grasped the gospel of the cross, and to that extent we have not shared fully in the saving act.

Jesus did not give us what we really ask: a rational explanation of the existence of suffering, and a demonstration how the terrible waste of human resources which suffering involves really contributes toward the fulfillment of man. He said that the Son of Man had to suffer; he did not say why. He accepted it and made it the medium of salvation; but he left it mysterious why this is the only means by which the saving act can be accomplished. His own death illustrates better than anything else his principle of not resisting evil (Mt 5:39). That evil is overcome by nonresistance has been comprehended by very few Christians. These few were convinced that Jesus presented in his words and life not only a good way of doing things, not only an ideal to be executed whenever it is convenient, but the only way of doing what he did. They did this in pure faith, because there is no reasonable motive for acting in the way which he shows.

The themes which we have encountered in this chapter, we think, answer the question of what Jesus was. The answer was novel in Judaism, and it is still novel in Christianity; for it is never so well understood that its meaning is exhausted. The new Israel must be an Israel which is an instrument of the Reign of God through its suffering. This is the declaration which removes all ambiguity from the messianic mission of Jesus. It removes all ambiguity also from the mission of those who call themselves his disciples. They know to what they are called; they do not know how they accomplish that to which they are called; but if they are one with Jesus they do not really need to know.

VI THE SAVING ACT OF JESUS

The Old Testament and the Gospel

We have reviewed the titles of Jesus in order to see in what character he appears in the gospel; and we find that he is the suffering Son of Man who through his resurrection is revealed as Messiah and Lord. We must now look more closely at the nature of the saving act which he performs; for this saving act is the key to the way of life which Jesus communicates to men. The saving act of the Servant in Isaiah 53 is vicarious suffering of the innocent; through his suffering the guilty are healed from their unrighteousness. The writer of Isaiah 53 shows no insight into the mysterious bond between the innocent sufferer and the guilty for whom he suffers, nor how the suffering of the innocent becomes efficacious on behalf of the guilty. The gospel supplies these missing elements, and reveals the fullness of the healing and saving act.

The whole background of Old Testament history and prophecy is presumed in the gospel. The Old Testament can be summed up as the documentation of the sinfulness of man. It is the story of the encounter of Israel with God, an encounter in which God is more and more fully revealed as righteous and man is more and more fully revealed as wicked. The disasters of Israel arise from Israel's refusal to submit itself to the will of God; and ultimately man is proved helpless in the face of the evil which he himself has wrought. He has no hope of recovery or of survival except in the saving act of God. This is the basic flaw in man, his tragic fault; and no other cause can be assigned to explain the tragedy of the human condition. Man cannot deliver himself from sin —

which is to say that man cannot deliver himself from himself. He must become something other than himself if he is to live.

Judaism and St. Paul

The sense of universal guilt was deepened in Judaism. St. Paul in particular, a true disciple of the rabbinical schools, begins each exposition of the saving act of God with allusions to the sinful condition of man, whether Jew or Gentile. To St. Paul we owe the somewhat difficult passage in Romans 5:12 ff. in which the guilt of man is traced back to the beginnings of the race; for Paul more than any other New Testament writer speaks both of the universality of guilt and of man's helplessness in his guilt. All the New Testament books show the desire to convince men that they are in need of deliverance, and of deliverance from sin, not from something less than sin. They all show likewise the desire to convince men that there is only one deliverance from sin, and that is Christ Jesus. The first two chapters of Romans are a classic expression of this theme. The summary description of the religion and morality of the pagan world (Romans 1) discloses an atmosphere so sordid that it is depressing. But Paul did not exaggerate; he said nothing which cannot be documented from contemporary sources. Nor does he spare the Jews, in spite of the fact that Jewish morality was far more elevated than Hellenistic morality. The sins of the Jews were more subtle and more easily concealed by self-righteousness; Paul said no more about the Jews than we read in Matthew 23, where Jesus utters a terrible indictment against the Pharisees. The account of the internecine strife in Palestinian Judaism during the Jewish War found in the history of Flavius Josephus is a shocking story of the collapse of the most elementary humanity within the Jewish community even toward its own members. All have sinned, wrote Paul (Rom 3:23), and lack the glory of God.

Sin and Death

In Romans 7 Paul continues and expands the theme of man under judgment. Here he personifies the two enemies, Sin and

Death, who dominate man. Within the very nature of man there is a law of Sin which issues in a condemnation to Death. Against these two enemies there stands Law, the Law of Judaism, impotent to deliver man from Sin and Death, and indeed only making man's condition worse by imposing obligations which man cannot meet. The association of Sin and Death runs through much of the exposition in Romans. For Paul no other demonstration of man's hopeless condition is needed than man's mortality. The sinner is doomed, and every man dies. There can therefore be no real deliverance unless it delivers man from the hostile twins, Sin and Death. This deliverance is effected by Jesus Christ alone.

From Paul's exposition there emerges the awful necessity of deliverance through death. In a striking line he writes that God made "him to be sin who knew no sin, that through him we might become the righteousness of God" (2 Cor 5:21). When Jesus is made sin, he by that very fact is subject to death. He is made sin by his humanity; nothing else is required to put him under the curse of death. But when Sin and Death consume the innocent, they overreach themselves and lose their power. Sin and Death can rage among men because this is their proper field of operation; but when they attack him who knows not sin, they put themselves into his hands. The thinking of Paul here is so imaginative that it approaches the mythological; and in what other terms could he think of the mystery of the saving will of God? A merely philosophical exposition was not within his power; nor would it be adequate.

Saving Power

The saving acts of God throughout the Bible are inbreaks of divine power. The Old Testament in many respects is the heir of ancient Near Eastern mythologies, even though it transforms them. In these mythologies the cosmos is seen as a power struggle. There is unceasing conflict between light and darkness, order and chaos, life and death, good and evil. In the myths the struggle is perpetual, because neither pole of force is ever completely victorious; nature runs in cycles, and one cycle elicits the next. The Old Testament shares this view of the cosmos and of human history as a power struggle; it shatters the myths by its affirmation of the supremacy of light, order, life and good over darkness, chaos, death, and evil. We have seen that the eschatological interpretation of nature and history affirms this belief (Chapter III). The saving act of Jesus Christ is the beginning of the eschatological act of power.

But the idea of power is transformed in the gospel. The theme of power is more subtle than many other themes; a study of a concordance will show that it recurs more frequently than we notice in a casual reading. The person of Jesus is endowed with power, and his words are power. The conception of miracle in the New Testament is primarily a conception of power; and the Greek word for "power," *dynamis*, is the common word in the Gospels for the events which we call miracles. Neither in Old Testament nor in New is there any idea of miracle as an event which surpasses the laws of nature; for the Bible has no idea of laws of nature. Wonders were readily accepted in the Hellenistic world; the temple of Asklepios at Epidaurus had its votive tablets with testimonials of cures more wonderful than those related in the Gospels. A wonderworker of the first century A.D., Apollonius of Tyana, is the hero of legends in which fantastic miraculous powers are attributed to him. The New Testament writers credit the Jews with possessing powers of exorcism like those of Jesus. A modern apologete would deny the historical reality of such wonders; the primitive Church would regard this as unimportant. These wonders are not exhibitions of the saving power of God, and therefore they are meaningless. The miracles of Jesus are exhibitions of the saving power.

The Power of Jesus

We have noticed that Paul pairs Sin and Death as the powers hostile to man and to God. The inbreak of the saving power in Jesus attacks these. Wherever illness and death strike man, they are the work of Sin and Death. Whenever Jesus heals or raises from the dead, the powers of Sin and Death are rolled back. Each healing is an exorcism; for the diabolical power of Sin and Death is manifested when men suffer physical infirmity. The Gospels accept the popular belief of the connection between Sin-Death and physical suffering, indeed they emphasize it; for the popular belief expresses a theological truth which is central in the gospel. This is the truth that man's basic sickness is sin and nothing else. The appearance of Jesus reveals the power that will destroy sin and death. The final defeat of Sin and Death is eschatological; but already Sin and Death suffer defeat when they encounter the saving power. Less frequently in the Gospels the power of God in Jesus operates on nature; for nature also is unredeemed.

The power revealed in Jesus is always beneficent, and this is to be noticed; the power is not only revealed, but it must be recognized for what it is. The power of Jesus is not used on his own behalf nor on behalf of his associates. In the passion accounts we see the wonder of the primitive Church at the utter freedom with which Jesus surrenders himself to hostile powers. "Resist not evil" they remembered as his words. The beneficent power which he wielded could not be used even in self-defense. He would have been unfaithful to his own teaching and example if he had employed what is called legitimate self-defense; and no one has yet arisen to say that Jesus was not better entitled to legitimate self-defense than any man who ever lived. The use of his power for this purpose would have denied the whole course of his life up to this point. It is not coincidental that Luke relates the final exhibition of the saving and healing power in the arrest of Jesus (22:51), a detail missing in the other Gospels; but all agree that the power of Jesus in the passion was fully manifested as a power to save and not to destroy.

The Power of Love

For the power revealed in Jesus is a new power, not conceived in these terms even in the Old Testament. The power which destroys all other powers is the power of love, the love of God revealed and active in Jesus Christ. Where the Jews might have expected an apocalyptic display which would shatter kingdoms and shake the heavens, God revealed in Jesus that he loves man and will deliver him through love and through nothing else. Hosea *may* have written: "I led them with the cords of man, with the bonds of love" (11:4); the text of the verse is extremely difficult. Whether he did or not, we can take our lead from the traditional text and observe that the power revealed in Jesus is a humane power as well as divine power. It commands a humane response. To power in the vulgar sense one renders submission, admiration, obedience, and other such responses; the response to the love revealed in Jesus must come from the person, and it must come with utter freedom. The power of love has its own way of action, and it is not the way of compulsion. One would think that this revelation would have expelled compulsion from the Christian community once and for all.

The Power of Communication

The power of love is not the power to dominate but the power to communicate self; and the response is communication, tending toward complete identity. The incarnation is God's communication of self in Jesus Christ. Jesus said that he came not to receive service but to give it (Mt 20:28; Mk 10:45), and the supreme service, his own life as a ransom for many. "Ransom" has beguiled many interpreters into thinking of an exchange which is more commercial than amatory; a vigorous metaphor is misunderstood when it becomes a metaphysical principle. The life of Jesus was the price he paid for full identity with men; unless he shared the common human portion, he could not be in all things a man. He experienced even the reality of sin, for he lived in the sinful human condition which issues in death. All metaphors break down when one attempts to formulate this communication of self in proper language. Ultimately one always returns to the aggressive movement of the love of God toward its object.

For the response of communication is what brings man within the reach of the saving act; man loves God who loves him, and he is thereby saved. This may seem to oversimplify the process of salvation; but it does not oversimplify the process any more than the New Testament does. There is, however, an element in the response which needs reaffirmation. Man cannot love God in response. This object of love is above his powers, and man in his sinful condition is alienated both from the love of God and from the love of his fellow man. The saving act must enable man to do what is beyond his powers. Jesus is the communication both of the love of God for man and of the love of man for God. We have said that God finds identity with man in Jesus Christ; it is the identity of Jesus with man which enables man to respond to the love of God.

Union With Jesus Christ

For it is clear in the New Testament that salvation consists in union with Jesus Christ; this idea is so fundamental that the exploration of its fullness will occupy much of our exposition. The love of God which is beyond the power of man becomes possible when man identifies himself with Jesus Christ. We return to the idea of corporate personality; man can do in Jesus what he cannot do by himself. The power which breaks into the world in Jesus is communicated to all those who become one with him, and it continues active in them. Identity with Jesus Christ means in the first place that the Christian shares in the saving act which Jesus performed; and now at last we must look more closely at what this saving act was.

The Atoning Death

Paul wrote that Jesus was put to death for our trespasses and rose for our righteousness (Rom 4:25). The second half of this sentence has usually been less understood than the first. We can understand that one dies for another; this is a type of heroism more common than we know, and we esteem it. The hidden trap in this apparently facile explanation is that we may reduce the death of Jesus to mere heroism, if one will pardon the expression; and then one does not know what to do with his resurrection, which is easily and insufficiently explained as a repair of injustice. The death of Jesus was more than a good example, more than a ransom, more than satisfaction, more than a sacrificial offering; all these phrases, some biblical and some nonbiblical, are efforts to interpret the saving event. They do not express its fullness, and this exposition will not express it either; some things defy expression. But we can attempt to bring out some biblical elements which have received less attention; and the first of these is that the saving act is death-resurrection, not "the redeeming death." For the saving act is more than redemption and forgiveness of sin, more than atonement; and these are elements which we associate with the death.

Let us observe first, although it may not seem to follow from the observations just made, that the saving act of Jesus is an act of love of the type which he recommends in the Gospels; he loves God by loving his fellow men. He accepts their life and submits himself to their mortality in order that they may be delivered from Sin and Death. Theologians distinguish the "Godward" and "manward" aspects of the saving act, and such distinctions are useful in avoiding philosophical misconceptions; but the New Testament does not use such distinctions. The saving act is all Godward and all manward; it moves to God by moving toward man, as Jesus tells his disciples they also must do. And he leaves no room for man to move toward God except through his fellow men. The saving act is unitive; it establishes man in a new community of which God himself in Jesus Christ is a member. There is a subtle Christian logic in John 13:34: "A new commandment I give you, that you love one another as I have loved you"; and in 1 John 4:11: "if God so loved us, we also ought to love one another." A more reasonable logic would conclude: ". . . that you love *me* as I have loved you," and "If God so loved us, we also ought to love *him*." And this we would conclude, were not the New Testament so insistent upon its own logic.

The Death of a World

And from this we begin to see why in St. Paul the death of Jesus is the end of an era, the end of a way of life — in its own way the end of the world. Death is the death of the old man, the man of sin. For the basic sin is the refusal of love. The division of our eras into before Christ and after Christ has a deep theological basis. That the old world dies slowly is a theological and spiritual problem which can cause anguish; we who live in a world of quiet perpetual terror can be tempted to ask whether the saving act has truly saved. I think St. Paul would not share our terror. He was convinced of the victory of Jesus over Sin and Death, of their final defeat which is now being accomplished. A new power has entered the world, and that power is dominant; it is the power of love, and against love Sin and Death are helpless. One could despair only if Christ had died and not risen. It may be tediously repetitious to say once more that we experience the tension of history and eschatology, but it seems the only thing to say. If we do not believe in the death of the old man of sin, we really do not believe in the death of Jesus.

I observed in the first chapter that the Roman Empire was for the men of its time a cosmic rather than a political force, a component of nature. We possess a book written by an heir of Roman civilization who witnessed the beginning of its collapse: *The City of God* of St. Augustine. He is one of a number of splendid examples of Christians who blended genuine Christianity with their citizenship in the Roman state, now Christianized. The collapse of Rome and the visible prospect of a world turning barbarian were a dreadful shock to men like Augustine. For them it was the end of the world, the world which they knew. Very few men have taken the trouble to write a work of two fat octavo volumes to restore and reaffirm their faith; Augustine did. He would be no stranger to our quiet terror; *The City of God* is evidence of his own private hell. He was able to see that Rome was not a cosmic force, that the world and man would outlive Rome, that the Reign of God was eternal and the reign of Rome a mere phase of history. He achieved the rare insight that the collapse of Rome was the death of the old man of sin; and his solid Christian faith enabled him to see that life comes from death. *The City of God* is not the most widely read of his works, and it is strange that it is not; it has a very contemporary tone. We have not yet realized as well as he did what the death of the old man of sin can involve. It is more than a merely personal affair.

The Personal Revolution

But it is a personal affair. St. Paul is insistent that the saving act means a complete revolution in the personal life of the Christian.

What can the Christian retain? Paul's dearest possession was his Judaism. We read his words that circumcision and the law profit nothing more casually than he wrote them; he knew that to his own people he was the great renegade, fit to take his place in Jewish history with Ahab, Manasseh, and Jehoiachim. When Paul spoke of the death of the old man he knew that of which he spoke. For the old man of sin is not an entirely hateful fellow; he has many lovable traits, and he clutches some of the things we value most. We do not know how much we love them until the old man is threatened with death. The death of Jesus is more than the death of sin, as we have noticed; it is the end of a way of life, the end of a world, and one cannot be sure that anything will escape. The adage "Grace builds on nature, it does not destroy it" is true but by itself misleading; for what is nature? A practical working definition, I suggest, would be that nature is those things which we have persuaded ourselves we cannot do without. Yet for centuries Christian ascetical writers have been telling themselves and their readers that nature reduced to the destitution of Jesus Christ is capable of salvation. What is the scandal of the cross, except that it reveals how total the death of the old man is?

The Death of the Past

The words of Jesus in the Gospel make it so clear so often that a man must leave his past behind him that they need no express quotation. This does not mean, of course, that the Christian literally pulls up all his roots at once — although there are many who have done just this. It means that he allows nothing in his past, his cultural situation, his involvements in family, social, political or economic life to inhibit the act of love, the love of his fellow man in Jesus Christ. A list of the accepted inhibitions of love would be familiar and tedious; we can mention race, nation, property, job, ambitions, the duty of supporting one's family — or perhaps in one word, the duty of protecting the investment. It is not easy to see that the investment may be precisely and without doubt the old man of sin to which we must die. We know that "death" here is a metaphor; but the metaphor is biblical, and while we ought not to lay on metaphors more than they can bear, it does seem that phrases like "spirit of detachment" are rather feeble substitutes for "death."

The Death of the Flesh

I have not discussed the more obvious meanings of the death just because they are obvious; the Christian knows that in Jesus he dies to such things as murder, adultery, theft, and covetousness. Yet Jesus took some pains, as he is quoted in the Sermon on the Mount, to show that a narrow understanding of these grosser vices is not what he came to teach. Nor, we think, did he come to teach by how narrow a margin one may approach these vices and still be identified with him. St. Paul spoke of the other law, the pseudo law of the flesh, which wars against the Law of the mind. It is the next thing to an article of faith that man cannot achieve perfect sinlessness; but it is worth noticing what Paul says about the law of the flesh. He is delivered from the body of this death (Rom 7:24–25). The law of the spirit sets him free from the law of sin and death (Rom 8:2). God has condemned sin in the flesh, in order that the just requirements of the law might be fulfilled in us (Rom 8:3–4). A careful reading of the entire passage (Rom 7–8) shows that St. Paul conceives the death of the old man of sin in more vigorous terms than we are accustomed to do. The personal revolution means that a life governed or even notably motivated by carnal desires is ended; and I do not use carnal desires, as Paul did not, in the technical restricted sense of desires for sexual pleasure. The flesh in Paul is the principle of desires which we can sum up as human: motivated, that is, by human and secular goods with no reference to the Reign of God. In the death of Jesus the flesh dies.

The Power of the Resurrection

Up to this point we have considered the first of the two elements of death-resurrection, the element which we said was the easier to apprehend — and to misapprehend. We return to the idea of power. The power of love is seen in the death of Jesus; it is seen more fully in his resurrection. For love is a communication of self; and the Christian is not identified with God in Jesus Christ unless he is identified with Jesus risen. Death is the end of a life and of a world; the resurrection is the beginning of a new life and a new world. If Christ has not been raised, you are still in your sins (1 Cor 15:17). The Christian shares the saving act; he dies with Christ, he rises with Christ. Only then is he fully identified with Christ. For Christ lives. The life of the Christian is not the imitation of a dead hero — and it is worth noticing that it can become just that. The Christian lives in Christ, and Christ lives in the Christian.

The theological value of the resurrection, it must be confessed, has been somewhat obscured by its apologetic value; the resurrection has become the major weapon in the apologetic armory. On the hypothesis that we need apologetics, this is a useful treatment of the resurrection; but it is not the New Testament use. The resurrection of Jesus is attested entirely by a few chosen witnesses; the risen Jesus did not reveal himself to the same public which had known the historical Jesus — if I may use the term here. If Jesus had wished an apologetic demonstration, a public manifestation would certainly have done it; and it would have made the task of the apologete much easier. The resurrection is the climax of the saving act, and it must be seen as such before anything else. It is an object of faith before it is an object of demonstration.

Jesus Living in the World

The resurrection is, we said, the beginning of a new life and a new world; and the first element we may notice is that it is a world in which Jesus is living. The revolutionary point in the Christian event is the enduring presence of God's love in Jesus Christ, the enduring presence of the power which entered the world in the incarnation. This presence is associated with the Spirit, and to this theme we shall have to return (Chapter VII). Jesus living is the incarnate Reign of God. We touch once again the tension between history and eschatology, for we cannot make of the living risen Jesus a historical factor. Faith in him is still faith and not reason. But the primitive Church believed that he lived and that the world had entered upon a new era because of his presence. It believed that the course of events had begun which would issue in the subjection of all things to the Son and of the Son to the Father (1 Cor 15:27–28). And the Church which is one with the primitive Church must live in the same faith, confident that in the power which lives in her the Church can do what she has to do. And what she has to do is no more beyond the reach of mere human power now than it was for the primitive Church.

A New Life

The resurrection is the beginning of a new life. Christ raised from the dead will not die again; death no longer has dominion over him (Rom 6:9). The life of Jesus risen is a new life; he is established in the glory which belongs to him. The Christian who shares his risen life is also free of the dominion of sin and death. The Christian, of course, does not become immortal; but death has dominion over him no more than it had over Jesus himself. The Christian is liberated from the fear of death; death is not, as it was to the men of the Hellenistic world, the final frustration of all human endeavor. The Christian has a principle of life which is proof against death; his life, like the life of Jesus, has permanent value. Because he is identified with Jesus he can intend a lasting achievement. The resurrection is the creation of a new human life; it is a reenactment of the story of Genesis 2. God again breathes into man the spirit of life (Gn 2:7), but this is the spirit of eternal life. It is a new beginning. The past, as we have seen, is wiped out. The potentialities of man are no longer inhibited by the dominion of Sin-Death.

The new life conferred upon man is the life of Jesus. We have noticed that Jesus was an ordinary man among ordinary men; at the same time his life reached a sublime level. He has enabled any man through incorporation into himself to render human life sublime at any social level. The new life does not depend on those factors which make human life more or less respected in the world of convention. Incorporation into Jesus Christ renders all merely human factors supremely unimportant. The power which was revealed in Jesus is communicated to all his members without respect to their social or economic standing. Because of this power, man is enabled in any condition to live the life of Jesus and to continue in his own person the love which is the saving act.

The New Power of the Christian

The Christian who receives the new life must not measure his potentialities by the standards of the old man. We know that the natural man is capable of nobility, even of heroism. Men who live by the ethics of reason and nature have often put believing Christians to shame. We must confess that when this happens Christians have not lived up to their capacities. Unless the Christian is enabled to rise above the ethics of reason and nature, Christ has risen in vain. The power of love is beyond the capacity of the natural man. This is the power, we have seen, which overcomes sin and death; this power the Christian has, and he must recognize that he has it. To say that this power is impractical in any given circumstances is to say that there are circumstances in which Jesus could not have been himself.

This new life, we have said, is independent of the social or economic status of the Christian. It is also independent of the historical situation of the Christian; and here the tension between history and eschatology is resolved. The Christian is no more dependent on these external factors than was Jesus. Jesus lived as a Galilean peasant; but one cannot imagine him in another situation in which he could have fulfilled the potentialities of life in a better manner. Had Jesus announced a new stratification of society he would have announced nothing new. And so the life which he communicates is revolutionary in this also, that it annihilates all differences among men. The primitive community seems to have accepted this novelty more fully than the Church has succeeded in doing since. Yet if it is not accepted, then some Christians are by that very fact deprived of the new life which Jesus confers. No one is better equipped by nature or by state to be a member of Christ than anyone else. Jesus was criticized because he liked low company; his followers have sometimes succeeded in rising above this criticism.

The saving act of Jesus is an act of atonement through which man is granted forgiveness of sins. This is done through the mystery of solidarity; because God has identified himself with man through Jesus Christ man can be forgiven. And it is as an act of atonement that the work of Jesus is most easily seen. But when we think of the saving act as death-resurrection, we see that the act goes farther than atonement and reconciliation. The union of the Christian with Jesus risen confers upon the Christian powers beyond the powers of nature. The fundamental power conferred, as we have seen, is the power of love; here we must reflect on the fact that this is a power against sin. The New Testament speaks of the victory of Jesus over sin; he destroys the dominion of Sin and Death. The Christian shares in this victory; and dominion over sin means more than forgiveness. It means that the Christian is not under sin unless he submits himself to it; it means not only that he can be forgiven but also that he can overcome sin. He lives not in the flesh but in the Spirit. He is not in the condition of the natural man who struggles against the law of sin with the modification that his sins are forgiven; he is a new man in whose life sin has no place. Unless he is such a new man, the power manifested in the resurrection of Jesus has been frustrated by refusal of faith in the power. How often are Christians unwilling to believe that they have been transformed and that the impossible has become possible?

The Resurrection as Victory

We have noticed that the apologetic treatment of the resurrection has obscured its theological value. It is a kind of apologetic value, however, which the New Testament presents when it sees the resurrection as the sign of the victory of Christ. When he rises he has surely overcome death, and hence he has overcome the hostile pair of Sin-Death. The resurrection is the convincing proof of the saving power and will of God. It is, as we saw earlier, the act by which Jesus is established as Messiah and Lord (Chapter IV). We must notice also that when the resurrection is considered as the sign of victory it is rarely considered as the victory of Jesus alone. In him the new man whom he has created rises in victory also. It is the proof not only of the power of Jesus but of the power communicated to those who are incorporated with him. With him they reign.

The Resurrection of the Christian

The resurrection is also the sign of the hope of the Christian in his own resurrection. The place of the individual person in the eschatological process in the New Testament is practically limited to the resurrection of the individual person. In the Gospel of John there is no other eschatological reference. I have written elsewhere that the belief in the resurrection is an affirmation of belief in the essential goodness and permanence of man. The Greek philosophical doctrine of the immortality of the soul has been incorporated into Christian thinking, but this doctrine is not perfectly harmonious with belief in the resurrection. The immortality of the soul is Greek thinking, the resurrection of the body is Hebrew thinking. In the Greek philosophical schools where the doctrine of immortality was elaborated the doctrine was a statement of the impermanence of the bodily component of man. Man in Greek philosophy is really the soul, not the animated body; only the soul can be preserved and is worth preserving. The original sin of man in Greek philosophy was really the incarnation of the soul in the body; and the salvation of the soul consists in its liberation from the body.

Such a view of man and the world is removed from the biblical view that man rises, and that nature also is the object of redemption. A renewal of nature would be a blunder in Greek philosophy; it would be a restoration of the sinful condition of man, a new fall. The belief in the resurrection takes man as he is and does not hint that God made a mistake in creating such an animal. The life of the risen is human, although St. Paul does his best (1 Cor 15) to show that it is not the mortal life which we know. It is a transformation, and the term of the transformation lies beyond experience. Man has a fulfillment as man which is not yet achieved; it is the object of faith, but the risen Jesus is an indication of what this new life may be. There is a vast amount of popular mythology concerning the risen body, and some of the finest of this mythology is found in the writings of St. Thomas Aquinas. If one adheres to the biblical evidence, one will be very careful in making affirmations about what happens in the transformation. One thing is clear, and that is that the resurrection is the fullness of life, of human life. Man is saved by becoming fully man, and not something other than man.

The Paradox of the Resurrection

In Acts 17 is related a discourse of St. Paul at Athens. It is not couched in the style of the proclamation; it is dressed up in bits of erudition for one of the most sophisticated cities of the Hellenistic world. The speech went well until Paul reached the resurrection; the response of ridicule at that point seems to have stopped the discourse. Obviously Paul had better luck in other Greek cities, and he must have altered his presentation somewhat; but he certainly did not attempt to "demythologize" the resurrection. The belief is unpalatable to the sophisticated mind, for it seems to deny all the most obvious facts of experience. Whether it is the antinomy between the belief and experience which creates the greatest difficulty is not clear; perhaps as significant is the lingering doubt in the minds of most men that man has essential and permanent value. It is a paradox of Christianity that it is more humanist than any humanist system; no humanist system affirms the indestructibility of the individual person.

Philosophically it is difficult to affirm the indestructibility of the person; philosophical argument may be able to arrive at the indestructibility of the soul, which is not the same thing. The Christian affirmation is not based on philosophical reasoning; it reposes on the identity achieved between God in Christ and the individual person. Certain theological problems arise from this consideration which it is not our business to solve here; for if one were rigorously logical no one would live except those who are incorporated with Christ. Fortunately the New Testament is not rigorously logical; and it considers the resurrection as a resurrection to life, for a resurrection to death would be more illogical than the New Testament could tolerate. Hence the essential goodness and permanence of man can be said to repose on man's capacities for the new life in Jesus risen. That is the way God has made man, and the New Testament carries the analysis no further.

Resurrection in History and in Eschatology

There is an interesting ambivalence in the New Testament concerning the resurrection which deserves more than passing interest. The resurrection, of course, occurs on "the last day"; it is an eschatological event. But once again eschatology touches history. Even in John, where the resurrection is most emphatically placed in "the last day," the principle of eternal life is already communicated. The principle is faith in Jesus, which assures the resurrection. "He who believes in me, though he die, shall live; and whoever lives and believes in me shall never die" (Jn 11:25-26). For Jesus is the resurrection and the life (11:25), and faith unites the believer with resurrection and life. It might seem that John's statement goes beyond the realities; but he is not talking about the realities of experience. The meaning of physical death has been transformed by faith. Eternal life is not proof against physical death in the sense that the believer does not experience physical death. It is proof against death because eternal life has made physical death an incident through which eternal life enters into its fullness. The believer need not fear death, nor does death terminate the genuine life which has been communicated to him.

In John the Eucharist also is a principle of eternal life (Jn 6). In this discourse the Eucharist is united with faith as the bread which assures against death. The Old Testament theme of the manna is echoed; the manna was "bread from heaven," given by a deed of wonder, but it did not protect the Israelites against death. The eternal life which is the certain foundation of the resurrection is communicated by the Eucharistic bread consumed in faith. The sacramental bread is likened to the daily food which sustains physical life; and physical life is possessed by man, it is not an object of hope or anticipation. Eternal life also is possessed in reality and not merely in hope.

Paul sees the resurrection as an eschatological event, particularly in 1 Corinthians 15 and 1 Thessalonians. But the new life which is exhibited in the resurrection is already present in the Christian. It is, as we have noticed, a life of the Spirit and not of the flesh; the Christian thinks the thoughts of the Spirit and does the deeds of the Spirit. The power which will raise his body from the dead has already raised his body from sin. The first step in the victory over Sin-Death is achieved when the Christian believes and is baptized. It would be no more than a slight exaggeration, if it were even that much, to paraphrase Paul's thought by saying that the transformation effected in the resurrection is less revolutionary in personal life than the transformation effected by faith and baptism. In baptism, the new man is born; in the resurrection a life already existing reaches maturity.

The Central Reality of the Saving Act

In this chapter we have merely looked at the outlines of the New Testament presentation of the saving act of Jesus Christ. Almost everything we shall consider in subsequent chapters is related to the saving act; it is indeed the central theme which brings the New Testament together. It is evident that the New Testament treatment of the theme is not systematized; numerous approaches are found, and systematization may lose some elements of the total presentation. Here, for example, we have not been able to speak of the saving act as an enduring reality; this we must look at more fully. Nor have we been able to speak of it as a social act; this likewise must be more fully explored.

But we have tried to lay the foundation for this treatment. When one brings together the New Testament elements, it becomes clear that Jesus is never alone in the saving act. The identity of Jesus with those whom he saves is often explicit, always implicit; for it is this identity which communicates salvation to them. The full meaning of the reenactment of the saving event in the personal life of the Christian and in the life of the Church as a whole we have not yet seen in the fullness it deserves. But it should be clear that Jesus acts as a corporate personality.

It should not surprise us that the New Testament does not synthesize these ideas, so vital to Christian faith. The New Testament, we have seen, is a record of the growth of the Church in faith and understanding of who and what Jesus Christ was and is, and of what the Church is. The growth of faith and understanding in the Church is a paradigm of the growth of the individual Christian. The Church grew by experience of the reality in which it believed. The first generation of the Church was not a group of men with speculative minds. They were profoundly aware of the life of Jesus in the Church, and they were able to see him in places and situations where a less profound faith would miss him. The value of the New Testament lies in no small part in this, that it constantly reveals the possibilities of new insights based on the experience of the living Jesus. It is, as we have said, a faith which reposes on events; and it grows by engagement with events, seeing in events the development of the Reign of God in Christ Jesus.

VII *THE KNOWLEDGE OF GOD*

Knowledge

"This is eternal life, that they know thee the only true God, and Jesus Christ whom thou hast sent" (Jn 17:3). In these words of the priestly prayer a theme prominent in John appears: the theme of knowledge. Matthew 11:27 (= Lk 10:22) is called by some critics "a meteor fallen from the Johannine heaven": "No one knows the Son except the Father, and no one knows the Father except the Son and him to whom the Son is pleased to reveal him." For the theme of knowledge is less common in the Synoptic Gospels. Yet the knowledge of God is a fundamental Old Testament theme. But "knowledge" in the Old Testament does not signify intellectual apprehension; it signifies experience, and in particular the vital experience of possession. In Hebrew a man is said to know his wife; and this expresses the Hebrew idea of knowledge better than anything else. The theme of knowledge in John is an echo of the Old Testament and not of the knowledge sought in Greek philosophy. The saving act of Jesus, as we have seen, is a means by which God identifies himself with man in a new way; God is therefore "known" in a new way, and this knowledge, communicated only by the Son, is eternal life.

The continuity between the gospel and the Old Testament here is unbroken. Nothing in the words of Jesus or in the words of the Jews who opposed him suggests that any one thought that Jesus was proclaiming another God than the God of Israel. He was charged with claiming messiahship, and with something more which was not clearly apprehended, for the charge is not clearly and uniformly reported in the Gospels. Let us say that the Jews charged him with claiming a unique and more than human relationship to God. But he was not charged with idolatry. The God whom Jesus proclaimed was recognized as the God of the fathers.

Jesus and the Father

When we approach this question, we take the final step toward determining the identity of Jesus. It is a step at once easy and difficult: easy, because no theological problem has been the object of so many declarations of the Church as the relations of Jesus to the Father; difficult, because these relations escape comprehension more than any other biblical truth. Jesus did certainly reveal God in a way which was revolutionary, more revolutionary than was perceived in the primitive Church. Yet one realizes at once that this relationship is incapable of comprehension from the outside. The declarations of the Church had as their purpose to reject false statements of the relationship; they were not intended to be comprehensive statements, for the Church has always recognized that no comprehensive statement of the relationship is possible. The declarations were uttered in the language of Greek philosophy because the false statements were uttered in that language. If a philosophical statement of the relation of Jesus to the Father is necessary, the Church is faithful to its mission if it affirms its exclusive right to make such a statement. The New Testament is not written in the language of Greek philosophy. Its basic vocabulary is drawn from the Old Testament. Its language here in particular is inadequate for its object; one should not assume that philosophical language is adequate for the same object. There are times when precision can be a vice rather than a virtue; and when one speaks precisely about something which one does not "know" in the philosophical sense, one is saying more than one knows. If this seems tautological, it is one of the rare instances when tautology seems necessary.

"My Father and Your Father"

In the Gospels Jesus habitually refers to God as "the Father" or "my Father." This title is not entirely new; it occurs in the Old

Testament perhaps about two dozen times, but it never receives a thematic treatment. The idea of God the Father is the dominant idea of God in the New Testament; it cannot be called dominant in the Old Testament. "Lord Yahweh," the most common invocation of God in the Old Testament, is the dominant Old Testament idea. God does not cease to be lord when he is called father; but there is an obvious shift of emphasis. The shift was less obvious in New Testament times than it seems to us. The father of the family in most ancient legal codes and customs was a lord of his family; indeed, to call him an owner would not exaggerate his position. One could speak of fatherhood at length in the ancient world without conveying any of the emotional overtones which the word conveys to us; and no one would be surprised. It was not enough that Jesus should speak of the Father; it is the kind of fatherhood of which he speaks that is decisive.

The terms in which Jesus speaks of the Father are so well known that no listing of passages should be necessary. The tone is without fail one of tenderness, affection, and solicitude. Is this a notable departure from the Old Testament? We think not. The wrath of God is not an exclusively Old Testament theme. It appears in the New Testament also; and wrath is not the prevailing Old Testament tone. The change, if we can pinpoint it, is a change in depth and not in quality. Jesus speaks of the Father with an intimacy which appears nowhere in the Old Testament. This flows from his own unique relationship with the Father, of which we shall speak shortly. His own intimacy is communicated to those who are identified with him. Were it not for this, the idea of "the Reign of God the Father" would be too paradoxical to bear. But a reign of the Father with whose Son men live on such close terms becomes an idea which flows from the gospel without any disturbance.

The Love of the Father

The danger in the conception of God as Father is sentimentality. We are here concerned with the self-revelation of God; and sentimentality, if it intrudes, comes from us and not from the gospel. It is impossible to associate sentimentality with Jesus as he is in the Gospels, although we know it is quite possible to make the association if he is detached from them. There are certain realities in life which the revelation of the Father does not remove; the revelation permits us to view them in a different way. Sternness is not alien to the image of a loving Father; and the words of Jesus express sternness without taking away any of the love. It would not be without fruit to explore those passages of the Gospels where the Father appears stern; one would find that they are passages in which love is refused. Either men will not admit that God is loving, or they refuse to love their fellow man. The Father appears nowhere in a more stern visage than at the conclusion of the parable of the unforgiving slave (Mt 18:23–35). The sternness is elicited by the lack of mercy in the slave; and Jesus concludes with the words, "So will my heavenly Father do to you, if you do not forgive, each one of you, your brother from your heart." John wrote that God is love; and he who denies love denies the reality of God. This, we think, does not detract from the image of the Father as loving. The Father cannot permit men to remove him from the world; and this they do as effectively as they can when they refuse love to others or when they come between the Father and those whom he loves. If the Father does not exhibit sternness in this situation, he cannot exhibit sternness at all.

The Revelation of the Father

There is a temptation, after one has been reading the Gospels for some time, to put the sublime revealed religious truths in very familiar language. This may be a temptation to do what is right; Jesus himself has spoken of the Father in the most familiar terms. It is difficult to point out any difference in tone between the way Jesus speaks of his Father and the way any man would speak of a father whom he loves and respects. Jesus himself, who dealt with his associates on such easy terms, is the medium of familiarity. In the Gospel of John one of the disciples asks Jesus to show them the Father; such a response is natural enough after the glowing terms in which Jesus talks about his Father. The answer of Jesus is unexpected: "I have been with you so long and you do not know me? When you see me, you see the Father" (Jn 14:8–9). Jesus reveals the Father in another and a more intimate way than by talking about him. There is an identity between Jesus and the Father which makes any further personal manifestation of the Father unnecessary for full knowledge — as full, that is, as is possible for man. And thus at once all efforts to rise to some form of super-Christian gnosticism are confuted. The Father has spoken in Jesus, who is his word.

Titles of Sonship

Jesus has a unique relation to the Father. He is a man among men, but when he speaks to men he uses "my Father" and "your Father." This relationship he shares with no one. When men are identified with Jesus Christ in the New Testament they are adopted as sons of God; but adoption does not put them on the same plane with Jesus with reference to the Father. Jesus is the only-begotten Son, in the language of John; when men are called his brothers, the term is used in the loose sense of kinship in which it is habitually used in the Old Testament. I have already quoted the saying in which Jesus speaks of a personal knowledge of the Father possessed by him exclusively.

This relationship is designated by more than one term. The New Testament here faithfully reflects the growth of faith and understanding in the primitive community. The Epistles, particularly the later Epistles, and the Gospel of John show a development of Christology which is not seen in the Synoptic Gospels. We have seen that the Church proclaimed Jesus Messiah and Lord in terms which he did not use himself; the Church also proclaimed Jesus Son in terms which he did not use himself. Here, as in the question of messiahship, many critics have said that the Church not only used language which was not the language of Jesus, but that it also made statements which did not reflect the teaching of Jesus. If this be true, one can only say that it is strange that the Church wrote and preserved in the Synoptic Gospels the only evidence which the critics have for asserting that the Church in other New Testament books was unfaithful to the teaching of Jesus. It is almost as strange that the Church should not know the difference between the Christology of the Synoptic Gospels and the Christology of John and Paul. If this were true, then the primitive Church would have been so muddled that it could not be a witness to anything. These consequences are so unpalatable that it is far simpler to take the obvious course: that the New Testament is a document of growth, not of static assertions.

Son of God

We must remark that there were certain linguistic barriers to the New Testament use of the terminology of Nicaea and Chalcedon. The New Testament could not say simply that Christ was God until a development had been reached which is reflected in John 1:1 and not certainly in any other passage. "God," in Greek *ho theos,* always means that Father whom Jesus revealed, identical with *ho theos* of the Old Testament, Yahweh. To call Jesus *theos* would be to identify him personally with the Father, a step which the primitive Church knew it must not take. When John 1:1 was written the relations of Jesus and the Father were grasped with enough security to permit John to call Jesus *theos,* a divine being. Earlier the phrase in a Jewish or Hellenistic context would have implied that the Word was another god. Hence Jesus can only be related to the Father obliquely; and the most common designation, which rests upon the words of Jesus in the Synoptic Gospels, is the Son of God. This title affirms personal distinction. It does not affirm identity of nature, for this philosophical term was not in the minds of the writers of the New Testament. It was sufficient for them that the title affirm a unique sonship which is not the sonship of adoption communicated by Jesus to believers.

Father and Son

The title is exposed to that misconception which is called subordinatianism, and this misconception appears early in the postapostolic Church. In its most explicit form this heresy reduces Jesus to a level of being above the human but below that of the Father. It makes Jesus not only the unique Son but also a unique being; he is likened to the demigods and heroes of Greek mythology, impossible beings but so romantically and vividly portrayed in Greek poetry that they are accepted as real almost before one notices it. The New Testament did not encounter the danger of subordinatianism and therefore did not couch its language deliberately in such a way as to neutralize the danger. Jesus speaks of his relationship to the Father in words which imply an intelligible conception of sonship: he is sent by the Father, he has a commission from the Father, he receives power from the Father, he does the will of the Father, he is the mediator between men and the Father. In fairness to the subordinatianists, the relation of sonship should not be rationalized into mere metaphor or rendered so abstractly metaphysical that it is emptied of content. Jesus was not an angel; he is the Son. It is the Father who is the initiator and the term of the process of salvation, and Jesus is the intermediate agent in both directions. Salvation is from the Father through Jesus and to the Father through Jesus; if one does not maintain this, one confuses the persons, in the words of the Athanasian Creed. And this must be maintained, whatever be the risk of subordinatianism.

Sonship in the Gospels

If, then, we use the critical razor and limit ourselves to the Synoptic Gospels as the source of the words of Jesus — a procedure which does not by any means authenticate itself — we find not that Jesus spoke of his unique sonship in the words of John and Paul, but that he assumed a position in the world which is unintelligible except as an exercise of unique sonship. I have observed the obvious fact that he speaks of the Father as one who knows the Father personally to those who do not know the Father personally. His teaching, in the words of the Gospels, was invested with power and authority; this authority he takes no trouble to prove, but simply asserts. He is the one authoritative interpreter of the mind and will of the Father; he is the herald and the executor of the Father's plan of salvation. He treats the Law of Judaism, the traditional revealed will of God, with a casual independence and assures those whom he addressed that the Law is insufficient to lead them to the Father.

In addition to these habits of behavior, we have the saving act performed by Jesus. In this saving act Jesus is the corporate personality not only of the Jews but of men. The act is performed and is effective because of his solidarity with men and his solidarity with the Father. He belongs to all men in a way in which no other man did or could belong to them; he belongs to the Father likewise in a way which is proper to him. The simple assertion that the Son of Man can give his life as a ransom for many (Mt 20:28; Mk 10:45) should not be read casually. What lies beneath this tremendous claim to power to act as an agent of salvation for men? When Jesus said this — and it appears in Mark — was he saying anything less startling than we read in the prologue of John (1:1–18) or in Philippians 2:5–11? These later passages — if indeed Philippians is later than the Gospels — make some attempt to show what lay beneath the claim that the Son of Man could be a ransom for many. But the words of John and Paul are not placed in the Gospel of Mark for the good reason that they do not represent the words of Jesus. It is a fair conclusion that what Mark has does represent his words.

We have seen that Jesus exercised some reserve in the use of the titles of King and Messiah to designate his mission. It should not be surprising that he exercised even more reserve about his personal identity; but he did not exercise so much reserve that the Church could not discern that it gave its faith to a person like no other. Since the faith he demanded was the kind of faith given to no other, one can only say that there was a proportion between the two. In the sturdy Galilean peasant of wit and eloquence the disciples could discern a person of depths which they could not explore. To this person they committed themselves totally, and they did their best to convey to others the impact of the personality to which they had surrendered. The New Testament is the witness and the product of their faith. Jesus bore himself as the Son of his Father in a manner which was its own vindication. They who saw him saw the Father, and they knew that they had.

The Church's Profession of Faith

It is not surprising that the apostolic Church began to profess its faith in the person of Jesus as well as in his mission in more explicit terms. The teaching, we have seen, was the instruction given to the baptized about him in whom they had believed (Chapter II). The earliest statement of the New Testament in which the preexistence of Christ is affirmed appears in St. Paul, and this is early enough; the major epistles of St. Paul are earlier than the Synoptic Gospels. The preexistence of Christ is not affirmed even in the infancy narratives of Matthew and Luke. It is not found everywhere in the writings of Paul; but Philippians 2:5-11 is so clear and so much in harmony with the language of Paul elsewhere that there can be no doubt that it belonged to his teaching. This is not a point on which there is any discussion recorded in the primitive Church. Paul was not proposing any idea excogitated by himself; while he is the principal literary witness, there is no reason to think that the entire Church was not saying the same thing. The Church perceived that the Father had to have an eternal Son. If the Son were not eternal, then it would be impossible to see how he could have a unique sonship not shared with other men. The sonship of Jesus could not be acquired by a man, no matter how nearly that man approached to God. Jesus was, in the words of Philippians 2:5-11 (a classic of primitive Christian belief), in the form of God and equal to God. The Son was not merely designated by the Father or commissioned by the Father; he was sent from the Father (Gal 4:4).

The sonship revealed the meaning of the saving act of Jesus and explained the solidarity which made the saving act possible. Sonship was a revelation of the love of the Father; for God was mysteriously involved in suffering. The power manifested in Jesus was not conferred upon him; he possessed it by eternal nativity. He was in virtue of his person the creator of the new man. The dignity of lordship which came to him in his resurrection was an actualization of a dignity of which he had, again in the words of Philippians, emptied himself in his incarnation as a slave. But in all this he is the Son; the Father works in him, and Jesus does nothing which the Father does not accomplish through him.

The Attributes of the Father

Jesus is related to the Father obliquely and not by personal identity, as we have observed, and sonship is the usual designation.

But the New Testament employs other titles also to express the unique personal relationship of Jesus with the Father. Many of these titles have some affinity with the language of Judaism of the New Testament period. Jewish literature shows a practice of personifying the divine attributes and making them intermediary between God and man. No affirmation of real personality is intended; this was impossible within rigid Jewish monotheism. But in Jewish thought God himself had become more remote than he was in early Israel; even the divine name of Yahweh had become too holy to be pronounced. The attributes personified connected God with man; and it was the attributes which man experienced.

When Jesus is called the power of God and the wisdom of God (1 Cor 1:24) or the reflection of his glory and the stamp of his nature (Heb 1:3), the language but not the thought of the personified attributes is used. Jesus does not render the Father more remote, nor does he appear as a substitute for the Father. He brings the Father nearer; and men encounter the Father in him. By the use of these titles the identity between Jesus and the Father is more firmly stated, an identity which is everything but personal. Jesus is not any one of the attributes; he is all of them. The author of Hebrews takes some pains in Chapters 1–2 to show the superiority of Jesus over the angels, as he goes on to show that Jesus is more than Moses. Jesus is a mediator, but not an intermediate being. He stands definitely and by right in the world of men, and the same Jesus sits at the right hand of the Father. Were he less than this, he would not be capable of the saving act which God worked in him.

The Word of God

Two of these attributes demand particular attention; one will show us more of Jesus himself, the other will lead us into a more difficult area. The two attributes are word and spirit. Word as designation of Jesus is used only by John, and rarely by this author; the peculiar force of the term is seen in the fact that although the term is rare, it has become almost the technical designation of the Second Person in theology. The term has a long history not only in the Old Testament but in the religions of the ancient Near East. The word is conceived as a projection of the person. Once emitted it acquires an enduring reality of its own. It is a power-laden entity proportionate to the power of the speaker, and it effects what it signifies when it is a word of command. It gives identity to the thing when it is spoken as a name; and it reveals the identity of the thing to him who knows the name. The divine word is a creative force; this is particularly clear in Genesis 1, where God creates simply by uttering a word of power.

John's use of the term is clearly the "fulfillment" of the Old Testament in the finest sense of the word; and it owes nothing to Platonic or Stoic conceptions of the *logos*. In the world of thought which I have summarized above Jesus as the Word of the Father takes his place easily. He is the revelation of the Father and the embodiment of his power. He is the projection of his personality as an enduring reality. He makes the Father intelligible; in him men experience a personal encounter with the Father. He is the creative word, bringing into being a new man and a new world. It is no wonder that the term has acquired such significance in theology, even though the rich Old Testament background of the term has not always been considered. And as well as any other term it expresses the divine preexistence of Jesus.

The Spirit of God

The Old Testament background of spirit is also rich; but Jesus is not called the spirit, with the possible exception of 2 Corinthians 3:17; if Jesus is called spirit here, it must mean Jesus as the Christ supremely glorified. In the Old Testament spirit meant originally the movement of air, the breath, or the wind. It is a principle of life and of vital activity. The wind is the breath of God; and then spirit becomes an instrument of power, a divine dynamic entity. Like the wind, the origin and the course of the spirit cannot be traced; man can see its effects, but it remains inexplicable to him. Spirit is contrasted with flesh; but spirit does not designate immaterial being in the sense in which spirit and spiritual are used in scholastic metaphysics. Like the word, spirit is a creative power. But the peculiar effects of the divine spirit are seen in men. Spirit is a power which moves men to do that which is normally impossible and enables them to rise above their capacities. It is a charisma; by the spirit the Judges of Israel achieve their victories, and the spirit rests upon kings, enabling them to rule. In particular the spirit rests upon the King Messiah. Spirit is not frequently associated with prophecy until the postexilic period, for the charisma of the prophet is the word; but the association of spirit and inspired speech was made before the New Testament, and it appears in the New Testament. Spirit, then, is a mysterious divine force or impulse which explains the sudden and the unpredictable in human behavior; it is God at work in ways which are peculiarly his own. We must note that in the Old Testament this force is impersonal.

The Spirit in the New Testament

We observe a development of the idea of the spirit in the New Testament similar to the development of the idea of the person of Jesus. The word spirit is used much less frequently in the Synoptic Gospels than it is in the Acts of the Apostles, the epistles, and the Gospel of John. Furthermore, most of the uses of the word belong not to Jesus but to the narrators or to others who speak in the Gospels. If we again use the critical razor, we shall have to say that the reason the spirit is more prominent outside the Gospels than within them is that Jesus himself spoke less of the spirit than did the primitive community. But there is a passage of the Synoptic Gospels which could be called another meteor fallen from the Johannine or Pauline heaven. The theophany of the baptism (Mt 3:13–17; Mk 1:9–11; Lk 3:21–22) is represented as a revelation of the Father in a voice, of the Son in the flesh, and of the Spirit in a dove. This incident stands out in the Synoptic Gospels; for it is extremely difficult to point out passages in these Gospels where the spirit is conceived as anything else than the mysterious divine impulse or power which it is in the Old Testament. Jesus himself is "driven" (Mk 1:12) or "led" by the spirit (Mt 4:1; Lk 4:1). Even without the appearance of the Spirit in the epistles and the Gospel of John we would have difficulty in explaining the theophany of the baptism in the usual sense; for the theophany of the spirit has no parallel in the Old Testament. What is more important, it has no parallel in John and the epistles either.

When we speak of the Spirit in these other books it is necessary to write the noun with a capital letter. The use of the capital is an implicit theological declaration; but the same declaration is made in the New Testament books. We can begin our discussion by saying without any hesitation that the novelty of the New Testament is as clear in its conception of the Spirit as it is anywhere. The prominence of the Spirit, the functions of the Spirit, the relations of the Spirit to the Father and to Jesus are not derived from Judaism, and even less from any possible Hellenistic source. This must be taken into account when we come to the question of the personality of the Spirit, the most difficult point in the theology of the Spirit.

The Spirit in the Primitive Church

It is obvious that Luke deliberately has written the Acts as a companion piece to the Gospel; it has been called a gospel of the Spirit, and the term is not a distortion. The apostolic group must carry on the life and mission of Jesus, but they are unable to do this until they have received the Spirit (Lk 24:49; Acts 1:4–8). As the Gospel of Luke begins with the nativity of Jesus, so the Acts begin with the theophany of the Spirit; and this is the beginning of the Church. A careful reading of Acts shows that the activity of the Spirit moves the apostolic group at every turn of events. In the Spirit they proclaim their witness to Jesus, and they show eloquence and courage which is out of character with the traits which they show in the Gospels. Luke wished to make clear that the growth of the Church was not the work of men. Men were instruments of God through the divine force of the Spirit which dwelt in them. The Spirit was the answer to the warning of Gamaliel to see whether this undertaking was of men or of God (Acts 5:38–39). The Spirit was not limited to the apostolic group; it was conferred upon each believer at baptism or shortly after by the rite of the imposition of hands. The Spirit reposes not only upon the Church as a whole but upon each individual member. In Luke the Spirit is primarily the principle of the apostolic activity of the Church; in Paul the functions of the Spirit are enlarged.

The Spirit in Paul

Paul's theology of the Spirit is the most elaborate of all the New Testament writers; but it is unstructured and not altogether logically consistent. Paul can and does speak of the spirit in Old Testament terms. But the frequency of the word in the Pauline writings, where it occurs several hundred times, is out of all proportion with other biblical books. The Spirit has a unique relation with Jesus, as Jesus has with the Father; and the relation is seen most clearly in the risen Jesus, who enjoys the fullness of his power and glory. It is Jesus in the Spirit with whom the Church is one as members and body or members and head, not Jesus in the flesh. Jesus in the Spirit lives on a divine and heavenly plane; the phrase is difficult and may distort the complex thought of Paul, but it seems that he conceives Jesus in the Spirit as having a larger existence. But because Jesus is one with the members of his Church, the Spirit dwells not only in the Church but in each individual member of the Church. This means that the believer too lives on a divine and heavenly plane; he is the new man of whom we have spoken in the preceding chapter.

The Spirit as the Principle of Life

In the Pauline writings the Spirit is the operative principle of the Christian life. The effects of the Spirit may be such exotic phenomena as prophecy and the gift of tongues; but Paul does not treat these as important, and they were not a durable effect of the Spirit in the Church. The Spirit enables the Christian to pray. It is the Spirit of faith which illuminates for the believer the mysteries of God. It is the Spirit of hope; and most important, it is the Spirit of love, the living power which was incarnate in Jesus and now works in his Church. In the moral life of the Christian the Spirit is opposed to the flesh, the principle of sin and corruption. The moral life of man is war between Spirit and flesh;

the Spirit is the principle of eternal life which overcomes the flesh. In Paul's celebrated enumeration of the fruits of the Spirit (Gal 5:22–23) he does not mention prophecy and tongues. The enumeration lists the virtues which should ornament the man who walks according to the Spirit and not the flesh. In Paul the idea of the Spirit reaches its fullness in the New Testament; the Spirit becomes in a proper sense the life of the Church.

The Spirit in John

The Spirit in John differs sufficiently from the Spirit in Paul to demand our attention. The identity between Jesus and the Spirit in John is closer than in the other New Testament books. This is not an identity of person, nor is the Spirit a metaphor for Jesus himself; the two remain quite distinct. But it is no doubt because of this close identity that where Paul conceives the Spirit as dwelling in the individual believer, John describes the Spirit more as an external reality which operates upon the believer. John is extremely explicit that the Spirit is the successor of Jesus who continues the work of Jesus; the Spirit cannot come until Jesus is glorified, which is exactly parallel to the conception of Luke.

Peculiar to John is the Spirit as "Paraclete," the advocate, the intercessor or helper. It is as the Paraclete that the Spirit is sent by Jesus; that he is sent by both the Father and by Jesus is the historic point of doctrinal difference between the Greek and Latin Churches. It is also as the Paraclete that personal actions are more frequently attributed to the Spirit; the Spirit is the revealer, the teacher, the witness. Indeed, the functions of the Spirit in John are not too closely differentiated from the functions of Jesus himself. As we have noticed, the Spirit carries on what Jesus initiated.

The Person of the Spirit

It is an article of Catholic faith that the Trinity of persons exists in unity of nature; the personal reality of the Spirit is not subject to debate. Nor is the distinct personal reality of the Spirit from the Father and the Son subject to debate. Yet the New Testament can and does speak of the Spirit in impersonal terms because of the Old Testament background of the word; it does not and could not speak of the Father and the Son as impersonal. Certainly Christians have always found some difficulty in thinking of the Spirit as a person. Perhaps they ought. The innumerable portraits of a venerable old gentleman and a handsome bearded young man have made it easy for us to think of Father and Son as persons; it is much more difficult to personalize a bird or a tongue of flame.

But if we think of Father and Son as venerable old gentleman and handsome young man we are not thinking of the personal reality of Father and Son at all. We can and do humanize Father and Son; we cannot do this to the Spirit. And the revelation of the Spirit serves this useful purpose among others, to warn us that human personality can be a misleading analogy when we think of God. If we cannot assimilate the Spirit as he is revealed to a human person, does this show that the Spirit is less a person, or that man is less a person? The personal reality of God is mysterious; and the Spirit reveals this.

Knowledge and Experience

This chapter was begun with the statement that Jesus revealed God to man. It is evident that it fails pitifully to improve on the revelation as we have it in the New Testament. For it is a revelation that must be lived as well as studied. The encounter with God which is related in the Gospels must be lived by every Christian before he can have a mature faith. Jesus has shown us who it is that we encounter. The richness of the divine life of Father, Son and Holy Spirit is no longer hidden. God remains mysterious, indeed we know now that he is more mysterious than we suspected; but Jesus has put us on familiar terms with him. We know the Father as the one who initiates and wills the salvation of man, the Son as the one who executes it in the flesh, and the Spirit who endures as the living reality of salvation effected.

Knowledge and Mythology

Later in this book we shall touch upon the now famous question of demythologizing the New Testament. Here it may be noticed that precisely in the knowledge of the divine persons there is a considerable amount of false mythology in circulation; images have quietly become reality. We say that Jesus lives in the Church; do we mean it? Our mythology of spatial geography persuades us that God is really present in heaven, and that Jesus really lives only in some heavenly point seated at the right hand of the Father. We forget that heaven as a geographical reality is nonexistent, and could only be conceived as existent in a Ptolemaic universe. When we say that Jesus is in heaven we mean that he does not exist on earth — more properly, that he does not exist on earth as he did when he lived in Galilee. It is an unwarranted assumption and not faithful to the New Testament to say that he is less really present now than he was then; this is to measure reality by the corporeal existence of the human body. Spirit is power; and Jesus in the Spirit has power which he did not exhibit in his incarnational existence. St. Paul tries to tell us this in many passages of his writings; naturally he found it difficult, and his readers have found it even more difficult to believe him. We think the real Jesus is remote, only less remote than the Father; and perhaps that is where we prefer him to be. If Jesus revealed anything, it is that God is near; and surely this does not mean that he himself is remote.

The Mythology of the Spirit

We shall have to look more closely at the Church which Jesus founded; but we cannot speak of the Church without speaking of the Spirit, the personal reality with which we have just been engaged. Spirit, we have said, is power; as contrasted with the flesh it is enduring and incorruptible reality. What do we mean when we say that this powerful and enduring reality endures in the Church? Is the Spirit as powerful and as enduring in our thought as the external and visible reality which we can see, hear, and touch? In popular mythology the Spirit is not a bird or a tongue of flame; it is a kind of fog, a luminous haze. And what power, what activity can we attribute to vapor?

Yet Jesus revealed that the Spirit is the principle of life and activity in the Church and in the individual Christian. Our geographical mythology makes it easy for us to locate the Spirit every-where. We do not have to imagine that the Spirit is really existent only in heaven; our problem is rather to imagine the Spirit as really existent anywhere. Yet the Spirit is a greater reality than the hier-archical structure of the Church. Luke, we noticed, planned his work so that it would be evident that the Church was the work of the Spirit and not of men. Where he introduces the Spirit as active at every turn of events, we are inclined to think that the Church is no longer guided and impelled in this way, forgetting that if it is not, it is not the Church of Christ. The apostles, we think, must have had the Spirit present at their meetings invisibly; and every now and then a voice from no perceptible source said things like, "Pick out Saul and Barnabas, because I have a job for them." This is mythology again, and not sound mythology. One may ask where the Spirit was when Paul and Barnabas quarreled over John Mark or when Peter and Paul had a deep misunder-standing about the position of Gentiles in the Church. The early Church did not think the Spirit had left the Church at such mo-ments; the Church knew that even her officers could escape the guidance of the Spirit when they tried. But they had assurance in the enduring power which had entered the world through the Church, and which cannot be frustrated even by the pettiness of mankind. The Spirit will assert itself in its own way, and it may not be the way in which the members or the officers of the Church would like to have it done. There was a moment in the history of England when the Spirit asserted itself in no public figure except Thomas More and in no bishop except John Fisher.

Similarly the New Testament teaching that the Spirit dwells as a living force in the individual Christian is subject to mythology. What is the Christian doing which manifests the Spirit? We should prefer more frequent exhibitions of the gift of tongues and faith healing, or handling deadly serpents and drinking poison without harm. Would these things convince us if they did happen? The fruits of the Spirit enumerated by Paul seem pedestrian; and we wonder what he could possibly have meant by such a statement as "No man can say Jesus is Lord except in the Holy Spirit" (1 Cor 12:3). But Paul, we know, like so many brilliant speakers and writers, made his case by overstatement. This is a magnificent overstatement, and we admire it as such. What Paul meant was that we do not fall to the moral level of pigs only by the Holy Spirit. He could have added that to rise above the moral level of pigs is scarcely the fullness of life in the Holy Spirit.

The Spirit is power, and each Christian is endued with power from on high. But if he does not know he has it and is afraid to use it, the Spirit will assert itself in him more slowly; or it will be more difficult for him when the Spirit does assert itself. He is like a man who cannot convince himself that he has really recovered from a long illness; the mere effort of getting out of bed fatigues him so much that he feels he must crawl right back in. The gift of tongues is much less impressive than the fruits of the Spirit enumerated by Paul; but many of us feel that we will speak Swahili before we exhibit the fruits of the Spirit. The war between Spirit and flesh must be fought in each individual man. God has left man the freedom to make up his mind not only who will win the war, but even whether there will be a war at all.

But Jesus lives in the Church whether we think of it or not, and the Spirit is his life in the Church whether we think of it or not; for that is the nature of reality, to be independent of our thinking. God has entered the world and exists there — one is tempted to say lurks there — as an explosive revolutionary force. This is what Jesus revealed, that God is near and active, that he has broken into history to stay, and that his presence assures that the world will not be the same. It does no man any good to say that the explosive force will not touch him; and least of all can a Christian pretend that it will not affect his private world.

VIII THE NEW LIFE IN CHRIST

The Christian, we have seen, is saved by sharing in the saving act. The saving act is the death and resurrection of Jesus; and the sharing consists in a rebirth into a new life of union with Jesus in the Spirit through which one comes to the Father. Our question now is: How does the Christian enter into this new life? The requirements in the New Testament are simple: repent, believe, and be baptized.

Repentance

We have already touched on the idea of repentance and we have noted that it means more than regret for one's sins. Repentance is a declaration against sin as a constituent part of life and of the human condition. It is a radical change of attitude, of habits, ambitions, and ideals. It is a putting off of the old man so totally that one life is ended and another is begun. In the preceding chapters we have seen how the character of this new life emerges, and we shall turn our attention to it again. Once the radical effects of repentance are grasped, it is clear why the gospel issued a call to repentance which no one could think did not apply to himself. Elsewhere Jesus used the phrase "to deny oneself," to end one's former existence. Repentance is a departure from the morality of reason and nature that one may live on a higher moral plane. This does not imply that a morality of reason and nature is necessarily bad and that a kind of nobility cannot be produced by human nature. Both the ancient and the modern world afford examples of men and women whose moral character must be called admirable. They exhibit faults, but so do Christians; when one meets such people, one sometimes wonders in despair what Christianity would add to them. Our despair arises because we do not see the full potentialities of the Christian life clearly enough; and because Christians have not risen to the level of the life of the Spirit, we are inclined to doubt the efficacy of the Spirit which dwells in Christians. The morality of reason and nature is not the morality which continues the life of Christ; and therefore the Christian repents of this morality also.

Totality of Repentance

I have spoken of the "moral" level of Christian living; and I should not leave the impression that repentance and faith are merely a moral change. Christianity is not just another and better system of morality. In the preceding chapter we have tried to see that the change worked by the saving act is real and more than a change in attitude. Through the saving act God has made himself present and active in a new way. The Christian is transformed in his being, not merely in his habits and acts. His habits and acts will be affected by the change; but a transformation of his habits and acts arises from the real change worked in him by the present activity of God and not only from his own personal choice and determination. The power to choose to live like a Christian is not granted to man in virtue of his natural endowments, but by the work of the Spirit within him. Repentance means that he leaves no obstacle to the power of the Spirit, that he renounces any personal security which reposes on his own endowments or achievements or on any achievement which is purely human and secular. He is resolved that he shall substitute nothing for the power and work of the Spirit, no matter how good, how attractive, how beneficent the substitute may seem to be. In the baptismal formula a renunciation of Satan and all his works and pomps is pronounced just before baptism. The Christian needs to look carefully at what the works and pomps of Satan may include. They do not mean only sin; the Church knows the word for sin, and if it wished to use it in this formula it could have done so. The works and pomps of Satan are all those things which are alleged to be just as good as the power of the Spirit, and far more realistic and practical.

The symbolism employed in the apostolic and postapostolic Church was much more candid than the later Church would tolerate, and I am not suggesting that it be restored. But in the original practice of baptism the candidate was plunged into the water naked. Nudity was so common in the Hellenistic-Roman world that this practice was not shocking. Perhaps through this symbolism the candidates for baptism understood what total repentance is better than the modern Christian does. The baptized emerged naked as the newborn babe; and the exhortation that an old life was ended and a new life begun was stoutly supported by the ritual. The candidate symbolically left his entire past behind him. He renounced what he had been to become what he was not.

Faith

With repentance comes faith to fill the void which repentance created. Here it will be necessary to set our consideration against a recent theological background. One of the points of division between Catholics and Protestants in the sixteenth century was the nature of faith. The Protestant thesis emphasized the element of confidence so much that faith seemed, at least in the writings of some Protestant theologians, to be reduced to confidence in forgiveness through the merits of Christ. The Protestants asserted that their position was a return to the New Testament and to the teaching of St. Paul that grace was given by faith and not by works. The Council of Trent opposed to the Protestant position an article defining faith as an act of the mind, an assent to truth. In the Catholic position a theological tradition which had found its best exponent in Thomas Aquinas was crystallized. The issue seemed to be clearly drawn between faith as an emotional experience, the Protestant position, and faith as an intellectual experience, the Catholic position. Actually to put the question in these terms is not only to oversimplify but to falsify. The theological development in Catholicism since the Council of Trent has followed the lines laid down by the Council; and faith has been treated in theological teaching and literature with an excessive emphasis on the intellectual quality of faith. The Council of Trent never intended that its declarations should be taken as a complete and final exposition of the nature of faith; it is a theological axiom that the statements of ecumenical councils are always to be read in the context of the controversies which elicited the statements. As a consequence the idea of faith often presented in Catholic instruction does not bear a very close resemblance to faith in the New Testament. There is not one New Testament passage in which faith is clearly described as an intellectual act. This does not mean that it is described as a nonintellectual act, a pure sentiment; it means that the New Testament does not make philosophical distinctions but views the complex act of faith as a psychic unity. When this complexity is expressed in philosophical distinctions, it is possible to state it falsely. Faith is indeed an assent to truth, but it is more than an intellectual assent. The statement is misleading if truth is conceived as propositions drawn up into a body of doctrine. In the New Testament faith is not given to doctrine but to something more.

Faith in the Gospels

Jesus often demands faith; faith is sometimes made a condition of healing. Jesus could not work deeds of power at Nazareth because of the unbelief of the Nazarenes (Mk 6:5–6; Mt 13:58). If we could grasp the connection by which unbelief inhibits the power of Jesus and faith releases the power, we should have a much better understanding of what faith is in the Gospels. For faith is certainly connected with power. Anything is possible to the one who believes (Mk 9:23). Even a grain of faith can move mountains and do other wonders (Mt 17:20; 21:21). But the object of faith is not stated in the Synoptic Gospels. The whole context shows that the object of faith is Jesus himself. One who believes accepts him as genuine. We have already seen that the person and mission of Jesus were presented with some reserve. Thus one who believed committed himself to something which he did not know and see clearly. He accepted the word of Jesus that in Jesus the Reign of God had come; and he undertook to submit himself to the Reign, whatever that submission might involve. Faith here is the acceptance of a person, not of a doctrine. It is surrender to the call of Jesus, and it is a surrender the totality of which is still unexplored at the moment of faith.

Faith as Union With Jesus

The passages quoted in the preceding paragraph should surprise us by the connection they establish between faith and power. We have seen that the incarnation is an inbreak of power; and we might expect that the response to power would be submission. But faith is less a submission to the power than a communication of the power — which, of course, does not exclude submission. The emphasis, however, does not fall so much on submission as on the result of submission. One is reminded of the classic Old Testament passage in which Isaiah recommended faith as the only practical policy for Ahaz and the kingdom of Judah in an hour of national crisis (Is 7:1–9). The crisis was a power struggle; and Isaiah advised that military and political power could be met only with faith. The men of Judah did not believe in faith as a power against armies and diplomacy, and they countered power with like power; their action is not surprising. The Gospels echo this theme when they treat faith as that which joins the believer to the power manifested in Jesus in such a way that the same power is exercised in him.

And thus faith appears as the act which establishes a personal conjunction between the believer and Jesus. Jesus is the corporate personality of redeemed man; this means that men must be incorporated into him and that they must accept his headship. The incorporation included more than a psychological act performed by the believer, as we shall see shortly; but it must include that act. As we look at the act of faith, we see that the degree of surrender to Jesus grows; faith is much more than acceptance of the teaching of Jesus — which in the Gospels is not emphasized much more than acceptance of his claims, or much more than submission to his commands. It is surrender of self to the extent that one buries one's personal life in the life of Jesus and ceases to exist as a detached unit of humanity.

Faith in the Acts

In the rest of the New Testament faith remains faith in Jesus, despite all the elaboration which the idea receives, especially in the Pauline writings. In the Acts of the Apostles "believers" is a usual designation of the community; for it is faith that makes them members of the group. And here we must note, although we shall have to take it up again, that faith is not an act of personal union and incorporation as an isolated personal act (Chapter IX). Faith occurs only within the community which is identical with Jesus; one cannot believe alone. Faith immediately identifies the believer not only with Jesus but with the community in which Jesus lives in the Spirit. With the coming of the Spirit it is impossible to detach Jesus from the group which is incorporated in him. That the object of faith in the Acts of the Apostles is usually the apostolic proclamation (when it is not Jesus himself) does not alter the concept of faith; for the proclamation, we have seen, is what renders Jesus present to those who hear it.

Faith in St. Paul

The treatment of faith in Paul is more extensive and more complex; and like the other theological topics treated by Paul, it is not systematized. Paul's conception of faith was one of the major points which emerged from what we shall study later as perhaps the most decisive episode in the life of the apostolic Church, the controversy over the relations of Christianity and Judaism (Chapter X). The antithesis between faith and works, which was the pillar of the Protestant thesis, is a genuinely Pauline theme; but it suffers when it is taken in isolation from the current of Paul's thought. The works to which Paul denied saving value were the works of the Law, the observance of the obligations of Judaism. These had no power to save, because nothing except Jesus Christ had power to save. Christ had annulled the validity of the Law — or rather, as we have seen, he brought the Law to its fullness (Chapters IV–V). The Law as observed in Judaism was an arrested development. Hence a man is constituted righteous by faith and baptism; and it is to be noticed that he is constituted righteous, not endowed with a capacity to acquire righteousness. He receives a capacity to maintain the righteousness which he did not earn by his merits. The one act by which a man becomes righteous in the Pauline teaching is faith; and it is evident that the faith which achieves this is much more than an assent to a body of doctrine. Paul can sum up the object of faith in one proposition (Romans 10:9): that Jesus is Lord and that God has raised him from the dead. This, we have seen, is a summary statement of the proclamation. Paul is rather insistent that there can be no faith without the proclamation (Rom 10:14–17). Jesus Lord is not learned from the Law nor from the reasonings of philosophy. His reality is revealed, and the proclamation is the sole vehicle of revelation. It is the only way in which men can experience Jesus.

The Power of Faith

It is difficult to grasp the power which Paul attributes to faith and baptism, the power to convert a man from unrighteousness to righteousness, unless we take a view of faith as broad as his own. Neither intellectual assent to doctrine nor simple confidence in forgiveness through the merits of Jesus Christ can effect this radical transformation, nor both put together. Neither idea comes near exhausting what Paul thinks faith is. Faith is a total acceptance of Jesus Lord with the totality of one's person. One neither withholds any part of one's person, nor any element of one's resources and activities; nor does one believe with reservations about how far the commitment will take one. One accepts Jesus totally, entirely as he is, and accepts the salvation which he works in the way in which he works it. One looks for salvation in no other, nor does one look for a different type of salvation. It is precisely as the Messiah of Judaism and the Suffering Servant that Jesus is recognized as something other than a culture hero, a political savior, an economic prophet, a scientific sage, a psychotherapeutic bearer of life. By such an acceptance one goes to the depths of one's personality and there destroys in order to rebuild. Such an engagement is as profound a personal revolution as a man can make; and he can contribute nothing more to the establishment of himself in righteousness.

The Permanence of Faith

Faith is a personal revolution, but it is not a single act. It sets up an enduring and stable condition. The righteousness which is granted to faith is maintained by faith. The personal conjunction with Jesus achieved in faith remains; Paul uses the obvious analogy of growth from infancy to maturity. By faith and baptism one is born; by the same faith one lives in the new life to which one is born. Paul makes his own the text of Habakkuk: "The righteous man lives by faith" (Hb 2:4; Rom 1:17; Gal 3:11). The Revised Standard Version has an interesting interpretation in its rendition: "He who through faith is righteous shall live." This interpretation says less clearly that faith is the principle by which a man lives in his righteousness. The personal conjunction with Jesus established by faith puts the believer into the life of the indwelling Spirit. Paul has not in mind a faith which is a mere inoperative sentiment. Faith is operative through love (Gal 5:6). That faith which did not issue in love would be proved spurious by that very fact. For it would be clear that the effect of faith, conjunction with Jesus, had not been achieved.

The Act of Faith

Can we look more closely into this complex psychological process? Here we go beyond the New Testament, which does not engage in psychological analysis. But we shall be on safer ground if we adhere to New Testament language and ideas as closely as possible. Faith arises from an experience; in modern language it is called an encounter with Jesus. The encounter in the New Testament involves either Jesus in the flesh or Jesus in the proclamation; for the same response is given whether Jesus is encountered in the one or in the other. The proclamation was intended, as we have noted often enough, to render Jesus present in such a way that a confrontation with him could not be evaded. I use the word *experience* of set purpose; for how can one describe a personal encounter? One realizes that one meets a new reality in one's life; but this is a daily experience. One realizes that this new reality demands a new response of a type which one has never given before. In what is this conviction rooted? Ultimately in the compelling power which the person manifests; and it is a part of this compelling power that one recognizes that the person responds to needs and desires which we have long had, perhaps without being fully aware of them. The encounter awakens us to possibilities which we have never seen; and we know that this person is what we have been seeking. This awareness is not without anxiety. We know that we are now faced with a decision, that evasion or postponement are themselves decisions. We know that after this encounter our lives will never be the same again.

Recognition

This is the experience; and faith is our response to the experience. Certainly the basic element seems to be recognition. We recognize that the person whom we have encountered speaks to our innermost being, supplies our needs, satisfies our desires. We recognize that this person gives life meaning; I do not say a new meaning, but meaning simply, for we realize that before we encountered this person life had no real meaning. We recognize that this person has revealed to us not only himself but our own true self as well. We recognize that we cannot be our true self except by union with this person. In him the obscure is illuminated, the uncertain yields to the certain, insecurity is replaced by a deep sense of security. In him we find we have achieved an understanding of many things which baffled us. We recognize in his person strength and power which we can sense passing from him to us. Most certainly if most obscurely, we recognize that in this person we have encountered God; and that we shall not encounter God in any other way.

I have used the word recognition to put under a single term psychological responses which are almost as many and varied as there are persons. For some the recognition of faith is the term of a long process of reasoning and argument, of study and investigation. For others it is an insight so sudden that it seems easy. Faith is one thing in the intelligent and educated, another in the simple. But it is important to notice that when I speak of it as the term of a process of reasoning and argument, I do not mean that recognition is the conclusion of the reasoning. There comes a point where reason and argument break down before an object which is above the grasp of reasoning and argument. Here the intelligent and educated are reduced to the same state as the simple. Hence I have called recognition an element in the process and not a step; for the second element exists with the first.

Surrender

The second element is a movement toward the person recognized. The movement, one might say, is accelerated as the recognition grows in clarity; and the movement contributes to the clarity of the recognition. I call it movement rather than desire, for desire in its usual sense means a movement toward something which can be possessed. This is a movement toward a person by whom we wish to be possessed. We have spoken of total personal surrender; the totality is a response to the recognition. For when one moves, one observes that the person recognized has moved to us, that he awaits us, indeed that it is he who moves us rather than we who move ourselves. What we recognize makes us move toward as close and as total a union with that person as is possible. As we approach the union, we see that the union will achieve a totality which no other personal conjunction admits. And so we accept him as we have never accepted anyone before and will accept no one else. His demands surpass all others; his communication of himself likewise surpasses all others. And so we believe in him.

The Sacramental Experience

This description, I trust, does no more than paraphrase in modern language the things we read in the New Testament about faith. I trust also that it presents faith as a revolution in one's personal life, which I have said it must be. We now return to an idea uttered earlier, that the Christian united with Jesus is saved by reexperiencing in himself the saving act; with Jesus he suffers, dies, and rises to a new life. This process is not simply a psychological process. In the primitive Church it was signified and effected by the sacramental ritual. Faith alone does not incorporate the believer in Christ, but faith and baptism. For if it were faith alone, the salvation of man could be conceived as his own personal achievement. The sacramental ritual not only reminds man that his salvation is the work of God; it is the means by which his salvation is effected, and the Church is the agent of the ritual. The salvation of the believer is accomplished in and through the society of the Church.

Myth and Ritual

The sacramental ritual reflects an ancient pattern which is called the pattern of myth and ritual. This pattern was found both in ancient Near Eastern religions and in the mystery cults of the Hellenistic world. The pattern consists in the ritual recital and reenactment of the myth which relates the saving event. The sacramental ritual differs in one respect, and that a vital respect; the saving event which is recited and reenacted is not a mythological event but a historical event. It has become universalized; it is enduring, and not a recurring event like the mythological event. But it is eternally present, for Jesus lives eternally. Were it not eternally present, there could be no effective reenactment; there could be only a commemoration of the event.

The sacraments which are most clearly described in the New Testament are baptism and the Eucharist. It is not relevant to our discussion to deal with the seven sacraments, which as seven were not enumerated until the tenth century. Each of the sacraments is in its own way a recital and a reenactment of the saving event; for each of them is a confession of faith and an incorporation into Christ. But we need look only at baptism and the Eucharist to grasp the sacramental idea in the New Testament.

Baptism: Initiation

Baptism is a rite of initiation; and in this it can be compared to other rites of initiation in the ancient world, particularly in the mystery cults. There is no obvious dependence on any of the

mystery cults; but the idea of ritual initiation was common, and
Christianity would have been eccentric if there were no external
official cultic act by which members were inducted into the
group. Judaism had its rite of initiation, circumcision. It is interesting to notice that circumcision of the proselyte was regarded
by the Jews as legal death. The proselyte took a new name to
signify the appearance of a new individual in the Jewish community. Theoretically the proselyte was relieved of all existing
obligations as completely as if he had died. These included the
marriage bond, family duties, and debts, and it is doubtful that
the theory could be carried into practice completely. It is not at
all unlikely that some aspects of Christian baptism are related to
the Jewish idea of circumcision; the initiatory rite of Christianity
would not be conceived as less effective than the rites of Judaism.
St. Paul insists that circumcision becomes meaningless with the
incarnation; but baptism is as vital in the life of the Christian
as birth in the life of the individual person.

I have called baptism a rite of initiation. By it one becomes a
member of the group which in its origins had no name; the group
was first called Christians at Antioch. But the rite effected more
than membership in a group; it identified the candidate with Jesus
in his saving act. Baptisms attested elsewhere in Judaism were not
so clearly rites of initiation. The Qumran community practiced
baptism as a part of the rite of initiation; and the baptism seems
to have been repeated, perhaps annually. It has not the major
significance which baptism had in the primitive Christian community. The symbolism of the Qumran baptism was the obvious
symbolism of purification; the symbolism of Christian baptism, as
we shall see, was much more complex than this. John the Baptist
attached unusual importance to the baptism which he administered,
and this was recognized by the Jews; otherwise it is difficult to see
why they would have called him "John the baptizer." The symbolism of John's rite was clearly purification from sins; to submit
to the rite was a public profession of repentance. The difference
between John's baptism and Christian baptism is noted in Mark
1:8; John's baptism was done with water, but the baptism of
Jesus was done with the Holy Spirit.

The Necessity of Baptism

That baptism is necessary is stated occasionally in the New Testament (for example, in Jn 3:5), but its necessity is assumed rather than argued. The commission to baptize goes back to Jesus himself. It is rather startling that it is noted that Jesus himself did not baptize, but only his disciples (Jn 4:2). Possibly this reflects the belief that baptism was an encounter with Jesus, and that a personal encounter rendered the rite superfluous. The New Testament knows no way of becoming associated with the group of Jesus' disciples except baptism. The necessity of baptism rests on the fact that baptism is an act of God performed through the Church; man cannot substitute his own efforts for the act of God. Not even the baptism of John, who had himself led some of the disciples to Jesus, was accepted as a substitute for the baptism of initiation (Acts 19:1–5). For the ritual act effects what it signifies; and the simple act of bathing has a potentially multiple symbolism which must be more precisely determined before it can become effective.

The Symbolism of Baptism

The symbolism of Christian baptism is determined, but it is not single. The obvious symbolism of the rite is the purifying bath, and this is mentioned frequently. The Christian has his sins forgiven when he submits to the rite. We have seen that the beginning of the Christian life is the annulling of the past. That which needs annulment most is the sins of one's past. What is notable about this symbolism is the totality of the forgiveness. There is no condemnation for those who are in Christ Jesus (Rom 8:1). By the rite the Christian is rendered holy; and holiness should not be taken in the negative sense of absence. It is a positive relation to God the Father through Jesus Christ; the holy appertains to the sphere of the divine. The newly baptized is innocent. The bath is compared to a new birth; the Christian emerges without any guilt and with his powers to live unimpaired as the infant begins his life with no encumbrances from his past. Here baptism is manifestly the act of God. Simple forgiveness does not itself imply the rebirth of man into a new life. God gives the new life as he gave life in the first place; and he does this through an act which is manifested externally. The rebirth of the Christian should be as much a concrete event as the birth of a new human being.

Baptism as Reenactment

But the act of God is also a reenactment of the saving act performed in Jesus. Baptism is the ritual reenactment, and the symbolism expresses this; Paul especially dwells on this feature. Baptism is death, burial, and resurrection with Christ. Immersion signifies the death and burial, and emergence signifies the resurrection. For the new life to which the Christian is born is the life of the risen Jesus; and this life is conferred when the Christian enters into the experience of Jesus. The rebirth demands a preceding death, the death of the old man of sin. This death also is not effected by a simple act of the will; it is the work of God achieved through the sacramental ritual. Paul introduces Old Testament typology when he represents baptism as a reenactment of the passage of the Israelites through the cloud and through the sea (1 Cor 10:1–2); baptism is the act by which God delivers the Christian as he delivered Israel from the oppression of Egypt. The author of 1 Peter employs a somewhat quaint typology when he makes Christian baptism the reenactment of the voyage in which Noah and his family were saved by passage through the water. In both of these the New Testament is seen as the fulfillment of the Old in a way which is peculiar to the New Testament. Both writers wish to make it clear not only that baptism is a saving act, but also that it is an act of God.

The Formula of Baptism

It is an ancient and famous theological problem what words the primitive Church used in baptism. The Trinitarian formula of Matthew 28:19 has become the official formula not only in Catholicism but also in every Christian community. This formula, however, appears in the New Testament only here. Elsewhere baptism is usually said to be done "in the name of Jesus." Both of these are ancient; and it is not certain that either formula is really a formula in the sense that it reports the words that were employed, although this is very likely. The New Testament, it is now known, contains a large number of allusions to liturgical formulae. But it is doubtful that the primitive Church thought that an exact formula had the importance which is attributed to it in recent theology. As we shall notice, the Eucharistic institution is certainly a liturgical formula; but it admitted variations. Both formulae express the effect of baptism, which was to identify the Christian with Jesus; in biblical language this would be to receive the name of Jesus, not as a personal name but as the name of the Lord to whom the baptized person now belonged. The primitive Church would have seen no difference between baptizing in the name of Jesus and baptizing in the name of Father, Son, and Holy Spirit. We have seen that it was aware of the relationship of the three and of their engagement in the work of salvation (Chapter VII).

The Eucharist

The Eucharist was also a ritual recital and reenactment of the saving event. Unlike baptism, which was performed once — for a man can be born only once — the Eucharist became the distinctively Christian act of worship with the beginning of the Church. That this rite was instituted by Jesus himself is one of the best attested facts in Gospel tradition. The account of the institution, while it varies in unimportant details, has a uniformity which is not usually found in Synoptic parallels. The Eucharistic food and drink have the symbolism of the death of Jesus, explicitly stated concerning the wine in all four sources, explicitly stated for the bread only in Paul (Mt 26:26–28; Mk 14:22–24; Lk 22:17–20; 1 Cor 11:23–25). Of these Paul is almost certainly the earliest literary source; the phrase concerning the body (and the precept of commemoration) should not be regarded as more recent developments. The word "commemoration" is open to some misunderstanding. To us it suggests the honoring and the preservation of the memory of a person or an event. The event commemorated is merely historical. The death of Jesus, we have seen, has more than historical dimensions. Memory in biblical terms, as the study of B. S. Childs has shown, is not mere retention, recollection, and recall. Memory in the biblical language makes the person or event again present, or preserves their presence. I have chosen the term "reenactment" because it renders better than "remember" or "commemorate" the Greek word *anamimnēskein*.

The Eucharistic Rite

The primitive Church chose the day after the Sabbath for the celebration of the Eucharistic rite because this was the day of the week on which the Lord had risen. In addition the primitive community was Jewish, and they continued to worship in the synagogue or the temple on the Sabbath. The service was modeled closely on the synagogue service. It consisted in readings from the Old Testament, a homily, the singing of psalms and hymns, and the blessings. Into this structure the Christian community incorporated a recital of the passion and resurrection; and the reading of Christian documents, such as the Gospels, began as soon as they were written. Some of the written sources of the Gospels came from written recitals prepared for the Eucharistic service. The Old Testament passages no doubt were chosen for their relevance to the Christian event, and the homily dealt with their interpretation. Very early also the homily must have become an explanation of the words and the deeds of Jesus.

The service was climaxed by the recitation of the Eucharistic formula and the distribution of the species. We know from 1 Corinthians that the Eucharistic food was combined with a communal dinner; Paul speaks of certain abuses which occurred at this banquet. The Qumran documents have acquainted us with the messianic banquet, eaten in anticipation of the banquet which God prepares for the elect (Is 25:6), also alluded to in Luke 14:15. The Christians, with or without the influence of Qumran, conceived their weekly service as the messianic banquet. Paul calls the banquet a proclamation of the Lord's death "until he comes" in the Parousia; it is a pledge and an anticipation of the eschatological fulfillment.

The Eucharist was very probably also conceived as the Christian Passover banquet, although scholars are not agreed on this typology. The Jews commemorated the deliverance from Egypt by a ritual meal and a recital of the event. Jesus died either on the day of the Passover or on the day before; this involved controversy need not detain us here, for in either case Jesus celebrated the Passover the night before his arrest, however one explains the variation in dates. The Eucharist was instituted at this meal. Paul has the only explicit reference to Christ as the Christian Passover sacrifice (1 Cor 5:7), and this is not necessarily a reference to the Eucharist. But the association is so near and so obvious that it has long recommended itself to Christian interpreters.

The Symbolism of the Eucharist

The symbolism of the Eucharist is rich. The significance of the rite in the formulae of institution and in Paul's Eucharistic passage (1 Cor 11:17–34) is the significance already mentioned: the reenactment of the death of Jesus. Sharing in the death is signified by the striking symbolism of partaking of the food. Thus the Christion is identified with Jesus as the suffering servant who by his death saves. This symbolism is related to the symbolism of baptism, and one may ask what the one rite was thought to add to the other. The symbolism of food and drink gives the obvious answer. The Eucharist does not imply that the saving act performed in baptism is not efficacious. A new life is created; and life must be sustained. The Christian lives in Christ and Christ lives in him; his life should exhibit the mind and the character of Christ. The Christian cannot live in this way without a constant conjunction with Christ which will render him proof against those things which threaten the integrity of his Christian life. This symbolism is more explicit in the Eucharistic discourse of John 6. John makes no reference to the themes of reenactment of the death. The Eucharistic food is the food of eternal life. Through its consumption Jesus abides in the Christian, and the Christian abides in Jesus.

The Eucharist is the sign of the enduring union of the Christian with Christ and of the vitality of the union. The symbol of food and drink is of its nature repetitive; the symbol establishes the lasting reality of the transformation of the Christian. The lasting reality is also signified by the "blood of the covenant," found in all four sources. In Exodus 24 there is related a covenant ceremony in which the elders, representing Israel, eat a ritual banquet in the presence of Yahweh. The blood of sacrificial victims is smeared on the altar, the symbol of the presence of Yahweh, and on the elders. This community of blood establishes the covenant relationship between Israel and Yahweh. The blood of Jesus is the bond of the new covenant relationship. The covenant theme is not common in the New Testament, for reasons which will appear in a later chapter (Chapter X). It is expressed in the Eucharistic formula. The drinking of the wine obviously is the Christian ritual successor to the sprinkling of the blood. The Eucharist continues the covenant renewal festivals which most Old Testament interpreters now believe were celebrated in ancient Israel, although no explicit record of them is found in the Old Testament. The renewal of covenant was a part of the covenant conception in the ancient Near Eastern world.

The Eucharist as Sacrifice

This leads us to the question of whether the primitive community conceived the Eucharist as a sacrificial rite. Here it seems we must say that it would have to conceive the death of Jesus as a sacrificial act before it could conceive the Eucharist as a sacrificial rite. The death of Jesus as a sacrificial act is explicit in Hebrews; it is striking how the author of this work deals with Old Testament themes in one of the best Greek styles of the New Testament. The death of Jesus has voided the Levitical priesthood and the Jewish sacrificial cult. The total effectiveness of the death renders any other sacrifice impossible; it is the one great saving act which cannot and need not be repeated. The author of this letter was not introducing an entirely new theme. The traces of the sacrificial character of the death of Jesus and of the Eucharist are numerous and clear enough to remove doubt that this theme belonged to the primitive faith of the Church. But no formal exposition of the theme appears in the New Testament before the epistle to the Hebrews. The participation of the primitive Jerusalem community in the temple worship suggests that they had not arrived at the theological development expressed in Hebrews.

The allusion to the covenant ceremony of Exodus 24 is an allusion to the blood of sacrificial animals. The blood of the victims is the symbolic bond of the covenant; but it is also an atoning blood. The words of institution combine the sacrificial blood with the theme of the Suffering Servant. Paul states that participation in the Eucharist renders the Christian incapable of participation in pagan sacrifices (1 Cor 10:14–22). Christians would be incapable in any hypothesis; but Paul chooses this motive, and he alludes to the sacrifices of Israel which make those who participate in the altar partners in the sacrifice. The most significant sacrificial theme is not explicitly called such, and is not recognized except against the ancient conception of sacrifice. The effect of sacrifice was to establish and to maintain communion with deity. This is patent in the death of Jesus, and it is the death which is reenacted. The communion was symbolized by a ritual banquet to which the deity was a party; and the Eucharistic meal fulfills this function of sacrifice in a way which is unique to this rite. Jesus is the bond of communion. Jesus is man, and man is a body. Communion in this case must be achieved on the level of bodily existence, as it is by the partaking of the sacramental food.

The Eucharist is nowhere in the New Testament conceived as a ritual killing of Jesus. Attempts to relate it to the mystery cults break down completely. Modern theological attempts to interpret the significance of the rite have sometimes moved in the direction of a ritual or symbolic killing. This type of explanation rests on a somewhat mechanical conception of sacrifice, in particular on a mechanical conception of the efficacy of the shedding of blood. The Eucharist is not a ritual shedding of blood, and this is not implied by the ritual reenactment of the event. The event was much more than bloodshed. It is communion with the Father, it is life conferred through atoning death.

The Symbol of Christian Unity

The Eucharist is for Paul the sign and the symbol of Christian unity. He finds fault with the Corinthians (1 Cor 11:17–34) because they have introduced divisions into that ritual assembly which is above all things the place where Christian unity is effectively signified. The ritual banquet loses its purpose when the goods brought to the banquet are not shared among the members of the community. This does not reproduce the sentiments with which Jesus made the Eucharistic banquet possible. We shall see that Paul was a stout spokesman for Christian unity; and the abstract idea was for him best realized concretely in the Eucharistic assembly. The disruption of Christian unity seems to be what is most prominent in his mind when he speaks of those who eat and drink of the table of the Lord unworthily and thus eat and drink their own judgment (1 Cor 11:27–29). The unity of the Eucharist — one loaf — is a symbol of the unity of Christians in one body (1 Cor 10:16–17). When Christians partake of the one loaf and the one cup, the body and blood of the one Christ, they declare that they are one with each other in this body. Thus the Eucharist becomes the effective symbol of that which marks the Christian community and the Christian individual as one with Christ: love. This is the fruit of communion.

Liturgy in the Church

"The liturgical revival" has established itself as a factor of primary importance in the modern renewal of the Church which we are witnessing. The revival is not intended to be a return to the ritual practices of the primitive community, although a return to the practice of performing the liturgy in a language native to both ministers and participants deserves serious attention. A study of the sacramental life of the primitive community can be very rewarding; here we have done no more than touch on some aspects of this life, and I believe we can see even from this that our sacramental theory and practice must never lose touch with the New Testament. The sacramental life is the power of God in Christ communicated to the Church. It is the effective sign of the vitality of Christian life. There can be no doubt that in the primitive community all the members were participants in the action, not spectators. When one thinks of strengthening Christian unity in the modern Church, one might think of a somewhat neglected point: the unity between clergy and laity. The focus of this unity, one would believe, would be the focus of the whole of Christian unity, the altar where all Christians join in worship and where all experience the effects of the reenactment of the saving event. In this act all members of the Church can profess together the words of Romans 3:22–23: "There is no distinction. Since all have sinned and lack the glory of God, they are made righteous by his grace as a gift."

IX

The Enduring Reality of the Saving Act

The saving act which God accomplished in Jesus Christ is an enduring reality, we have said more than once. Reality need not be sensible, but it must lie within apprehension of some kind. When we use the word reality, we are talking about something which is more than an object of thought or an image created by the mind of man. We are not speaking of the lasting effects of the saving act. If this were all we meant, the saving act would have no dimension of reality which is not found in all acts to which we give the name historic. Caesar's crossing of the Rubicon still endures in its effects, more faintly now than it did two thousand years ago; it is the nature of historic acts that their effects become overlaid with the effects of other historic acts. When we speak of the enduring reality of the saving act, we mean that its reality has not dimmed in the course of time. The saving act occurred in history, but it is more than historic; for it is the act of God.

I shall attempt no demonstration that the enduring reality of the saving act in the New Testament is the Church. If this is not evident in the New Testament, nothing is evident there. The dimension of the Church corresponds to the dimension of the incarnation. The Church occurs in history, but it is not the product of history. It is the act of God, the inbreak of divine power. It has an identity with Jesus Christ of an order all its own. Wherever we examine the saving act in detail, we find that salvation is communicated to men through the Church. The Church is a perceptible reality; it even belongs to the order of sensible objects, although its full being is not observed by the senses. It belongs to the divine level of existence and to the human level of existence, as Jesus Christ belongs to both levels.

What Is the Church?

I shall not begin with a definition of the Church, although there are standard theological definitions. The Church is beyond definition in the usual sense of the term, just as Jesus Christ is beyond definition; to attempt to define him in logical categories would imply a denial that he exists in the mysterious order of divine reality. No definition of the Church is more than an abstraction of some features of the Church, and these not always the most vital and the most characteristic. The definition of man as a wingless biped does not miss the essential features of man much more widely than some definitions of the Church fail to miss her essential features; only we should not speak of "essential features" where the Church is concerned, for such words place the Church in logical categories. The Church is a mystery, and let us not forget it. It is to be experienced, not defined. For in the Church one attains God; and if one has not attained God, one has not attained the Church.

Jesus and the Church

Did Jesus himself ever speak of the Church? And if he did not, are we not somewhat bold in assuming the connection which we have just assumed? The Word *Church* goes back from English through Anglo-Saxon to the Greek *kyriakon,* "belonging to the Lord," not a biblical word for the Church. *Church* translates the Greek *ekklēsia* in the New Testament; and *ekklēsia,* at the time when the first letters of Paul were written, was the common designation of the community of those who believed that Jesus was the Messiah. The Greek word represents the Hebrew word *kāhāl,* one of the words used in Judaism to designate religious assemblies; *kāhāl* also went into Greek as *synagogē,* our word "synagogue"; and it is very probable that Christians chose the word *ekklēsia* to distinguish themselves from Jewish assemblies.

The assembly intended by the word is a cultic assembly. There are only two Gospel passages, both in Matthew, in which *ekklēsia* occurs in the words of Jesus (Mt 16:18 and 18:17). It is highly unlikely that Jesus used either the Greek or the Hebrew word to designate the group of his associates and followers.

One may not conclude from this that the Church was invented entirely by the disciples of Jesus with no foundation in the works and words of Jesus himself. We are dealing with realities, not with words. The question is whether Jesus was in any way responsible for the formation of a group, and whether the Church is continuous with that group if he was responsible for its formation. Scarcely any interpreter would deny the first of these; many have denied the second, and furthermore, they assert that the break in continuity came in the New Testament itself. The break came, they have said, when the group became structured. We are not concerned now with the complex structure of the modern Church; we shall have occasion to see that except for a few elements the structure of the modern Church is entirely the work of the Church herself, and that the power which erected the structure could alter it or remove it tomorrow if it wished to do so. Our problem lies deeper. But it has to be stipulated that Jesus did not establish a church or a group which became a church simply by gathering disciples.

The Spirit and the Church

We noticed in a preceding chapter (VII) that the coming of the Spirit is a decisive step in both Luke and Paul. We can now say that the decisive step is that the Church comes into existence with the coming of the Spirit. This is more than superficial; for these two writers the Church did not exist as such in the historic career of Jesus. A new reality emerged after his resurrection, and we shall see why it could not emerge until after his resurrection. The other New Testament books do not make this point explicitly, but neither do they make any other point. When we say that Jesus founded the Church, we must not leave Luke and Paul out of calculation. They speak for the faith of the early Church that the Church was constituted by the coming of the Spirit.

The Disciples and the Church

I have said that Jesus did not found the Church merely by gathering disciples. The group of disciples appears in the Gospels as a small rabbinic school of a type familiar in Palestine of the first century. The group had, as we have seen, no clear perception that they were a group with a messianic faith. They were not a cult group. This means that of the three classic elements, creed, cult, and code, two were missing. And the third, code, was not fully developed. They had no awareness during most of the Gospel narrative that they were anything more than a rabbinic school; and the Church is much more. If we try to trace when the awareness of the Church blossomed in the minds of its first members, we find that we cannot improve on the account of Luke; the Spirit revealed the Church to them.

But it is important, nevertheless, that Jesus assembled a group of disciples. For in them the fulfillment of certain Old Testament themes is discerned. Jesus was the new Israel and the corporate personality of the new Israel. This at once places him outside of solitude. The number of the apostles was twelve, the number of the tribes of Israel, and they are promised twelve thrones from which they shall judge (that is, govern) the twelve tribes of Israel (Mt 19:28; Lk 22:30). The new Israel is not to have the same structure as the old. Jesus showed no intention of assuming the presidency of existing institutions and leaving them unchanged. Israel was a society; and the new Israel must also be a society. The disciples are the nucleus of the society.

The Bond of Discipleship

What held the group together? They had no bond other than their personal allegiance to Jesus. He was the center of the group, but the center in a novel way. We have seen that he demanded a total commitment from his followers which had no parallel in the institutions of Judaism or Hellenism. Their relation to him was not the relation of disciples to a rabbi. When the name "Christian" was applied to them (Acts 11:26), it signified the personal allegiance to Jesus which was the bond of the group. Other bonds would arise in the course of time; but the original and vital bond of the group could not be replaced by any other social link. The group was one in Christ from its beginning.

The Twelve and the Apostles

The group was not entirely unstructured. There appears early in the Gospel narratives an ingroup called the Twelve who enjoy a peculiarly close association with Jesus. The Twelve, we noticed, were a new form of the twelve tribes of Israel; and the number had a certain sanctity. Many writers have noticed that the Eleven elected a replacement for Judas Iscariot; they did not elect a replacement for James the brother of John, who was executed under Herod Agrippa in 42. Judas had failed to fulfill his mission as one of the Twelve and therefore had to be replaced. When the Eleven replaced him, they looked for a man who had been in the company from the baptism of Jesus to his "taking up"; and this man should be with the Eleven a witness of the resurrection. The Eleven thus defined membership in the group. The Twelve are not always called apostles, and apostle is a wider term than the Twelve. Paul is sure that he was an apostle, and probably Barnabas also had the title, and some others as well. An apostle can be defined from New Testament allusions as one who had seen the risen Jesus and who had a personal commission from Jesus to proclaim the gospel. When these elements are put together, it is possible that Matthias, although one of the Twelve, was not an apostle.

The Office of the Twelve

Apart from these differences, we can take the term apostle as it is usually taken and include in it the Twelve and those outside the Twelve who were recognized as commissioned to proclaim their personal witness. It is clear that the leadership of the group falls on the apostles with the ascension of Jesus and the coming of the Spirit. The apostles themselves conceived their mission to be the proclamation of the gospel; whatever became necessary in the fulfillment of this primary duty was done with regard to the primary duty. In the primitive community of Jerusalem before it was attacked by Herod Agrippa — which happened between ten and fifteen years after the death of Jesus — we see the Twelve proclaiming the gospel, baptizing, accepting the goods renounced by the members, and administering the distribution of the goods, and presumably presiding over the celebration of the Eucharist; there is never any suggestion that the Eucharist could be handled by just anyone. They appear not too unlike those who have exercised pastoral duties in the Church ever since the apostolic age.

With the rapid progress of the primitive community we see the Twelve making decisions: about the proclamation of the gospel outside Jerusalem, about those who claim to share in the apostolic mission without accreditation, about the relation of Jews and Gentiles in the Church. This last decision was of such moment that we must give it special treatment in a later chapter (X). Indeed, with the growth of the Palestinian community we see the Twelve engaged less in the proclamation of the gospel and more in the administration of a community of believers in the gospel. It is Paul who in the New Testament best illustrates that diffusion of the faith by preaching which we associate with the word "apostolic."

But whether in proclamation or in administration, one cannot miss the fact that most of the Twelve never appear by name. In Acts 1–12 only Peter and John are the heroes of stories of individual action. Quite suddenly a person named James appears as nothing less than the presiding officer of the Jerusalem community. This is difficult to contest; but nothing is related of how he became presiding officer, or how the community became aware that it wanted a presiding officer. Nor are his relations with "the apostles" at all clear. Most intriguing of all, we are not altogether certain that he is the second James mentioned in the lists of the Twelve. Much charming legend has grown up about an apportionment of the world to the Twelve, their preaching and their martyrdom in remote regions. Distressing as it may seem, there is not a shred of historical evidence for any of these legends. We have no certain information about the further career of any of the Twelve after the first dozen chapters of Acts. We are sure that James the brother of John was killed in Jerusalem, and that is all.

There is an old local tradition that Peter died in Rome; that no visit of Peter to Rome is mentioned in Acts is no refutation of this tradition. But the tradition that Peter died in Rome is much less well documented than the tradition that Paul founded the church of Corinth. Setting Peter apart, there is no reason to affirm or to deny that any of the Twelve ever left Palestine.

Apostolic Missionaries

If the Twelve did not, certainly others did. The Twelve admitted other men into the mission of proclaiming the gospel. The anonymity of the first missionaries of Christianity is almost annoying. Who founded the churches of Antioch and Alexandria, which were so great in the early history of the Church? Who founded the church of Rome? Paul even found brethren in the insignificant port of Puteoli (the name survives in the modern Pozzuoli near Naples). Legend has supplied founders (usually apostles or evangelists) for the ancient churches of the Mediterranean world; these legends need not be false, but they are unhistorical. The gospel was carried about by a large number of people, and many of them were not important enough to be remembered. It is absurd to think of the Jerusalem group operating a Bureau of Foreign Missions; but we should not think that no one knew what was going on. The letters of Paul are clear evidence that he exercised some supervision over the churches he founded and over the men who were the officers of these churches. They are also evidence of a surprising amount of communication, both by travel and by letter, between the churches. Paul seems to assume that members of one church will know members of another; and when he wrote his letters it had become nearly impossible for anyone to present himself as a representative of another church without accreditation. This is clearly implied in 2 Corinthians 3:1–3.

The Structure of the Apostolic Church

Thus we find at an early date that the Church has acquired structure. We cannot describe the structure in detail; but the Church was organized, or at least not disorganized. And we can speak of "the Church," not only of "the churches." Karl Rahner has written well and beautifully that each local church is the whole Church, since it contains the fullness of the Christian life. This is entirely a New Testament idea; but the New Testament is aware that the local churches constitute a single larger whole, which even in the New Testament is called simply "the Church." When we ask what holds this community together, we have more than personal allegiance to Jesus Christ, more than a common faith in one gospel, more than a participation in the same sacraments. These would indeed furnish a base for a certain type of unity; but the unity of the apostolic Church is closer.

The Seven

We must look at those whom the apostles associated with themselves in the work of the Church; for the structure of the Church is revealed in these officers. The first whom we find are seven who are chosen to assist the Twelve in Jerusalem. They are called simply the Seven; they are not called deacons. The apostolic Church had deacons, and the office may have arisen from the charge given to the Seven; but the title is not used of the Seven nor any officer in the Book of Acts. The purpose for which the Seven were chosen is clearly stated: they are to take care of the distribution of food and thus to free the Twelve for the ministry of the word. Yet in spite of this clear division of labor, both Stephen and Philip of the Seven proclaim the word and baptize. Certainly the appointment of the officers to the "service" of tables was not understood to exclude them from the "service" of the word. Luke may have compressed here a longer development in the character and functions of the office.

Lists of Officers

Paul speaks in more than one passage of functions or offices within the Church; but it is difficult at times to say whether he is speaking of functions which could be discharged by anyone or functions which were attached to a particular office. Thus in Romans 12:6–8 he enumerates several "charismata," gifts: prophecy, service ("deaconry"), the teacher, the exhorter, the distributor [? of alms], the "president," the almsgiver. All of these could indicate an office; none certainly do, even "president." If they do, almsgiving was evidently an important function. The question turns on whether *charisma* had acquired the meaning of "office." On the other hand, Paul was here writing to a church which was unknown to him personally: and it is doubtful that he would speak of its offices and functions with familiarity in particular terms. These functions are probably described in general terms; they were things which would be done in any church.

Two lists appear which are somewhat parallel, one in 1 Corinthians 12:28, the other in Ephesians 4:11, which is less certainly written by Paul:

1 Corinthians	*Ephesians*
apostles	apostles
prophets	prophets
teachers	evangelists
wonder-workers	shepherds
healers	teachers
helpers	
governors	
speaker in tongues	

The Nature of Church Office

These, Paul says (1 Cor 12:28), God has appointed in the Church. Most of the titles are clearly designations of an office, but here there is an obscurity; it is difficult to believe that the speakers of tongues constituted an office. Similarly one is slow to concede the existence of an official class of wonder-workers or healers. Furthermore, the context of 1 Corinthians is a long discussion of the *charismata:* and there can be little doubt that for Paul the apostolate, prophecy, teaching, and governing were as much *charismata* as miracles and tongues. If this were his mind, then he had not the same understanding of ecclesiastical office as we have. Of this I feel fairly certain anyway. Paul's use of the word *charisma* to designate various functions shows that the primary element in these functions is the gift of the Spirit which empowers the person to fulfill the function. The idea echoes the "charismatic" leader of the Old Testament, the judge or the king, who is impelled to his function by the power of God. The Spirit does not look for human qualifications. Human qualifications are not unimportant, but they are insufficient for the officer of the Church. The function is a grace given for the service of the Church, the building of the body of Christ. Every office is an operation of the Spirit. The Church has no need and no room for offices which are anything else.

Episkopos and Presbyteros

Besides these we have two titles which are less common. *Episkopos* (the Greek word from which *bishop* is derived) meant "overseer"; the word is used in Hellenistic Greek of the officers of a religious community. The word appears once in Acts, once in Philippians, twice in the pastoral epistles (which show a more developed structure); once it is used in 1 Peter in reference to Christ. The technical use of the word for the head of a local church, which was established by the time of Ignatius of Antioch (the end of the first century), is rather surprising in view of this slender biblical basis; plainly the office had become the chief office by a process which we cannot trace. The other title is *presbyteros,* elder. This title in the apostolic Church shows nothing to distinguish it from the institution of elders in the Old Testament, in Judaism, and in most of the ancient world. The elders were the adult males of a town or city to whom local affairs and judgment of cases were committed. Although the word is the etymological ancestor of the English word *priest,* the elders nowhere appear as priests. The Greek word for "priest," *hiereus,* is applied to no officer of the Church in the New Testament; this is another instance in which the usual word was not suitable for a new institution. The word *presbyteros* occurs several times in Acts, nowhere in the Pauline letters, and several times in the other epistles. That these titles have a meaning of their own in the New Testament is clear from the fact that except for *episkopos* in the pastoral epistles, they are always used in the plural of a local church; and several writers have suggested that there was no difference in the office designated, or that the overseers were a kind of executive board of the elders.

An enumeration of these titles seems almost as bewildering to the modern reader as a list of the officers of the Roman Curia and the diocesan chancery would be to St. Paul; and the modern reader will wonder whether continuity in the Church can be traced through its officers. The modern reader is right; we shall essay to set forth the continuity of the Church in a way which is broader and deeper and in which the offices of the Church will be seen as part of a larger reality. Particular offices are of Church institution and can vary from time to time and from place to place; the continuity lies in that from which the offices arise and which the offices serve.

Structure and Order

Our point, however, was that the apostolic Church exhibited structure, and that type of structure which consists in the defining of functions within the organization. Of this there can be no doubt; the apostolic Church was not an anonymous mass of men moved by the Spirit each in his own direction. The identity of a community demands order within the community; it does not demand order of a certain type or a certain degree, and the apostolic Church gives no evidence of uniformity in its order. In Ephesians 4:4–6 the ideal of unity and order is proposed in these words: one body, one Spirit, one hope, one Lord, one faith, one baptism, one God and Father of us all. And it is in these elements that we find the unity and continuity which we are seeking.

For the Church is a unique society, so unique that the word "society" is applied to it only with some danger of misunderstanding. Human societies are recognized by their structure, which are the visible means adapted to the end of the society. A political society has a well-defined end, the common good. Political societies are all at one in their purpose; but they admit variety in the structure by which they intend to achieve the common good. Whatever the structure, it is a vehicle of political authority and can be recognized as such. A structure which is not suitable for the exercise of political authority cannot survive. The end of the Church is not defined by the Church herself; indeed, can one define the end of the Church in any way? Does the Church herself achieve the end she has, or does not rather the act of God worked in the Church achieve the end? And can the Church be recognized in her structure?

Development of Structure

The differences between the structure of the contemporary Church and the structure of the apostolic Church are obvious, so obvious that they can become disturbing. It is the teaching of the Catholic Church that the primacy of the Roman Pontiff and the structure of the monarchical episcopate are of divine institution; these are essential elements of the structure without which the Church would not be the Church. The monarchical episcopate was certainly in existence at the end of the first century, as we have noticed. There is not sufficient evidence to place the monarchical episcopate in the first years of the primitive Church, but this is not important; the monarchical bishops are successors of the apostles. But we have no evidence that the apostles themselves acted as monarchical bishops. The churches we know best in the New Testament are the Jerusalem church and the churches of Paul. Paul was not the "bishop" of any church; he was the apostle of the churches he founded, but identified with no one of them in particular. James in Jerusalem had a position of preeminence; he is not called the bishop of Jerusalem, but we should not quibble about titles.

Peter in the Apostolic Church

The position of Peter in the apostolic group was one of preeminence; this is a commonplace in Catholic theology, and it has within recent years been set forth very clearly by the Protestant scholar, Oscar Cullmann. It is also beyond dispute that to call Peter the "Pope" of the apostolic college is to imply a position of which the New Testament knows nothing. Here again the Acts of the Apostles and the epistles of Paul are our best witnesses; in these Peter appears as a leader, but not as endowed with supreme jurisdiction. We cannot define the position of Peter exactly in any of the terms which we use; and the New Testament has left his position undefined in its own language. The thesis of the primacy is weakened if one attempts to find in Peter the jurisdiction which has been exercised by the Roman Pontiff for some 1700 years. This is a long time, and it takes one back very near to the apostolic Church; but Peter lacks that position in the New Testament which he ought to have if he or anyone else thought of him as Pope.

The College of Bishops

Within recent years, and in particular at the Second Vatican Council, a theological thesis concerning the collegiality of the bishops has taken form. To the student of the New Testament this type of structure is much more evident in the New Testament than either the jurisdictional primacy of Peter or the monarchical government of the episcopate. When we speak of the structure, we ought to look for a central element which remains whatever be the variations in form which the structure may take. It is very probable that collegiality of the bishops is the element which should be so identified. For the Twelve always appear as a college, by which we mean a group to whom the proclamation of the gospel is committed as a group. The deliberations described in Acts 15 are more clearly the deliberations of a college than they are anything else; we are not sure who composed the college, but there is no indication that the decision was reached by an individual person possessed of exclusive authority. Paul supervised the churches he founded; locally each church handled its own affairs, but we find no individual officer whom Paul addresses as head of the church. We have noticed that "bishops" and "presbyters" always appear in the plural even when local churches are mentioned. These are all so many indications that the responsibility fell upon a group and not upon an individual officer; and this is what is meant by collegiality.

The primacy of Peter, then, is a primacy in the college. It is not to be conceived as if Peter were first established as primate and then given others as associates. First the college is established, and Peter is primate within the college. Peter could not be a primate except as a member of the college; he needs the Eleven, and the Eleven need him. He does not derive his position from the college, nor does the college derive its position from him. Indeed it has long been taught in theological schools, even before modern developments, that the bishops have no claim to apostolic succession except as members of the episcopal college which succeeds to the apostolic college. And it should be noted that the earliest method of selection of bishops was election by the congregation; appointment by a Roman bureau has suggested to some theologians that authority is delegated to the bishops by the Roman Pontiff. This position is supported neither in the Bible nor in history. The members of the apostolic college were not agents of Peter, nor are the bishops agents of the Pope.

The Central Structural Element

All these things suggest that the central element in the structure is the apostolic college with its primate. Apart from this central element the structure of the Church can be and has been modified to suit different needs in different times and places. Behind the central element of structure is a more central element, the life of the Church, of which the apostolic college is the agent, the channel, the expression. Through the proclamation of the word and the ministry of the sacraments the apostolic college communicates the life of the Church to its members. And here we can return to an element mentioned earlier: the power of God which breaks into the world in the incarnation. The apostolic college is the enduring center of this power. But when we speak of the power revealed and operative in Jesus Christ, we speak of a unique power that must not be defined as mere authority. It is the power to save; it is the power of love. This the apostolic college must manifest if it is the genuine continuation of the life and mission of Jesus. That which Jesus established as primary in the new life which he confers must be no less primary in the college on which his Church is structured. This power is the Spirit dwelling in the Church. The Spirit dwells in the whole Church and in all its members, and it can reach its full activity in any one of them. But if the structure of the Church means anything, it should mean that the life of the Spirit is centered in the apostolic college and in that body which succeeds the apostolic college. From the college the Spirit should be mediated to the rest of the Church, principally through the proclamation of the word and the ministry of the sacraments, but also in the ways in which Jesus communicated the Spirit: through personal influence.

Church Government

Up to this point I have studiously avoided the use of the word "government," or any word which would suggest the idea. It is a conventional thesis in theology that the triple office of the hierarchy is to teach (the ministry of the word), sanctify (through the ministry of the sacraments), and rule. I have no desire to remove this third office from the Church, but only to suggest that it be considered in the light of the New Testament. And the first thing one notices about the New Testament is that government is not a prominent part of the apostolic office. I have said that the mission of the apostles was to proclaim the gospel and to administer the sacraments, and to do all in the community which these two offices required. The proclamation of the word and the ministry of the sacraments are functions which have no parallel in any merely human society. Government is the function of the human society, and in particular of the political society. Must not the Church have a government which is uniquely ecclesial, dissimilar to any other form of human government? In a Church whose inner life is the Spirit can there be an exercise of authority which is not an operation of the Spirit?

Church Government and Secular Government

The Christian community has long been aware that the rulers of the Church rather easily imitate the external forms and structure of human government. No one is really sorry that the day of the prince bishop is over; we have trouble explaining how such an institution ever arose in the Christian community. It is, no doubt, only natural that when the Church emerged from her primitive condition and became gradually the dominant society in western Europe, she should have adopted the only forms of authority known. But how often can the Church afford to do what it is natural to do? Should there not have been someone to recall the Gospel account of the temptations of Jesus, in particular that temptation in which Jesus was shown all the kingdoms of the earth? Indeed there should have been and there were; the list of those who have wondered whether pomp and power exhibit the genuine image of the Church is long and includes many names which are venerated in the Church. The accretion of pomp and power to the hierarchy and clergy was surely the result of good faith and devotion, of a desire to present the Church to men in a manner becoming to her dignity. Such an impressive institution deserves, one would think, an impressive manifestation of itself. It is precisely here that a danger arises; the Church may present an image of herself which is more the image of a Renaissance princedom than of the suffering Son of Man and the Reign of God. For pomp and power are signs of success in human enterprises; they can be signs of failure in the life and work of the Church.

Power and Authority in the Gospels

The number of New Testament texts in which power and authority in the Church are mentioned is not great: and these texts have received at least their full value in theological treatments of the ecclesiastical polity. It is not my purpose here to demonstrate the existence of power and authority in the Church, for such a demonstration is altogether unnecessary; if theological argument has been active anywhere, it is in this area. But when power and authority are discussed, certain sayings of Jesus should not be omitted. In one episode (Mt 18:1–5; Mk 9:33–37; Lk 9:46–48) a dispute arose among the disciples as to who was the greatest in their group. Mark alone has the interesting note that when Jesus asked them what they were talking about they were silent; they knew his mind, and they were ashamed to reveal the topic of the dispute. The answer of Jesus was pointed. The one who wishes to be first among you should be the last and the servant of all. He strengthened his saying by leading a child into the group; if anyone wishes to be first, let him become a child, because the Reign of God is for children. The sharpness of this answer has not always been appreciated. Effectively Jesus says there is no "first" in the Reign of God. If you want to be first, become every man's lackey; return to your childhood and then you will be fit for the first place. Jesus leaves little room for ambition; and he leaves no more room for the exercise of power. Lackeys and children are not the bearers of power.

A second saying is placed by Matthew and Mark after the petition of the mother of the sons of Zebedee for the first places in the Reign for her sons; Luke transfers the saying to another context, but relates it to an unspecified dispute concerning precedence (Mt 20:25–28; Mk 10:42–45; Lk 22:24–30). Here Jesus compares the government of the secular state to the condition of the Church. He speaks of the secular government in harsh terms; the great men and kings of the nations lord it over their subjects and tyrannize — and for this, adds Luke with a touch of sarcasm, they receive the title of "benefactor." But you — not so; let the first among you become the lackey of others, as Jesus himself came to be the lackey of others. The antithesis between the exercise of power in secular states and in the Church could scarcely be drawn more clearly. But what is the antithesis? Jesus does not contrast the improper exercise of power with the proper exercise. One may say, and indeed many have said, that power exercised without "lording" and tyranny is the power which the state should exhibit; and that such power is not unworthy of the Church. If Jesus had wished to distinguish between the proper and the improper exercise of power he had the vocabulary in which to do this. It was unnecessary to contrast domination and tyranny with being a lackey and a slave.

A New Idea of Leadership

Such passages could seem to destroy authority within the Church and leave not even a democratic society, but rather a horde of rugged individualists, each self-propelled in his own direction. Such a picture is not the picture of the apostolic Church, nor can it be deduced from any of the sayings of Jesus. We encounter here a situation not unusual in the New Testament: a new reality which it is difficult to portray in the language of custom. The Church is unlike any other society; and when we attempt to make the Church intelligible, we easily fall into language which assimilates it to other societies. The point of the passages quoted, if they have any point at all, is that the leadership of the Church must not be exercised in the manner of secular leadership. There is no room for power struggles within the Christian community. Indeed, there is no power in the ordinary sense; those who occupy the top positions have a more complete dedication of service. "Service," like "charity," is a word which has lost much of its gospel connotations. Jesus and his listeners caught the full force of the metaphors of child and lackey which he used; the force is not so readily caught in a modern world where the title of "public servant" is given to public officials who are aware of their power to dominate others, and are usually quite jealous of it. Jesus left with his apostles and their successors the duty of arriving at a new conception of leadership corresponding to the new community which he created.

Here we can ask two questions: Did Jesus leave with his Church the resources to create a new concept of leadership? And has the Church created this new concept? One can scarcely doubt that Jesus left his Church the resources to accomplish all that pertains to her mission. But if one looks in the New Testament for something like a manual for executives, one will hardly find it — unless one wishes to call the pastoral epistles such a manual. Certainly these epistles deal expressly with the responsibilities of the leaders of the Church, and no one would suffer if they were taken as a manual. But they presuppose a great deal, and the presuppositions are not trivial. They not only presuppose that the leader will himself exhibit in a high degree the life of the Christian; they say it explicitly. They presuppose that his leadership, like the rest of his life, will be motivated by the principle which motivates all Christians: love. Leadership will be an act of love as much as any other act in the life of a Christian; and if one wishes a more precise definition of what love in leadership can be, a careful reading of 1 Corinthians 13 should be revealing. Or, to risk a summary statement: if one has learned what it is to be a Christian, one has learned what it is to be a leader in the Christian community. For successful leadership in this community is not measured by the usual standards of wisdom, prudence, efficiency, and production; it can be measured only by those standards by which the Christian life is measured, by the fullness with which the life of Christ flourishes in the leadership.

Leadership and the Spirit

Leadership in the Church is like the Christian life in another respect. The Christian life itself is not the work of man but the work of the Spirit dwelling in the Church. Successful leadership also is the work of the Spirit and not the work of man. The Spirit in the Church does not displace the human powers of intelligence and will; but these powers are helpless without the Spirit. The leader also is helpless if he is left to his personal and organizational resources, however abundant these may be. The Spirit does not supply intelligence, judgment, or courage which may be lacking. The Spirit does supply the fullness of faith, hope, and charity which should give form to leadership. Too frequently the leaders of the Church have counted on the Spirit for what the Spirit does not give and counted on themselves for what the Spirit does give. One wonders whether the Spirit is present with all its force in the Church when the words "obedience" and "due submission" and "duly constituted authority" are heard in the Church more frequently than the word "love." One could suspect an effort to substitute for the power of love the power of domination; and one is reminded of the kings and magnates of the Gentiles.

Yes, Jesus has endowed the Church with ample resources to create a new concept of leadership. Has the Church created such a new concept? If she has not, she has failed in a part of her mission which seems to be vital; and this conclusion is inadmissible. The history of the Church exhibits an imposing number of names of men who have known what Christian leadership is. That it exhibits an even larger number of names of men who have not had the slightest notion of Christian leadership is no more an affirmation of the failure of the Church than the fact that she has harbored so many mediocre Christians of all states. The Church has no guarantee against corruption either in her leadership or in her membership. She has had corruption in the past, she has it in the present, and there is scarcely any doubt that she will have it in the future. As long as the Church is a field for personal ambition for power or even for wealth, she can be prostituted for ambitions which are legitimate in another society. The conception of the Church as a means of personal advancement, and in particular as a means by which one can acquire vulgar power over one's fellow man, is such a shocking denial of Jesus Christ that it leaves one speechless. In fact it is probably because it is such a shocking deviation that it so often passes unnoticed.

Failure of Leadership

For this is the basic corruption of leadership in the Church, besides which other forms of corruption such as concubinage and the acquisition of personal fortunes, dishonesty and unfairness, mendacity, treatment of other persons as means and not as ends, are merely accessory or consequent. The leadership of the Church is corrupted when it is conceived in terms of power and not in terms of love. It is corrupted when the leader refuses to think of himself as a lackey who did not come to be served but to be a slave and to give his life for the salvation of many. I have likened it to the temptation of Jesus; for if it is permitted, men worship the evil one. Power corrupts love. Perhaps bureaucratic power corrupts love more than any other form of power does.

The Strength of Leadership

I said the Church has no guarantee against corruption in her leadership. I should add that she has more than sufficient means to prevent it. The most important of these means, surely, is the awareness which the Church has of her identity and mission. She is the body of which Jesus Christ is the corporate personality; in the language of St. Paul, she is the body of which Christ is the head or the totality. It is not insolent, I trust, to observe that in the New Testament the Church has no other head but Christ. In this body no one is more a member than anyone else. There are different charismata but one and the same Spirit. The same divine life moves in all the members. This body is recognized as the Church of Christ by her unity, not by her divisions. The unity of the Church is the love which unites the members with each other and with Jesus; it is not a unity of authority. Jesus has authorized no one to substitute control for love. This is the essential structure of the Church which her organization must reflect. At best the organization can reflect it no better than imperfectly; at worst the organization can make it quite difficult to see the identity of the Church with the body of Christ. When the Church ceases to be a community of love, it will have ceased to be itself. We believe this cannot happen; but we are aware that the Church need not be as far from her ideal self as she often has been. And it should not be her leaders who dim the image of the community of love.

Successful Leadership

The Church is guarded against corruption also by the awareness of her mission. One may readily admit that it is more difficult to be aware of the mission in some offices of the Church than in others. When one is engaged in the proclamation of the gospel and the ministry of the sacraments, one can be no closer to the actual living work of the Church. It is more difficult to see the ecclesial aspect of administration, particularly because administration tends to take on the form and substance of the administration of secular business. But no officer of the Church and no member can ever afford to forget that the enterprise in which he shares is the building up of the body of Christ. He is a part of the agency through which the saving act of Jesus Christ is mediated to men, both the members of the Church and those whom the Church wishes to gain as members. The success of the Church is solely and purely in the growth of the life of the Spirit in her members. No other statistically analyzed achievement has any relevance to her mission. She is not judged by the number of her members, the property she owns, the institutions she operates, the influence she has in the secular world of politics and economics. She may and sometimes must engage in all these things to fulfill her mission; but she has not accomplished her mission unless through these things men become one with Jesus in the Spirit. It is not therefore encouraging to hear Catholics speak of these activities as if they were an index of the flourishing condition of the Church. We simply do not know when the Church is flourishing because we lack the standards by which it should be measured.

Scarcely anyone, I think, would question that this is the mission of the Church. One wonders why our practice does not always reflect this conviction. When we Catholics adopt as our own the journalese jargon which gives the name of "top jobs" to administrative positions in the Church, we give occasion for the question where we rank the "jobs" of preaching and administering the sacraments. To speak of the mission of the Church in this language is to adopt secular values, which are good in their world but not in the Church. One is reminded of the analysis of ideate and sensate cultures made by Pitirim Sorokin. In Sorokin's terms the Middle Ages were an ideate culture. In this type of culture thought and the arts attract the best minds, and theology was the most respected employment in the Middle Ages. The modern world is a sensate culture in which production is our greatest achievement; and the best minds are attracted to executive positions in the world of commerce and industry. Sorokin's analysis does not satisfy all his fellow scholars; it does not, for instance, account for the prince bishop of the Middle Ages. But whether we think of the leader of the Church as a prince or as an executive, it is clear in either case that Church leadership takes the form which is most admired in the contemporary secular society. The mission of the Church in its purity is admired in no secular society, ever.

Leadership and the Led

The Church in the New Testament is described as a community of love in which the Spirit dwells; and through the indwelling Spirit of love it becomes the body of Christ. We must repeat that the Spirit dwells in the entire Church and in each of its members; it is not given exclusively to the leaders of the Church. No one is a purely passive member of the Church. The Spirit is power by which the Church fulfills her mission. She will do much less than she is able if the lay members of the Church are unconscious of their power, either through their own failure to observe it or because they have been told by their leaders that they do not have it. A genuine idea of the mission of the Church must include the functions of all her members in the mission.

Lay Activity

In modern times there has been for a number of years a restless stirring among both clergy and laity concerning the position of the laity in the Church. The feeling is widely expressed that there should be more lay activity in the Church, that the Church should be less closely identified with the clergy, that the laity can and must participate in the work of the Church. If the New Testament has anything to contribute to this problem, certainly we ought to study it closely; for it must be confessed that the active role of the laity is not yet clear. And the preceding paragraphs may seem to indicate that there is little to add from the New Testament; for I have emphasized the proclamation of the gospel and the administration of the sacraments as the essential mission of the Church.

The Laity and the Proclamation

That the layman can have no active role in the administration of the sacraments is clear beyond discussion; no such radical alteration of the structure of the Church is possible. That the layman can have no active role in the proclamation of the gospel is not clear at all. The proclamation of the gospel is the office of the bishop. The bishop commissions his clergy to assist him in this work, which is too much for one person. There is nothing in the structure of the Church which prevents the bishop from commissioning laymen as well. This does not mean that the laity would receive the commission of preaching in the formal sense, that is, of addressing the congregation in the church from the pulpit. But the proclamation of the gospel is a much wider function of the Church than the office of formal preaching. Every parent who undertakes the religious instruction of his children engages in the proclamation of the gospel. Every layman who takes up the work of theological teaching and scholarship engages in work which is closely related to the proclamation of the gospel. And there is now an urgent need for educated and devoted laymen and laywomen who are willing to accept a career in theological teaching and research. Every layman who has the opportunity or the obligation to speak as a Catholic in public, whether orally or in writing, is concerned with the proclamation of the gospel. We are all too familiar with utterances of laymen which show a profound ignorance of Catholic faith and Catholic traditions. The laity have far more occasions than the clergy when they can and must speak as Catholics to the world; when they evade the opportunity or distort the Church by what they say, something has been lost which cannot be recovered elsewhere.

Universal Lay Activity

The number of those who have such opportunities, of course, is limited; and we should not conceive an active laity in terms of a small elite group. Lay activity, if it is to be meaningful, must include every member of the Church. This activity we have not yet found. One may allege the institution of the seven helpers of the apostles related in Acts 6 as an example, and an example it is. The functions of the Church which are not directly executions of her mission of proclamation and sacramental ritual should be fulfilled by those who are not directly committed to this office. The activity for which the Seven were chosen was the distribution of alms. This is an office which the Church has recognized from the beginning as hers; and it is an office which is more properly fulfilled by the laity than by the clergy. Nor has the laity ever been unaware that this is one of the works of the laity; one may regret that it is not more widely recognized, but the laity as a whole do not fail in this respect. That almsgiving has been bureaucratized may have something to do with the limited recognition of the office; what is done by a central headquarters releases the individual person from doing it. Almsgiving in the New Testament is a personal communication; a doubtful increase in efficiency may be a small reward for the sacrifice of personal engagement with one's fellow man. The mere giving of money is a kind of purchase of release from the duty not unlike the older practice of purchasing a substitute for military service. Recent statistical estimates show that even the payment for release has not reached the point in the United States where pain is felt by the Catholic body as a whole. Efficient administration has brought us to the point where the giving of self rather than of one's goods has become the work of a small corps of dedicated specialists.

The Spirit and the Laity

The laity look for directions on how they should become active; and this itself may be a sign that we are slightly sick. The New Testament contains no directions left by Jesus on how the apostles were to fulfill their mission in detail. They were commissioned to proclaim and to baptize. How they were to accomplish this was left to their personal responsibility. Under the impulse of the Spirit they showed resolution and decision; it is slightly ludicrous to imagine them huddled in Jerusalem awaiting directions from on high. We, perhaps, expect the leadership in the Church to do what only the Spirit can do, the Spirit which dwells in all the members of the Church. The laity know their potentialities and their opportunities better than the clergy know them, or they ought to. They too have the resources to fulfill their mission.

For in the New Testament the laity are a part of the structure of the Church. This point is not so obvious or so trivial as to be passed without comment. The Church does not consist exclusively of her leaders. It is not without interest that in the New Testament the words which signify vocation are used only of vocation to faith, not to any particular state within the Church. The lay state is not a nonvocation, and a person is not a layman simply because he has not chosen to be anything more. He is called to be a Christian, and this means that he is called to be one in whom Christ lives. Christ scarcely lives in anyone, we would think, if that person were merely passive and nonresistant. And if the layman has a vocation, he, like the apostles, must find the way in which he is to accomplish it. The Spirit enables him to be directed from within. He will find what he can do if he is not told too often that he cannot find it, if he is not stifled by a mass fear that Catholicism may realize its power and become what it ought to be.

The Church as Witness

Therefore, no directions are offered here on how the layman can realize his potentialities. But I think we can return to an idea which was set forth earlier, the biblical idea of witness (Chapter II). This was one of the terms in which the apostolic Church conceived its mission, and it is applicable to laity as well as to clergy. There is no Christian who cannot bear witness to the risen Jesus. The Greek word *martyr* means witness; and we have perhaps admired the supreme witness so much that we have not seen so clearly that every Christian is a witness all the time. This is the fundamental vocation of the Christian, lay or cleric. The witness of the clergy is or can be quite clear to the clergy; the witness of the layman is more obscure. Yet he is the living Christ; and if he does not manifest Christ, no one else will do it in his state and condition. Yet often he does not do it because he has been told that there is no clear obligation for him to do it in this or that set of circumstances. There was a logical means of evasion for most Christians who have been faced with the choice of martyrdom. Possibly they refused the evasion because they saw that if they did not bear witness in this crisis they would never bear it anywhere. Lesser crises do not make this so luminously evident; and one can always find a reason for putting off the witness in any particular situation. Here we may be looking for a clarity of insight which we shall never have. Perhaps we shall evade less frequently if we remind ourselves that each man bears witness by his own independent and responsible choice. We ought to have enough confidence in the Spirit to let the Spirit work, and not to replace the movement of the Spirit by routine and discipline. There are some things which routine and discipline do not achieve. Love is one of them.

X CRISIS IN THE CHURCH

Saul

Within a few years after the death of Jesus the Jewish leaders had become bitterly hostile to the group of the disciples of Jesus. Several hearings before Jewish tribunals were held, and some of the disciples suffered legal punishments. At a date which cannot be determined, but which must have fallen between the removal of Pontius Pilate as procurator in 36 and the accession of Herod Agrippa as satellite king in 41, the hostility reached a peak in the stoning of Stephen. The Jewish authorities, taking advantage of a vacuum in the Roman administration, decided on harsh measures even outside of Judea; and they dispatched a commission to Damascus to arrest the disciples of Jesus there. The commission was headed by a young rabbi named Saul, a Hellenistic Jew of Tarsus in Cilicia, who had proved his dedication to Judaism by zealous hunting of the disciples.

Near Damascus an event occurred which was revolutionary in the career of the primitive Church. The event is related three times in Acts (9, 22, and 26) and is alluded to in Galatians 1:13–16. Saul saw the risen Jesus and was stunned into insensibility and temporary blindness. When he recovered he had become a disciple; more than that, as Paul he now began to proclaim Jesus as Messiah. It seems that he was not entirely acceptable to the Christian community, for the next few years of his life are obscure. He appears again in Acts 13 when he and Barnabas are commissioned by the Church of Antioch to the work for which the Spirit had selected them. This work was the proclamation of the gospel in Cyprus and Asia

Minor. Their procedure in each city was to proclaim Christ in the synagogues and to call the Jews to faith. At Antioch in Pisidia, however, the hostility of the Jews exhibited itself not only in refusal to believe but in harassments of the apostles. Paul and Barnabas then declared that since the Jews rejected the gospel they would proclaim it to the Gentiles. Thus began the career for which Paul was a chosen instrument (Acts 9:15), the apostolate to the Gentiles which God committed to Paul as he had committed the apostolate of the Jews to Peter (Gal 2:7–8).

The Mission to the Gentiles

I have called the conversion of Paul revolutionary not because the apostolate to the Gentiles was an idea original with him or because it would not have happened without him, but because the apostolate to the Gentiles received its form from Paul. The apostolate to the Gentiles caused the first crisis in the life of the primitive Church. From this crisis the Church perceived its true identity and mission; and in the resolution of the crisis it arrived at a statement of every important theological truth which it proclaimed. These statements appear in the Gospels; but the principal source of the statements is the Pauline corpus of epistles, which come from Paul himself and from the Pauline group or school. It is evident from the epistles that Paul was endowed with a fertile and active mind which was at once both rapid and penetrating. He was also endowed with a generous flow of language which can be so abundant that at times it approaches incoherence. The reader scarcely notices the incoherence; the language of Paul communicates the profound conviction of the truth of the gospel which Paul possessed, and the total personal dedication with which he gave himself to Jesus Christ. He has been called a second founder of Christianity, and by a few scholars of extreme views even the first founder: neither title is accurate. Paul himself is one of the strongest witnesses that Christianity had only one founder and no second. But these exaggerations are a tribute to the formative influence of Paul on the New Testament and the Church. This influence centers upon the crisis of the Gentile mission.

Jewish Christians

We have seen that the primitive community was a small group of Jewish "messianists" who added to Jewish belief and practice faith in Jesus Messiah. This faith they proclaimed within the Jewish community. They were not explicitly aware of themselves at this stage as the new Israel; it seems they rather thought of themselves as the agents of the renewal of Israel. Through faith in Jesus Messiah, Israel would accept the Reign of God, which God would then extend to the entire world with the Jews as his messengers. This was the destiny of Israel; and the task of the community, while not easy, was simple. The apostles seemed in this conception to be continuing the proclamation of Jesus himself, who had addressed the Jewish community exclusively. The community did not depart from Judaism and saw nothing in its proclamation which compelled a departure from Judaism. When the schism finally occurred, the community felt the Jews had expelled the Christians, not that the Christians had left the Jews. More profoundly, the Christians believed that the Jews in rejecting Jesus Messiah had rejected Judaism, and that the Christians were the true Israel, the remnant which God had left. But these things were not perceived in the first years of the primitive Church.

Gentile Christians

The ambivalent attitude of the primitive Church toward Gentile converts is further complicated by some ambiguity in the records. Critics have long noticed that the first fifteen chapters of Acts are historical narrative of a much more free type than the last chapters, which include the "We" passages. The author was personally engaged in the events of these later chapters. For the earlier chapters he depended on reports which evidently were scattered. The question of the reception of the Gentiles is raised in the story of Cornelius of Joppa and his household (Acts 11). Here Peter needs a vision to be convinced that he should baptize these Gentiles. Once he is convinced, he understands that God does not respect persons; the faith of any man is acceptable to him. The

Gentiles were baptized; and when Peter was taken to task by the Christians of Jerusalem for receiving the Gentiles, his account of his vision settled all objections.

The further developments in Acts and the epistles of Paul make it clear that all objections were not settled. A number of writers have suggested that the story of Cornelius is a narrative exposition of the theological truth that salvation is for the Gentiles and of the historical truth that Peter recognized this. Paul attests in Galatians 2 that Peter's principles were sound, but that his practice was inconsistent with his principles. One can conclude from the story of Cornelius and from the account of Paul that Peter's understanding of the position of the Gentiles in the Church was not as clear as the understanding of Paul.

The Judaizing Party

Whatever Peter's attitude was, it did not convince all the Jewish Christians. Acts 15 introduces us to some "from Judaea" and "of the party of the Pharisees" who taught that no one could be saved unless he were circumcised and accepted the obligation of the Law of Moses. The epistles of Paul, in particular Galatians and Romans, also attest the existence of this party. Paul even more than Acts attests that the party was quite strong. Johannes Munck has recently proposed the thesis that the adversaries of whom Paul speaks were not Jewish Christians but Gentile converts who had become Judaizers. This thesis is difficult to sustain; but Munck is surely right at least to the extent that many Gentile Christians were convinced that circumcision and the Law were absolutely necessary for the Christian. The issue was clearly joined. The Judaizing party claimed that one could not become a Christian unless he became a Jew first. Jewish proselytism was a long-established practice; the proselyte submitted to circumcision and the full obligation of the Law and, as we have seen, was reborn in the Jewish community.

James

This claim, it seems, could scarcely have been made unless the practice of Judaizing already existed. Paul, in spite of his principles, permitted Timothy to be circumcised because his mother was Jewish. It would be easier to understand this if Timothy's father had been Jewish; and we can gather from this how much pressure was exerted by the Judaizers. Paul's practice was very probably regarded as a deviation from established custom. But custom alone does not explain the strength of the Judaizing party; and interpreters have long wondered whence their power came, particularly since Peter cannot be included among them. Yet Peter also yielded to pressure and refused to sit at table with Gentiles, although he had eaten with them until emissaries came "from James" (Gal 2:12). On the basis of this verse a number of interpreters have elected James as the chief of the Judaizing party; no one else is mentioned, and it is difficult to account for the strength of the party unless the party included some respected Church leaders. From the tone of Paul's letters we gather that he felt beleaguered; and the tone is somewhat excessive if Paul had no one to deal with except a few eccentrics. Yet Paul includes James among those who accepted his Gospel (Gal 2:9). That James reversed his position is possible. One suspects a certain degree of politeness in all the documents by which the names of the adversaries are avoided; and such politeness is not shown except to important people. James is also cited in Acts 15 as supporting the position of Paul with unimportant reservations.

A reason why James might have reversed his position can be conjectured. It is clear from Galatians 2:7–9 that Jerusalem's approval of Paul's gospel was given under the condition that Paul should proclaim the gospel to the Gentiles only; the evangelization of the Jews was the exclusive field of the Jerusalem Church and its affiliates. Chronology becomes a pressing problem here into which we need not go; for there is no assured chronology of the period by which we can solve the problems. In the course of events given in Acts, Paul, even after the council of Jerusalem, continued his practice of proclaiming the gospel in the synagogues before he approached the Gentiles. This occurred in Philippi (Acts 16:16), Thessalonica (Acts 17:2), Berea (Acts 17:10), and Corinth (Acts 18:3). If these areas were evangelized after the agreement described in Galatians, Paul was rather careless of his commitments. He may have thought that since these cities lay in the entirely new mission field of Europe, they were not covered by the agreement. But it is easier and kinder to Paul to suppose that the agreement had not yet been reached. If it had been reached, James had excellent reason for reversing his position; but it seems very probable that the agreement had not been reached and that Paul is not to be charged with insincerity.

Two Churches?

The agreement as described in Galatians involved problems which we are surprised were not foreseen. Effectively the agreement created two churches, one Jewish and one Gentile. In large cities the two distinct churches would stand somewhat as national parishes used to stand in the cities of the United States. They would be a sign of division, not of unity. As such they were offensive both to the Jerusalem leaders and to Paul, who wrote of Christian unity more than any other New Testament author. Very probably again it did not take long for the consequences of the agreement to become evident. When they did, the Jerusalem group led by James desired the only unity they knew, the unity of all Christians in the parent Jewish community. Paul had by this time reached another conclusion; and it is this conclusion which lies behind the composition of the epistles.

The Problem of the Jerusalem Council

But when was the agreement reached? And how was the difference resolved? The Council of Jerusalem, we have seen, could not have been a final resolution of the debate; and some modern scholars have proposed a rather daring view which would solve most of the problems. It has been customary to identify the Council of Jerusalem with the meeting of Paul and the "pillars" described in Galatians 2, principally because the chronology will allow nothing else. But to solve the chronological problems here raises more problems. Paul nowhere alludes to the council nor to the decision set forth in Acts 15:20. If Paul had the support of a general assembly for his position, it is strange that he would not quote it, or that he would call it a private conference with the leaders. It is strange also, as we have noticed above, that Paul would be unfaithful to an agreement which he had accepted. Recent writers have sought a solution in the literary character of Acts 1–15. We have already noticed that the accounts in this part of the book are often narrative expositions of theology and not a literal account of events. It is noticed further that Luke, both in the Gospel and in Acts, is a conciliatory writer. He has less anti-Jewish polemic than any other Gospel; and here it should be remarked that the anti-Jewish polemic is not so much anti-Jewish as anti-Judaizing Christians. Luke moved toward a reconciliation, if indeed he was not writing after the problem had ceased to be acute. The Church had learned much from the question, and Luke wished to state what had been learned. In the hypothesis of recent scholars the Council of Jerusalem as it is described never occurred; it is a theological statement of an agreement which was actually reached, and of the position which the Church finally took on the question of the Gentiles. This hypothesis I have called daring; and it must stand or fall on the literary character of Acts 1–15. Acts 15 cannot be explained in this way as an isolated piece; but, to repeat, it solves most of the problems of the events.

The Final Resolution

In this hypothesis, the problem was not finally resolved by any of the agreements reached. It was resolved by the Jewish rebellion against Rome and the ensuing war which destroyed both Palestinian Judaism and Palestinian Jewish Christianity. But the problem was already speculatively resolved. The Church knew what she was and what she had to do, and Paul is the chief witness of her knowledge of herself. I say chief and not only; for the Gospels, both the Synoptic Gospels and the Fourth Gospel, show abundant reflections of the controversy. The Gospels are also witnesses to the thinking of Paul, which became the thinking of the Church. What is called in the Gospels "anti-Jewish polemic" should not be confused with vulgar anti-Semitism. I have observed above that the New Testament writers were more concerned with Jewish Christians who wished to put Judaism on a level with the gospel than with Jews who rejected the gospel. A close study of the Gospels will show that the controversy is conducted on a purely theological plane. Misguided Christians who have transferred the controversy to the social and political plane had no warrant in the New Testament for the transfer.

The Origins of the Controversy

I said above that Luke constructed his narrative from scattered sources. The New Testament student who attempts to continue the construction from scattered sources should have no trouble feeling sympathy for Luke; and he will not be inclined to suppose that Luke had a complete file of data from which he made just that selection which is most apt to confuse. But whatever Luke's data may have been, we are free to ask how the controversy arose; for we have no account of this. Like so many important controversies, it seems to have arisen without any planning. We can deduce — and we have deduced — that the original practice of the primitive Church, when it first received Gentiles, was to incorporate them into the Jewish community, as they themselves were incorporated. The number of Gentile converts was probably not so great that the practice caused any difficulty. This action, it seems, was taken without reflection; but it had theological implications. And we can remark by the way that the Church can take no action which does not have theological implications; this lesson from the controversy could have been better learned.

Theological Position of the Judaizers

What were these theological implications? First, that the Christian community was a part of the Jewish community. Second, that the process of salvation was initiated in Judaism and completed in Christianity. Third, that the work of the Church was conditioned by Judaism. Fourth, that the fulfillment of the Church would consist in incorporating all men into a Christianized Judaism. These are the more tolerable implications; some less tolerable implications were pointed out by St. Paul, as we shall see shortly. We should not think that the position of the Judaizers was entirely unfounded. The community was the new Israel, as we have seen;

this idea does not of itself signify any detachment from historic Israel. Jesus himself had been a member of the Jewish community and had spoken to Jews exclusively. A messianic community which was not a Jewish community was difficult to conceive. The revolutionary character of the gospel had not been grasped by the Judaizers.

Theological Position of Paul

It seems very likely that the original practice of Paul similarly had arisen without reflection. Gentiles were not Jews and they were called to faith in Christ and baptism. Paul saw no reason why more should be demanded of them. In the sources one can almost catch the shock with which Paul heard the statement that one could not be saved without circumcision and the Law. One imagines him asking himself, "Have I been doing this all wrong?" Reflection followed; and the fruit of the reflection was Pauline theology. To justify his own practice Paul gave the gospel a close scrutiny such as it had not yet received. There is scarcely any point of Pauline theology which is not directly or indirectly a response to the Judaizers. And for this reason the controversy over Judaism is more than a historical curiosity with as much interest for modern Christians as the Monophysite controversy. Out of the Jewish controversy were elaborated the fundamental ideas of Christian doctrine. If there is a key to the New Testament — and there really is not — it would be the Jewish controversy.

The Efficacy of the Saving Act

The central problem was the efficacy of the death and resurrection of Jesus. Paul had proclaimed the gospel of salvation through faith and baptism; by these one shared in the saving event. Now if circumcision and the observance of the Law were necessary, this was not the saving event. The efficacy of the saving act of Christ had to be total or nothing. Because it was unique it could not be combined with any other factor. Paul had accepted this without any question; now he had to ask himself what it was that made the death and resurrection a unique event. Ultimately it had to be the unique personality of him who had performed the saving act; it had to be his unique relationship with the Father and with other men. This relationship was shared by no one, whether Jew or Gentile. If Christ were the savior of all men, he could not be less the savior of some than of others. The saving death and resurrection therefore acquires in the epistles of Paul a prominence and a depth which it does not have in the Synoptic Gospels. The sonship of Jesus likewise emerges into greater clarity.

The Depravity of Man

The total efficacy of the saving act corresponded to the total need in which mankind finds itself. Was this need any less for the Jews than it was for the Gentiles? Paul had to reappraise Judaism; and what he found was not easy for him to assimilate. Judaism, we have seen, felt assured of its good relations with the one true God. It was secured by the Law against idolatry and against the moral collapse of the Hellenistic world. God has spoken to Israel and to no one else, and he dwelt in Israel alone. Now it became clear that if Jesus was the one savior of all, the need of the Jews was no less than the need of the Gentiles. The Old Testament is a statement of the sinfulness and the helplessness of man; but it is addressed directly to the people of Israel. Paul drew from the Old Testament his own conviction of the guilt which mankind as a race, including the Jews, has incurred. There is no man who is not under judgment and who does not need the fullness of salvation. This becomes a favorite theme of Paul. Faith is impossible without a confession of guilt.

The Mission of Judaism

If this be the human condition, does it not seem to evacuate Israel's function in the saving process? It is clear that Paul faced this problem; but he could not permit this problem to make void the cross of Christ. Paul's anguish is attested in Romans 9–11; and his anguish was rendered more acute when it became evident that Judaism as a community would not accept its Messiah.

Judaism must indeed have a function in the process of salvation which no other people has. Ultimately Paul recognized that this function was to produce the Messiah. Judaism was no less an object of the messianic salvation because it had produced him; for what it had produced was a son of Israel according to the flesh. It had produced a faith and a culture in which the Messiah could be recognized as the Messiah. The faith of Israel was a faith in the power and will of God to save man from his own guilt. But God had produced the Messiah. Israel had contributed nothing to his saving power. If it had, then there was another savior besides Christ.

The Newness of Christ

We have summarized the position of the Judaizers as the belief that the Gentile had to become a Jew in order to become a Christian. Paul had never affirmed that the Jew had to cease to be a Jew in order to become a Christian. Paul himself observed Jewish rites; and his epistles clearly attest satisfaction with his own Judaism. It seems that Paul never completely resolved this problem in his own mind. The total efficacy of the saving act creates the new man in Christ; and we have observed how entirely new the life in Christ is. No one expounds this novelty more clearly or more frequently than Paul. And he had to maintain this thesis; unless the saving act produced an entirely new life, Paul could not have defended his position against the claims of the Judaizers. They did not deny that baptism was a communication of the saving act nor that a new life began with the sacrament; but they did not conceive it as totally new. The new life was an addition to Judaism, and in their belief it was more than a superficial addition. The logic of Paul's position led him to the statement that in Christ there is neither Jew nor Greek (Galatians 3:28). This comes very close to a statement that the Jew ceases to be a Jew. If the Jew is saved by faith as much as the Gentile, and if baptism is a new birth in which the past is wiped out, what is left of Judaism? If the Judaizers were right, then Christ died in order that men might become Jews. If the rebirth of circumcision were required of Gentiles, then the Jews, who were already circumcised, must have experienced the saving act. One could then conceivably proceed to the argument that the Jew did not really need baptism. For Paul the efficacy of the saving act and the efficacy of baptism were one and the same thing; he could not tolerate the suggestion that baptism needed anything else or could be supplied by anything else.

Righteousness and the Law

The obligation of the observance of the Law followed upon circumcision; and this is the way the Judaizers conceived it. The Law was the revealed will of God governing life; and the Judaizers could not see how the revealed will of God could be omitted from the way of salvation. Paul can scarcely have reached the conclusion he did reach as easily as the epistles suggest. The revealed will of God cannot be dismissed lightly; of all the elements of Judaism this would seem to be the one which would most readily be retained. Yet Paul exhibits no wavering on this point from the beginning. Gentiles must not be obliged to observe the Law. It is unlikely that he came so quickly to the conclusion that Jews were liberated from the obligation to observe the Law. For if a Jew were freed from the Law, he had indeed ceased to be a Jew. Again the logic of Paul's position would not allow him to stop short of the full conclusion. The Law had lost its efficacy.

Here we encounter the Jewish conception of the Law of which we have spoken earlier. It is not much of an exaggeration to call this a quasi-sacramental conception. The observance of the Law was required and was sufficient to maintain good relations with God. To the Judaizers the saving act of Christ had altered the position of the Law in no respect. The Law was still what God demanded, and it was all that God demanded besides faith in Jesus Messiah. Against this Paul denied that the observance of the Law had any saving value at all. The Law would be in the hypothesis of the Judaizers an agent of salvation which had not come through Christ. Had Christ incorporated the Law into his own saving act Paul would have accepted it, but as the Law of Christ, not the Law of Judaism. Jesus had shown, as we have seen and shall see again, independence of the Law (Chapters III, XI).

Again we point out that Jesus did not die and rise from the dead in order that the Gentiles might become Jews. Had the Law been what the Judaizers claimed it was, Jesus need not have performed his saving act. Ultimately the conclusion could follow that the Jew did not need faith, which meant that he did not need Jesus as savior.

The proclamation of salvation through faith and not through works has become the object of one of the most critical controversies in the history of the Church; but this later controversy has no reference to the Pauline teaching which we discuss here. Paul attacked the Jewish conception of the saving power of the Law. We may and indeed should generalize from his teaching, and we shall see that this feature of his teaching has contemporary applications. One might have expected Paul to say that the observance of the Law with faith was a salutary action. We know that he tolerated observance of the Law by Jews and himself observed it, although it seems certain that he did not observe it according to Pharisaic standards. One can detect a certain ambiguity in his attitude; his teaching on the inefficacy of the Law is rigorous and uncompromising, but in his practice one can see manifestations of the desire to temper the wind to the shorn lamb. He may have been more severe with Peter than his own conduct entitled him to be. This surely needs no explanation. His mind was clear on the subject, and he acted according to his mind within the limits of his vision. He was ready to go as far as he could to avoid offending the Judaizers; but his conviction that his was the true gospel was so deep that he was ready to see the Church split on this question. We do not know that any other member of the primitive Church saw that this question could split the Church.

Christian Freedom

The allegation that the Law had a sacramental value was an implicit denial that the new life conferred by Jesus was really new, and that the Christian had received new powers which enabled him to live a new life. The Law placed a ceiling upon the saving act of Jesus and the work of the Spirit. If the Law was the fulfillment of the will of God, then Jesus had accomplished nothing; for the

Law was already in existence. Jesus had sent the Spirit as a new principle of action. The annulment of the Law was not intended to create a vacuum. Paul elaborated the idea of Christian freedom, which meant precisely freedom from the obligations of the Law. It did not mean Christian anarchy. In a sense it did mean freedom from all obligation; but this statement is so open to misunderstanding that it needs to be framed with great care. Freedom means that the person who possesses freedom is self-determined. To Paul, obligation was an external determination from which Christ had freed us. Obligation was replaced by another principle of action, the Spirit. The Christian is self-determined; but he has put on another self. He lives in Christ and Christ lives in him. He is endowed with a power which no obligation can give him. The Christian who lives in Christ and in whom the Spirit dwells needs obligation no more than the healthy man needs crutches. He moves by inner power, not by external compulsion. The Law was made for man under sin; when man is freed from sin, he is freed from the Law and from that kind of necessity which the Law imposes.

Therefore the manifold obligations of the Law — the rabbis counted 613 precepts — are annulled. The Christian is left with only one saving act which he can perform; this is the saving act of love. Love is not the fulfillment of an obligation but a spontaneous movement. The Christian would be incapable of this spontaneous movement were the spontaneity not given him by the indwelling Spirit. But it is given him, and words like law and obligation become meaningless. Freedom then is the exercise of a power communicated in baptism, the power to do that which is impossible for unregenerate man. As long as the Christian does not rise to the full exercise of his power, he is not truly free. He is a slave of the Law; and for Paul this is the same as being a slave to sin. This is a vitally new conception of morality to which we shall have to return at greater length (Chapter XI).

The Newness of the Church

Through the controversy Paul arrived at an understanding of what the Church is; and the Church has made this awareness her own. The Church is not an annex of Judaism. The Church is an entirely new reality with her own life, her own mission, and her own powers. This does not mean that the Church arises independently of Judaism. We have seen many instances of the connections between the Church and Judaism, and there are more which we have not had occasion to mention. The Church is the fulfillment of Israel, but not in the sense that Israel itself remains without transformation. The Church is the new Israel into which historic Israel must be incorporated; the Judaizers believed that the Church must be incorporated into Judaism. The mission of Jesus was no less decisive than the mission of Moses; indeed it was far more decisive, for it had a scope as wide as humanity itself. The apostolic Church was not, it seems, fully conscious in its beginnings of its universal mission; and it became fully conscious when it saw the consequences of viewing itself as less than universal. Jesus, we have noticed, lived and spoke within the Jewish community. The number of clear statements in the Gospels which refer to a universal mission is not large, and we can conclude that this was less emphasized than some other aspects of his proclamation. But it is not foreign to anything he said. More important is the inner dynamism of his teaching; it leads inevitably to an understanding of his mission which cannot be combined with the views of the Judaizers. The Gospels witness that Jesus did not tell his disciples everything; as we have already remarked, he gave them no manual of directions on how to go about their work. The Gospels assure us that the Spirit revealed much to them. We do not readily see how revolutionary the idea of a universal Church was to Jews. It was more comprehensible to Gentiles, whose religious world had already been leveled by the divorce of religion from political identity. The Jews resisted Hellenism by tightly uniting their faith and their identity as a people. The gospel demanded that this union be relaxed. That the Church had to learn this by steps for itself should cause no surprise.

Unity in Christ

The relaxation of the unity of religion and people demanded that another bond of union be supplied. Paul more than any other New Testament writer states that the bond of union is the person of the risen Christ. His is the figure of the body of Christ as a description of the Church. The similarity between this figure and John's figure of the vine and the branches (Jn 15:1–8) does not have to be pointed out. This conception of a person as the bond of union of a society was entirely new to Judaism as it was to the Gentile world; yet, as we have seen, it is an expansion of the idea of the corporate personality which appears in the Old Testament. But it is a development; it is not altogether the same idea. In the figures of the body and the vine life is communicated to the members from a living person risen and glorified. When this is contrasted with the unity of Judaism in one Law and one cult and one people, the implications are evident; and they touch the foundations of Judaism. The Church is Christ the new Israel. This understanding made the Church aware both of her power and her responsibility.

She must be recognized, then, by the way in which she reflects her identity with a person and not by her structure and her institutions. The Church understood that she could not live off the institutions of the past, even the venerable institutions of Judaism. As Jesus Christ was the new event which was the cardinal point of history, so the Church had to assert herself as something new and unique. As a society of men she could not be formless; but she had to evolve her own forms which would be determined first of all by her identity with Christ. Where the forms do not reflect this identity, they are useless at best and can easily become harmful. When one compares the apostolic Church closely with existing religions of the first century, one is constantly impressed by the way in which the apostolic Church almost without thinking created new forms or so transformed old ones that they can scarcely be recognized. We observed in the preceding chapter that the Church has not always been equally successful in preserving her distinct forms in her later history. For the apostolic Church realized fully that a universal Church can never become identified with any particular historical form, be it a race, a nation, a culture, or anything else. In the light of this conviction of the apostolic Church one must say that the idea of "Christendom" as a designation of a continent or a group of nations is a deviation from the idea which the apostolic Church had of itself. One wonders whether the identification of the Church as European is not a resurgence of the thesis of the Judaizers. Unless you are educated and adopt European forms of thought and European customs and culture, you cannot be saved. Perhaps the controversy over Judaism is much more than a mere historical curiosity.

Divisions in the Church

We have observed that James and the Jerusalem group may have regarded the development of Gentile churches as a divisive element which would produce two churches. Their judgment here was absolutely correct; it would be strange if Paul did not see this as quickly as they did, yet the agreement of Galatians 2 indicates that he was willing to compromise if he could save his Gentile churches from the Judaizers. Whether he was slow in foreseeing division or not, he became the most eloquent spokesman for the unity of the Church; and here he reached the full conclusions of his position. The unity of the Church is the unity of the members of the body of Christ. Does this unity annihilate all differences? Obviously it does not; at least historically it has not. When Christians can with good conscience conduct war against each other with no fear that they thereby become less Christian, they are at least as well aware of their diversity as they are of their unity in Christ. But Paul said that in Christ there is neither Jew nor Greek, slave nor free, male nor female, because we are all one in Christ Jesus (Gal 3:28). Paul or one of his school also wrote that there cannot be Greek and Jew, circumcised and uncircumcised, barbarian, Scythian, slave, free man; for Christ is all in all (Col 3:11). It reduces the impact of Paul's words notably if we say that "in Christ" means "in church" — although even in church, we are sadly aware, we still occasionally segregate barbarians, Scythians, and slaves. Paul here only echoes the parable of the Good Samaritan, which answers the question who is my neighbor (Lk 10:25–37). He happens to make it more specific; many of Paul's listeners probably could not tell a Samaritan from a Scythian. Modern readers of the Gospels also need to have the parable specified; that they are neighbors of the Samaritans, or one in Christ with the Scythians, bothers them very little.

It would be difficult to argue that Paul believed that the Christian lived in Christ only in church and that he returns to his normal state of Jew, Greek, Scythian, slave, etc., when he leaves the house of worship. Paul earnestly intended to say that the Church is much more than a cult group and that if Christ does not live in the world, he does not live anywhere. Differences between men are not annihilated, of course, in the sense that all Christians become one color and speak one language by the grace of baptism. Paul must mean at least that differences become totally irrelevant as determinants of how one man shall deal with another. This would be unity; and Paul's concern is that Christians should be aware of their unity, not of ways in which they can evade it. We are not ready for this unity, of course; neither was the world ready when the parable of the Good Samaritan was uttered or when Paul wrote Galatians. I think Paul would be quite surprised if he heard Christians say that their mission is not to promote total unity but to postpone it.

The Removal of Divisions

The insight which Paul reached as a result of the controversy was that the Church could not be one for Jews and another for Gentiles. This difference was in the mind of the Jew so profound that any other difference was minor by comparison. If Jew and Gentile were one in Christ and of equally good standing in the Church, one could conceive no difference which would discriminate the members. Of the examples Paul gives we can best appreciate the difference between male and female; we do not so quickly realize that this difference was far deeper in the mind of Paul than it is to us. Once the idea of difference itself is removed, all forms of difference go. From the difference between Jew and Gentile, which was ethnic, cultural, and religious, Paul proceeds to differences of nation, language, social class, even of sex. One cannot have several bodies of Christ and several lives of Christ and several Spirits. That the Church has not yet reached the destiny which is marked out for her is altogether too evident. Here perhaps more than anywhere she needs to keep in constant touch with the New Testament. It is terribly easy to rationalize unity out of existence;

for diversity is so natural that one might think it is a precept of the natural law.

I said above that Paul never completely resolved the question whether the Jew had to cease to be a Jew to become a Christian. It is a comfort to know that the spokesman for Christian unity had some of the same difficulty which we have in accepting the unity which he proclaimed. Yes, of course the Jew ceased to be a Jew; every man ceases to be what he was, for baptism is birth into a new life and annihilation of the past. The Jew here was no better and no worse off than the Gentile; he pays the price which is demanded for unity in Christ. Paul knew the renunciation which this price involved; he knew also that one dissolved a lesser unity for a greater. Salvation, we said, consisted in becoming fully human — not fully a Jew, a Greek, a European, or a white American. To choose to be these or any similar denomination is to choose to remain essentially small.

The Meaning of the Crisis

This chapter has been an attempt to summarize what I believe was the major crisis of the apostolic Church. It has also been an attempt to show that the crisis was a step forward of incalculable importance. Had the Church met all her crises as she met this one, many things would not have happened. She faced the crisis with candor and without human respect; and the Church was still too young to have any vested interests to protect. The only vested interest in question was Judaism; and one must stand in admiration and awe at the way in which the Church abandoned this vested interest, an interest far more sacred in the eyes of those who defended it than any vested interest which the Church has had since. The crisis exhibits the kind of restlessness which the Spirit creates in the Church, an impatience with things as they are; for things are never entirely as they ought to be. The Church could have closed her ranks in this situation; if she had she would have turned inward instead of outward, and she would have proved herself a merely human organization which protects itself by refusing risks — and runs the supreme risk of becoming a fossil. Because of the indwelling Spirit the Church can never become a fossil, despite the devoted efforts of many of her members to make her one.

XI

THE CHRISTIAN MORAL
REVOLUTION

A Christian Manner of Life

In the preceding chapter we saw that freedom from the Law was one of the ideas which was elaborated in the controversy over Judaism. Law and freedom deserve closer study; for the gospel in this respect initiated a moral revolution which has not yet worked itself out. That Christianity creates a new life is one of the truths of the gospel which Christians have found difficult to grasp in its totality. Or, if the creation of a new life is accepted notionally, it often seems impossible to reduce the notion to a manner of life which can be practiced. At times the desire to fulfill the demands of the new life has led to deviations which ended in some form of withdrawal from the world and from human society. Other ways of fulfilling the new life which are deviations by secular standards are approved by the Church as safe ways of leading a Christian life. Such are the monastic and other orders which profess a life according to a rule taken under vow. The rule is intended to institute a form of life in community which is called "evangelical," that is, according to the gospel. The essential features of the religious life are poverty, chastity, and obedience; the differences between one order and another are variations on the essential obligations. This is called the life of the counsels in contradistinction to the life of the precepts, to which all members of the Church are obliged.

An Evangelical Manner of Life

The traditional terminology here is not entirely fortunate. The difference between the life of the counsels and the life of the precepts is not intended to imply that the life of the precepts is not evangelical. If all Christians do not live according to the gospel, then Christ did not affect the moral life of man in general at all. Furthermore, the distinction between counsel and precept is not too securely founded in the Gospels. The usual base for this distinction is the story of the rich young man (Mt 19:16–30 = Mk 10:17–31 = Lk 18:18 – 30). This episode does not suggest an option between the life of the precepts and the life of the counsels. Jesus puts before the inquirer the Law and the gospel; and when the inquirer chooses the Law, Jesus does not invite him to an intermediate phase between discipleship and the life of the precepts. He observes that those who refuse the gospel will not enter the Reign of God. The primitive community of Jerusalem, which Luke idealized, urged candidates for baptism to renounce their wealth (Acts 2:44–45; 4:32–35; 5:1–11). They may have misunderstood the teaching of Jesus; and their practice did not endure in the Church. Before we say they misunderstood him we must look carefully to see whether it was not rather a failure to find a practical way of executing an idea which they understood very well.

The reader of the New Testament is not left with the impression that either Jesus or the apostolic Church conceived the plan of creating a spiritual elite within the Church. Even the apostolic college is not described as a spiritual elite. Jesus makes no distinction between the moral level of the apostolic college and the moral level of all who become his disciples. The epistles of Paul were written for the members of the churches he founded without distinction between members. There is only one gospel, as there is only one Lord, one faith, one baptism. We have seen in the preceding chapter that the Church could not tolerate a division into a Jewish church and a Gentile church. She can no more easily tolerate a division into one church for the spiritual elite and one for the spiritually mediocre. No such division has occurred, of course; but one may ask whether the Church has here reached the perfect unity which is her destiny. And one may certainly ask whether all her members desire this unity, or whether all of them even think it is possible. Some wit has said, not without cynicism, that in modern times it is impossible to be canonized unless one is a bishop or a member of a religious community. The cynicism is unpleasant; but it points to the fact that the Church needs in modern times some recognized saints who were married and had children. On the records of canonization, most of the laity have to be judged as spiritually mediocre. Obviously we need another standard of judgment. We shall have it if we recall that in the New Testament the fullness of the Christian life is not a matter of option. Jesus invited no one to become an unfinished Christian.

The Morality of the Law

Let us try to assess the Christian moral revolution. One may begin by pointing out that Jesus and the apostolic Church rejected the conventional morality of the world in which the incarnation occurred. The conventional morality of the day can be summed up in two systems of law: the Jewish Law and the natural law of Stoic philosophy. Of these the first is by far more prominent in the New Testament. We have already had more than one occasion to refer to the place which the Law had in Judaism and to the attitude of Jesus and St. Paul toward it. The attitude is summed up in the statements of Paul that the Law is inefficacious for salvation. The Gentile may not observe the Law, the Jew need not observe it. Neither Jesus nor the apostolic Church proposed another law to replace the Torah. To speak of the gospel as "the new law" is a misleading expression. It is the new law in the sense that it displaces the old law, but not in the sense that it is another and better law. That it is not a law at all will, I hope, emerge from this discussion.

The Morality of Stoicism

The second moral system in question is the natural law of Stoicism (see Chapter I). This is certainly not mentioned in the Gospels; and the allusions in the epistles are so few and fleeting that some scholars question whether it is mentioned there at all. I am convinced that it is. Stoicism was the dominant moral system of the Hellenistic world; it was so well known that it is difficult to see how Paul could have been unaware of it. If he knew anything about it, he knew that it was something which the gospel had to displace; he could not have left it alone. A review of Stoic morality will show that it was not an ignoble system. It was the morality of most of the more admirable figures of Hellenistic and Roman history, and it produced some men of greater than average stature. Marcus Aurelius, known vaguely to most people as one of the ten persecuting emperors if he is known at all, left a journal of his meditations which is a monument to an honest and fair-minded man who was fully aware of his duties and responsibilities. Stoicism was the best moral system of the Hellenistic world; one can guess that men who were convinced of it would be slow to believe that the gospel offered a better way of life.

A Morality of Reason and Nature

The morality of Stoicism was a morality of reason and nature. It integrated its cosmology and its ethics better than any other philosophical system of its time; and it had an attractive simplicity which made it comprehensible even to the unlearned. The universe itself is governed by law; and the law which governs the moral life of man is patterned after the natural law of the cosmos. The universe in Stoicism is logical; it is governed by a creative and unifying principle called Fire, Spirit, or Reason (Logos). This principle is the one true divine being; it can also be called Nature or God. It is the soul and the principle of the life of the universe; it does in the universe what reason does in man. Therefore the universe is governed by intelligence and providence. The good of reason is the moral good, and therefore moral good is prior in the universe, whence it is participated to man. The good life for man is to live "conformably," or "conformably to nature," or "conformably to the experience of the events of nature"; the Stoics had some trouble finding the best phrase to express this norm of morality. Nature, both of the individual and of the universe, is the common law, the right reason pervading all things. This law is above any human law; human law is valid only in so far as it is in harmony with the law of the universe. Justice is established by nature, not by ordinance; and the law of nature is eternal, immutable, and invariable. Local laws are necessary for most men because they do not participate sufficiently in Reason. The wise man does not need human law, for his own reason is the only rule which he needs and the only rule which he can accept with dignity. He is self-sufficient and has all he needs to live a happy life. No evil can disturb him, for the only true good is the moral good, which he can preserve.

Stoic Virtues

The Stoics insisted on the four cardinal virtues: prudence, justice, temperance, and fortitude. Their understanding of these virtues was sound; the system did not admit immorality in the common sense of the term. The Stoic conception of the brotherhood of man was quite unusual in the ancient world. The system arose in the Hellenistic period, when, as we have seen (Chapter I), political allegiance had been relaxed. In the Stoic system the world was one great city (cosmopolis), and all men were its citizens. The slave could be a wise man, and if he was wise he was free; for only the wise man is free.

Stoic Faults

There were soft spots in the Stoic system. The self-sufficiency of the sage is hard to distinguish from pride and arrogance. The ideal of apathy led to disengagement; the rise of the Hellenistic kingdoms and empires destroyed the ancient freedom of the Greek citizen, and the Stoic was inclined to accept the world passively. He could create his own little island of serenity; but to do this he had to be detached from the affairs of his fellow man. It recommended suicide, we noticed (Chapter I), as an honorable escape.

This was, as we have called it, a morality of reason and nature; and it is obvious that to the apostolic community it was a morality of reason without revelation for man without regeneration. It is hard to see how St. Paul could have been more sympathetic to the natural law of Stoicism than he was to the revealed law of Judaism. The law of Judaism was at least the revealed will of God. St. Paul, as we have seen, gives Stoicism little attention. He could not have used the word "law" of the norm of Stoic morality; for him there was only one law, and that was the Law of Moses. Anything else is called a law in a transferred sense. Hence he does not take the trouble to reject the law of Stoicism. He may have given the question no thought at all; or he may have thought that his rejection of the Law of Moses was enough of a rejection of law in principle to need no explicit extension to the law of Stoicism. If he thought this, it must be noticed that many of his interpreters have not. The suggestion that the gospel may reject law in principle is challenging; and an examination is in order to see whether this is a tenable interpretation of what the New Testament says about law.

Nature Without Regeneration

The Stoic natural law is based on nature as it is known by reason. Nature as it is known by reason is an unreality in the world of biblical thought. Man is not an abstract essence but a historical existent. As historical he is under judgment, the slave of sin and of his own demonic impulses. He lacks precisely what Stoicism boasted it gave, the self-sufficiency by which he can lead a happy life. He is incapable by his own resources of achieving moral good; he is desperate without the salvation which Jesus Christ alone brings. Whatever is deduced from nature as a code of conduct is deduced from the nature of this fallen lump of clay, who is a reasonable animal only when he chooses to be. The deductions are made by other fallen lumps whose limited vision is obscured by personal desires. Paul does not give man, enslaved to sin and death, any possibility of escaping his slavery by his wits. In the first chapter of Romans he has written a moral analysis of the Hellenistic world of his day, and his appraisal of this world is dismal. This recital of the vices of the world is Paul's estimate of the moral capacity of man led by reason and nature.

Reason Without Revelation

As a Jewish Christian Paul believed that the most important events in history were the revelation of God's word to Israel fulfilled in Jesus Christ. The Stoic system is innocent of any revelation. Man acquires wisdom by reason which he shares from the reason of the cosmos. He is his own master; indeed he cannot be truly wise until he is his own master, for the sage must be self-sufficient. What would Paul think of a system which expressly declared that we really do not need God's revelation of himself to devise an adequate code of conduct? He did not think it deserved mention. The only true wisdom is the knowledge of God which is acquired by the self-revelation of God. In biblical terms any other alleged wisdom is folly. To assert the self-sufficiency of reason is to deny man's dependence on God. To the Stoic claims on behalf of reason Paul could well have responded with the story of how man sought the knowledge of good and evil by eating of the tree of knowledge, and discovered only that he is naked.

Law and Obligation

Morality considered as a system of law imposes obligation. This is the only effect of law and it is the only motive for the observance of the law. This fits well into Paul's conception of the Law as made for man under sin. Other philosophies such as Platonism did not consider obligation as the motive for doing the good. The good is to be chosen because it is good and is intellectually apprehended as good; if the object of one's act is good, no other motivation for the act is either necessary or possible. Law and obligation make it unnecessary for the agent to apprehend the good. The agent is moved not by goodness recognized but by the threat of some external evil which is attached to failure to meet the obligation. This is the moral level of children: if you are not home by a certain hour, you will not be allowed to attend the party on Saturday. The only evil attached to tardiness is the loss of the party; whether tardiness is good or bad independently of the party is not known and is not important. For law does not look to motivation but simply to observance, which it does not reward, and to nonobservance, which it punishes. Is motivation important? Not to law, for the integration of personal life is not the purpose of law. The integration of personal life is the object of the gospel; for the gospel is directed to the creation of the new man who lives in Christ and in whom Christ lives. And it would be unfair to Stoicism to say that it did not have the integration of personal life within its purpose. The wise man is integrated with nature; strangely, neither Stoicism nor any other morality of reason and nature has been able to tell precisely what such a person is.

Morality of Duty

The morality of law is by definition minimal and negative. It is minimal because it is a morality of duty; and duty is that which is owed. It is unreasonable to go beyond your duty, and it can be annoying to others. The morality of law seeks not the good but the lawful; and the lawful is the permissible. The morality of law tends to look less at the observance of the law and more at the violation; and this morality easily becomes an ideal of moral goodness which is achieved not by doing what is good, but by abstaining from what is wrong. If one could list all the ways in which law is violated, one would have a model of perfection in reverse; one would know everything which one should not do.

Atomization of Conduct

The morality of law leads to the atomization of moral conduct into a multiplicity of individual acts; and each act becomes a case in itself. Acts are performed in concrete reality. The act in the casuistry of law is abstracted from living reality and analyzed as an isolated fragment hanging in the air dissociated from the person who performs it. Yet each individual act is a part of a continuous chain of one human life with relations to other individual human lives. The act arises from a living individual person with his own defined personality formed by his experience and his associations. It is his response to a concrete situation and to certain persons. It is a personal decision which forms his personality further. In a true sense each individual act is unique; it will not be repeated either by the same person or by another. No individual act is understood unless it is recognized that X did it in situation Y. This does not imply that each individual act creates its own moral standards by which it is judged; but it does imply that the moral judgment of the concrete act which abstracts the act from its situation in life can be notably distorted. When the act is considered in abstraction from the inner personal principles from which the act flows, one can recognize that it is wrong; but one cannot see what makes it good.

Chastity

The atomization of the individual act can be illustrated from an area which is notably more emphasized in modern moral philosophy than it is in the New Testament; I mean the virtue of chastity. The student finds the treatment of this virtue in the New Testament rather casual; in contrast, the morality of sex receives more treatment in modern literature than any other moral question. He may be tempted to ask himself whether chastity has not displaced charity as the basic Christian virtue. The difference in emphasis is hardly due to a deterioration of the moral situation from what it was in the Hellenistic world; no one who is acquainted with the history of Hellenistic culture could think that chastity needed less attention then than it does now. Corinth, where St. Paul founded a church to which he wrote at least two letters, had a reputation which can be checked in the Greek lexicon. In Greek "Corinthian girl" means prostitute, "Corinthian merchant" means procurer, and "to act like a Corinthian" means to visit a house of prostitution. The temple of Aphrodite at Acrocorinth had a staff of a thousand temple prostitutes. One would never deduce from 1 and 2 Corinthians that chastity was a particular problem in Corinth, and in a sense it was not; for chastity as a virtue was esteemed nowhere in the Hellenistic world. Paul had an excellent opportunity to write a flaming sermon on the subject to the Corinthians; instead he wrote the hymn to love (1 Corinthians 13). May one conclude that Paul considered that chastity would be a product of Christian love which needed no special attention? And may one ask whether he would have thought that it was possible to attend to chastity as if it were an end in itself, possible of achievement in some other way than as a product of charity?

In the Christian scheme chastity is not a way of life but a component of a way of life; and the consideration of chastity in a morality of reason and nature fails to present it as a part of a way of life. Chastity is found both in the celibate state and in the matrimonial state. The usual presentation of chastity describes it as a virtue which is achieved by not doing something. The Christian, if he takes the time and trouble, can be very sure what are the wrong things to do; he is less certain that by not doing them he has done the right thing. The use of sex is a fulfillment of the human person; concentration on single acts as permissible or prohibited has little or no reference to the fulfillment of the human person, and abstention from the use of sex without further qualification seems to be no more than a denial of fulfillment. That so many Christians, married and celibate, have found a positive understanding of their way of life is not due to the morality of reason, nature, and law. It is due to the movement of the Spirit which reveals the nature of Christian love even when love is obscured by a thorough study of actual and possible sexual deviations.

Fragmentation of Society

Law is a social phenomenon; yet a morality of reason, nature, and law tends to fragmentate the moral and social structure. For the isolated act is performed by an isolated person; and morality, when it is the morality of an isolated person, becomes self-centered. This is illustrated very well in the moral system of Stoicism. The end of Stoic morality was the perfection of the individual wise man; his success involved the success of no one else, and he was not concerned with the failure of anyone else. To become involved would disturb his serenity. Law is more a principle of regulation in society than a principle of morality; and morality reduced to law does not achieve much more than regulation. Where the Christian moral revolution has penetrated least is in the morality of society. It took some centuries for Christians to realize that one man cannot own another. Christians have not realized yet that what men may not do as individuals they may not do when enough of them are gathered in large numbers to form a political society. To tolerate and use a moral jungle in social relations while one strives to "save one's soul" in what private life is left is more or less the ideal of Stoicism.

Law and Responsibility

Law is an external regulating agency. It cannot possibly cover all contingencies; but in any contingency the law is there as a norm. The law is an abstraction, and it can often fail to touch reality. It is a general direction which must be rendered particular in each concrete action. But because law offers a certain security that what we are doing is right just because it is the law, we prefer not to incur the risk which a flexible interpretation of the law entails. Law offers a set of prefabricated decisions for every concrete situation up to a point. No reflection on the good or the better is necessary. One need feel no personal responsibility; for one has transferred all personal responsibility to the law. One has only to consult one's mental card file of the permissible and the prohibited and the decision comes out. It is all very simple up to a point, as I have said. The point of limitation is the point where a few crises occur. These crises, of course, are what make or break a person. What is to be expected from one who has trained himself not to make his own decisions but to look for the prefabricated decision? Anything can be expected, even the right thing; but the right thing will be done for the wrong reasons.

Reason and the Gospel

I have presented what I think are the implications of the principles of a morality of law based on reason and nature. The picture has not been altogether favorable, and I do not think it needs to be; were such a morality the supreme morality of man, the gospel need not have included a moral revolution. Our question was whether the moral revolution of the gospel is a rejection of the morality of reason and nature in principle. The answer will not be entirely clear until we have set forth the Christian revolution, if indeed it becomes clear then; but I think it is safe to say, at least as a hypothesis, that the gospel rejects those principles involved in a morality of reason and nature which have been set forth above. We shall find a direct antithesis between the gospel and these features of rational morality. One will, of course, ask whether rational morality can be rejected any more than one can refuse to have a head. Admitted that the gospel is a moral revolution, the revolution must be worked out by the personal decision of each Christian, as I have insisted. The gospel does not give specific directions for each situation either; and the Christian can make his moral decisions only by the intelligent use of Christian moral principles applied to particulars — which is a morality of reason.

With this there can be no quarrel. But Christian morality must be primarily Christian. Moral thinking cannot be based on an abstraction of what is convenient to human nature; it must think of historic man, fallen and redeemed. This means that man's potential is reduced by his fall and that fallen man is inevitably a moral failure. Redeemed man, on the other hand, is endowed with moral powers which he does not possess by natural endowment. Christian morality will consider what man can and cannot do; its conclusions will not be those of reason and nature. The moral ideal of the Christian is known by the revelation of God in Jesus Christ. The means by which the Christian can attain this ideal are the gift of grace known through the revelation of God. When reason considers nature and abstracts from these things, reason is not considering reality. This should seem obvious; yet solutions to moral problems are often alleged which are devised as if the incarnation had not occurred.

The Morality of Secular Goods

The Christian moral revolution overturns so many accepted ethical values that it is difficult to see how much of a rational structure of law based on nature could be left. Rational morality is the code by which man uses the goods of self and of this world in a way suitable to man living in society. The gospel does not so much reject secular goods as ignore them. The words of Jesus on wealth scarcely allow any room for a morality of the use of these goods. I have already noticed that the primitive community took him seriously. Does their failure to find a practical way to follow his teaching excuse other Christians from looking for a way? It is not without design that Matthew begins his account of the teaching

of Jesus with the words, "Blessed are the poor in spirit" — a phrase
nicely mistranslated for hundreds of years. It means those who are
poor of spirit, who have not much spirit, the helpless of the world
who have no power to resist. The gospel was proclaimed to the
poor whose masses constituted the vast majority of the population
of the Hellenistic world, and it was proclaimed by one of them.
He did not offer riches but congratulated them on their poverty.

Both Matthew (6:25–34) and Luke (12:22–31) preserve the sayings in which Jesus scoffs at concern for such basic needs as food
and clothing. This saying is so stunning that it has been simply
ignored except by a few who were regarded as fanatics. In the
story of the rich young man (Mt 19:16–30; Mk 10:17–31; Lk
18:18–30) Jesus concluded the dialogue by saying that it is very
hard for a rich man to enter the Reign, about as hard as it is for a
camel to pass through the eye of a needle. The history of the efforts
to interpret this as something else than what it means is pathetic.
The disciples understood Jesus better; they gave the obvious retort,
"Who, then, can be saved?" This was the opportunity for Jesus to
explain that the camel was really a rope and the needle's eye one
of the gates of Jerusalem, or that he was using Oriental metaphor
which is so popular in Oriental speech and need not be taken
seriously. Instead he observed that what is impossible with men
is possible with God — suggesting that resources were available to
achieve the impossible. Luke alone (14:33) has preserved the saying that one must renounce all his possessions to become a disciple
of Jesus. The saying is not out of character with other sayings;
and one finds it easier to understand how the Jerusalem community
did not treat poverty as an option in the Christian vocation. One
has a little difficulty in seeing how it is treated as an option.

In any case, the attitude of Jesus toward the use of wealth even
in the sense of the minimum material possessions is such that it
renders all the ethical treatises on ownership, theft, transfer of
ownership, contracts, etc. simply so much abstract speculation for
the Christian. When Paul appealed to the Corinthians for contributions for the poor in Jerusalem, he gave the example of Jesus Christ,
who impoverished himself for us although he was rich (2 Cor 8:9).
Paul's churches did not practice the communism of Jerusalem as
far as we know; but his teaching was that the abundance of one

should counterbalance the need of another so that equality should result (2 Cor 8:13–15). Paul was no more sympathetic to wealth than Jesus. The parable of Dives and Lazarus (Lk 16:19–31) does not recommend Christian communism; but it describes a man who is damned for doing nothing.

The Morality of Personal Dignity

The gospel focuses its attack on secular values against material goods because the need for them is so obvious and because they are so easy to justify. One hears it said that Jesus had rich friends, although the enumeration stops at Joseph of Arimathea; and it is conveniently forgotten that if Joseph joined the Jerusalem community he ceased to be rich. But the gospel attacks other secular goods with no less vigor. Jesus congratulates the poor on their poverty and his disciples for being reviled and persecuted (Mt 5:11; Lk 6:32). Jesus promises them no better treatment than he himself received (Mt 10:24; Jn 15:20). The disciple must take up his cross and deny himself (Mt 16:24; Mk 8:34; Lk 9:23). The sentence deserves scrutiny. In modern speech we can paraphrase the taking up of the cross only by some such phrase as "You have to become a gallowsbird." To deny oneself is to assert that one is not; it is to remove the self from the list of values. Whatever Jesus meant by hating one's self or life and thus saving it (Mt 16:25; Mk 8:35; Lk 9:24), he certainly meant a declaration against the ethics of survival which dominate the systems of rational morality. But much more than that is intended. The goods of the person are as unimportant in Christian morality as the good of wealth. The Christian can expect revilement and persecution for no other reason than his Christianity. Discipleship is not a way to honor and esteem; it is as certain a way as one can find to their opposites. Christians have found this as difficult as the sayings about wealth. They wish to be esteemed because esteem of them is an esteem of Christianity; and external honor paid to the Church and her prelates and members reflects honor on the Church. Jesus seemed to have expected something else. We can conclude that by these declarations ethical thought on the goods of the person is rendered otiose. The Christian needs no ethics on the use of the goods of the person because he will not have them to use. Against this background efforts to make the Church or her individual members honorable figures by secular standards seem dubious.

The Morality of Life in Community

The moral revolution of the gospel restores unity to isolated acts and to isolated persons. The moral life of the Christian is lived in and through the Church. Moral life is life not merely life in a community, but life which is fulfilled by means of the community. Salvation for Christians is a common effort. The members of the body in Paul's figure need one another; the life they share is shared fully by one when it is shared fully by all. When moral life is viewed as social and ecclesial, the decisive step is taken which removes the tendency of rational morality to be self-centered. The Christian does not look for his own fulfillment alone, nor does he think that fulfillment is possible alone. The self-sufficiency of the Stoic is foreign to Christian morality. What is impossible with men is possible with God; and it is through the Church that this divine power is mediated to the Christian.

Integral Personal Morality

The moral revolution of the gospel is directed toward an integral moral life. This we found lacking in ethical systems of reason and nature. One could if one wished compile a catalog of moral precepts and prohibitions from the New Testament; it has rarely been attempted because such a catalog would so evidently omit the central features of gospel morality. The gospel shows no interest in detailed directions, in cases and their solutions. Persons will live the gospel because of a revolutionary change in their personal life, their values, their habits, their attitudes. Once this change has been worked, detailed prescriptions become unnecessary; they could even inhibit the full development of the Christian life, well intentioned as they might be. We observed that each concrete individual act is a part of a vital chain; the gospel conceives a person's acts in this way, and it is concerned with the person who performs the acts. Given the personal qualities, the proper acts will follow. A good tree produces good fruit. The personal change is not conceived as the acquisition of habits of virtue; it goes deeper.

The New Testament frequently describes this personal transformation as putting on Christ, as living in Christ, as Christ living in the Christian, as the life of the Spirit in contrast to the life of the flesh. What Christ has done the Christian can do because he is a member of the body of Christ. He has the power of the Spirit which enables him to live in Christ. The language expresses a mystery which can never be fully comprehended; but the mystery is not penetrated more deeply by reducing union with Christ to the acquisition of good moral habits. In one passage (Phil 2:5) Paul calls it having the same mind among yourselves which you have in Christ Jesus. This verse is followed by the famous hymn in which Jesus is said to have emptied himself. We should notice that the mind of Christ is given to the Philippians as a guide to the way in which they should deal with each other. Their mutual relations should be governed by the personal transformation which has brought them to think like Christ, whose true mind is grasped in his emptying of self and his humiliation and obedience to death. This is the way in which the Philippians should attend to the interest of others. One can think like Christ because in the Church one is incorporated into Christ.

Imitation of Christ

The imitation of Christ is a form of Christian spirituality which rests on long tradition. Some recent writers have questioned whether the imitation as it has usually been presented is a correct interpretation of the New Testament. A mechanical imitation of Jesus is impossible, and where he exercises the unique power which he possessed it is scarcely conceivable. Actually the imitation of Christ is mentioned only twice in the New Testament (1 Cor 11:1; 1 Thes 1:6). One could say that the New Testament more frequently tells us that the Christian should be Christ than that the Christian should imitate Christ. And the passages where imitation is mentioned should be read against the passages in which living in Christ is stated as the Christian ideal. One lives in Christ not by aping him, but in the manner described in Philippians 2:5-7. The

Christian lives Christ when he shares in Christ's passion and death in the way in which God commits this share to him. Imitation could be again a question of isolated acts; identification with Christ touches the root of the acts, the principles by which one habitually judges and decides. When he becomes a disciple, the Christian denies that he is anything; and after this denial no future decision can ever be what it would be in rational ethics. There can simply be no morality of self-interest, enlightened or unenlightened.

The Centrality of Love

The personal transformation of the Christian is a mystery which cannot be pierced; but the effects of the transformation are set forth clearly — with such clarity, in fact, that Christians have some-times tried to make them more obscure than they are. The pivot of the Christian moral revolution is love. This is the entirely new and unique feature of Christian moral teaching; it is not the center of a moral structure, it is the entire structure. No one questions the centrality of love in New Testament morality; it is questionable whether Christians have always grasped how different it is and how total it is. I venture to state the difference by saying that it is not only a love which is known solely by Christian revelation, but it is a love of which only a Christian is capable. I venture to state its totality by saying that in the New Testament an act which is not an act of love has no moral value at all.

There are New Testament sayings which express the centrality and the totality of love. The first is a saying of Jesus found in the Synoptic Gospels with some variations: the saying about the great-est and the first commandment (Mt 22:34–40; Mk 12:28–31; Lk 10:25–28). The commandment of the love of God is called the greatest (Matthew) or the first (Mark) or the commandment by which one obtains eternal life (Luke). The commandment is named by Jesus (Mark and Matthew) or by the inquirer (Luke). The second is the commandment of the love of the neighbor. Matthew adds that the entire Law and the prophets (that is, the entire revelation made to Israel) depend on these two commandments. Luke adds to the discussion the parable of the Good Samaritan in answer to the question who is meant by neighbor. The answer,

which mentions the group most hated by Jews, is altogether in-
clusive. The second saying is found in Romans 13:8–10. Here Paul
says that one has no duty toward his neighbor except to love him,
that all the commandments are summed up in the commandment
to love one's neighbor, and that love of the neighbor is the fulfillment of the Law.

Love and the Moral Code

These passages, I think, support the statement that there is no
moral action in Christian life except the act of love. It is necessary
to add that the New Testament does not conceive the love mentioned in the two commandments as two loves but as one. What
is done to one's neighbor is done to Christ (Mt 25:40, 45). John
observes that one's love of God can be proved only by his love of
his brother (1 Jn 4:20). We have noticed (Chapter VI) that John
draws a paradoxical conclusion in 1 Jn 4:11: "If God has so loved
us, we also ought to love one another," where rigorous logic would
lead one to expect "If God has so loved us, we ought to love God."
But it is paradoxical only by ethical standards; John knew what is
so clear in the New Testament, that when one loves one's neighbor
one loves God. Matthew 25:31–46 contains a parable of an assembly
of all men before the Son of Man, who divides them into two
groups according to their merits. The sole question on which they
are divided is the rendering of service to others. I suppose one
would go too far in saying that this is the only point on which
men are judged, but one would scarcely go too far in saying it is
the chief point; for love is the fulfillment of the law.

The commandment of love, then, is the entire Christian moral
code. The commandments such as those which prohibit murder,
theft, and adultery are not voided; but it is fairly well assured that
one who loves his neighbor will not commit these crimes. One who
loves his neighbor with the fullness of Christian love is as assured
against sin as it is possible for man to be. He may make errors of
judgment and mistake love for something else. This is a risk which
cannot be avoided; but Jesus apparently was willing to trust the
mistakes of love more than the mistakes of reason. It would take
a rather bold moral philosopher to say that his system assures

infallibly against errors in moral judgment; and his errors will not be the mistakes of love. Justice under law is compatible with hatred.

Uniquely Christian Love

This is the centrality and the totality of love; the difference between this love and any other moral attitude I have said can be seen in the fact that only the Christian is capable of this kind of love. It is the love of God for man revealed in Christ Jesus, altogether other-directed with no return asked or expected and no limits placed on the demands it makes. Should love of the neighbor carry the Christian as far as Jesus' love of man carried him, the Christian has a better assurance that it is love and not something else which motivates him. It is always a help to reread Matthew 5, perhaps the best statement of the paradoxical folly of Christian love in practice in the entire New Testament. John said that the Christian cannot prove his love of God except by his love of man; Matthew makes it very clear that it is not really proved unless the person we love is an enemy. The Christian can be the object of enmity, but not its subject; one who is loved ceases to be an enemy. "Love of one's enemy" is a contradiction in terms; and Christians who think they are doing well when they love their enemies are often quite careful to make it clear that they remain enemies. The Christian loves his enemies as Christ loved man hostile to God. He is an agent of reconciliation, and a persevering agent. God has revealed to the Christian a value in his fellow lumps of clay which they do not have by their nature. Reason demands moderation in love as in all things; faith destroys moderation here. Faith tolerates a moderate love of one's fellow man no more than it tolerates a moderate love between God and man.

Among the condescending remarks which Europeans like to make about Americans is the statement that Americans like to be loved. One who is skilled in Mr. Stephen Potter's gamesmanship recognizes that this is a true ploy; to say that Americans like to be loved has as much point as saying that Americans have two feet. The Christian who begins to grasp the moral revolution of love begins to dream of a world, or at least a community, in which mutual love glows like the bright warm sunshine. Love returned is its own reward. It was necessary for Jesus to say explicitly that Christian love does not care whether it is its own reward or not; one should reread 1 Corinthians 13 for the classic statement of this principle. The Christian knows that his love is the active presence of God in the world; if he lacks it, he takes away God's presence from the only place where he can put it. He has come between his neighbor and the saving love of Jesus Christ. But if he is true to his Christian love, it may kill him, impoverish him, or disgrace him. In any hypothesis he is sure to lose at least some of those goods of this world or of the person which Jesus took some trouble to point out are of no importance.

Encounter of Reason and Gospel

We can now return to our question: Does the gospel reject a morality of law based on reason and nature? If the above exposition is based on the New Testament, it is difficult to see where there is room for it. If such a morality necessarily includes such elements as a morality centered on self, the atomization of the human community into isolated persons and of the moral life of the person into isolated acts, the minimal and negative morality of the permitted and the prohibited, and the partial or even total abdication of personal responsibility, then one must say that the gospel rejects any system which implies these things. Reason has its place in Christian morality in finding ways to fulfill these difficult and "unreal" commandments of love, not to evade them and substitute something else far more natural and practical and therefore just as good; at least no Christian has yet dared to say in so many words that rational morality is better.

But when one reviews the central theme of New Testament morality, one is depressed by a feeling of despair — despair of one's fellowman and of oneself. Is it possible? Is it practical? And one knows that one is asking God why he does not change the world into a community of love where it would not be so awfully hard to love one's neighbor as oneself. And one further realizes that the operation of this change is the mission God has committed to the Christian in that part of the world which is under the control of the individual person.

XII

THE CHURCH AND THE STATE

The Church in Society

The Church is a society. As such, it has relations with other societies. Its members are members of other societies. From the very beginnings of the Church these relationships, which can be the occasions of divided loyalties, created problems. The individual man has very little activity which is strictly private; and whenever he acts within a social framework, the framework is a condition and a determinant of his action. Other persons limit the area of his activity and turn it in certain directions; his Christian freedom and his personal freedom, when analyzed, are under numerous and constant restraints. Most of these social relationships have no direct reference to the Church and the Christian life; of themselves they are neither friendly nor hostile, but they can turn into one or the other. The Christian does not live in isolation from other social relations; he must be a Christian within a framework which he is unable to control.

The State

That other society which has bulked largest in the history of the Church is the state. The Church has always existed within a state; and she has never arrived at a final and definitive statement of her relations with the state. The history of her relations with the state shows a bewildering variation of arrangements. The history of her theological understanding of her relations with the state, as John Courtney Murray has set forth, shows scarcely less variation. The

Church has dealt with all kinds of states, and in each instance she has been concerned with what is vital, the preservation of her own identity. To this end she has been willing to make any adjustment with any state which leaves her what she is. Some of these adjustments in particular cases may have been more yielding than they ought to have been; one should be careful in showing hindsight, but at the same time we can be sure that the Church will not again follow some precedents from her past.

The Gospel and the State

In a matter of such profound importance we should look for guidance to the gospel as a theological source. It happens that the gospel does not afford much explicit guidance in the sense that a large number of passages can be assembled from which a doctrinal synthesis can be synthesized. This itself, as I hope to show, is significant. Furthermore, when we generalize from the Bible we must be careful to notice the differences between the concrete situation of the gospel and our own situation. The state in which the gospel arose has no parallel in the modern world; this could be significant, and one must advert to the fact before making any judgments. Nor is the historical situation of the Church today the same as the situation of the apostolic Church. The identity of the Church has not changed; but her concrete reality has, and her actions occur in concrete reality, not in abstraction. With these reservations, we should be deeply interested in whatever the New Testament has to say about the relations of the apostolic Church with the state.

The Roman Empire

The state in which the apostolic Church arose was the Roman Empire, which we have already surveyed (Chapter I). We saw that it was a cosmic rather than a political phenomenon, the first and so far the last world state, a political power without competition and seriously questioned by very few of its subjects. We saw that it governed better than any of its predecessors; the fact that this is not much of a tribute to Rome has nothing to do with the attitude of the subjects of Rome. It is, I think, safe to say that no state has ever governed with such a complete consent of the governed; in our own Declaration of Independence this is one of the conditions of a just government. There are other conditions which Rome did not meet quite as well; it was far from the ideal society, but neither in this chapter nor elsewhere in theological literature does the question arise of how the Church is to deal with an ideal political society which meets all conditions perfectly. This question is simply not practical. The practical question is how a Church whose leadership and membership in particular times and places is imperfectly Christian is to deal with a state which may be a polite gang of brigands. In historical situations discussions of the ideal Church and the ideal state have little reference to the realities. Neither the Church nor the state loses its rights when its leadership is corrupt; but they make it much more difficult to present a convincing case for their rights.

The Church in the Empire

Within the Roman Empire the Church in its earliest phase was, as we have seen, a Jewish sect as far as the Empire was concerned. The Church was therefore no particular concern of the government, which tolerated Judaism as a lawful religion. When it became evident that the Church was a community distinct from Judaism, the toleration of Judaism was extended to the Christians. This toleration endured throughout the New Testament period in the sense that Christianity remained a legal religion; the Empire made no deliberate general effort to destroy the Church, and the persecutions which occurred were brief and irregular. The persecutions are responsible for the sharp change in the attitude of Christians themselves which can be seen in the Apocalypse. There Rome has become the Beast and the Great Whore who sheds the blood of martyrs. But in the Gospels and the epistles Rome is still accepted as the world government, as much a part of the cosmic structure as the atmosphere.

Jesus and the Government

We have already noticed in discussing the kingship of Jesus that in John 18 Jesus expressly denies any relationship with the secular government (Chapter IV). His explanation was accepted by Pilate, who certainly did not take his claims seriously but recognized that he was not a rebel. All four Gospels are rather insistent on the fact that Jesus was not executed for any political offense; this insistence certainly reflects the image which the apostolic Church wished to project. The Church had nothing to contribute to the government and nothing to receive from the government. The activities of the Church and of the government were simply unrelated; there was neither friendship nor hostility. Christians were subjects of Rome and they could be expected to fulfill their duties as citizens — which in the Empire consisted principally in the payment of taxes. They were not lawbreakers and they had no complaint against the government; the government should have no complaint against them. Like the Jews, they could not take part in the Caesar cult; and in the apostolic period this was understood and tolerated by Rome. The kingship of Jesus was not of this world, and it took away nothing from the kings of this world. Nor did it demand anything from the kings of this world.

Tribute to Caesar

Besides John 18:36–37 there are only two New Testament passages from which a doctrine of the relations of Church and state can be deduced. The first of these is in the Gospels; it is the saying of Jesus in which he tells a questioner to render to Caesar what belongs to Caesar and to God what belongs to God (Mt 22:15–22; Mk 12:13–17; Lk 20:20–26). This is not the easiest of the sayings of Jesus; and its background must be looked at closely. The question asked was whether it was lawful to pay tribute to Caesar. This was a theological question in Judaism. For a Jew, to acknowledge an overlord by paying tribute could be a denial of the supremacy of God; and it was so understood by the fanatic groups in Judaism (Chapter I). In rigorous Pharisaic Judaism the use of a coin with a human image was a violation of the Second Commandment. The question was also a highly explosive political issue; as it was phrased, it seemed to leave Jesus no avenue of escape. He must either offend Jewish sensibilities or declare that Rome had no right to demand tribute.

In this situation the words of Jesus may be an evasion rather than an answer. When I speak of an evasion, I do not imply that Jesus withheld an answer from human respect; I mean that his answer tells us that his gospel has no simple answer to this question. Luke has preserved a saying in which Jesus refused to act as judge or arbiter in a question of inheritance (Lk 12:13–14). As far as the gospel is concerned, Jesus has nothing in particular to say about how inheritance should be divided. Similarly it is possible that he implied that his gospel has no answer to the question about tribute, which was actually a question whether the Roman government of Palestine was legitimate. It was a political question which he did not intend to settle. It should not be hard to understand why Jesus should refuse to become involved in a political issue.

The answer certainly seems to allow the payment of the tribute; but the permission is based on the practice of the Jews and not on anything in the teaching of Jesus. It amounts to this: as long as you use Caesar's money you accept his claim to it. You cannot answer the question about tribute by itself; and you have already answered it by your practice. Your answer raises other questions to which I have only one answer: Give Caesar what is his and give God what is his. We can hardly think that Jesus meant by this answer to divide the universe between God and Caesar. Caesar has nothing that is not God's. But God does not demand tribute; Caesar does, and he has the power to exact it. As long as you submit yourselves to his power, which you cannot resist anyway, you have no choice but to pay him tribute. Should Caesar demand something which God prohibits, or should Caesar prohibit something which God demands, you know what you must do.

What Is Political Power?

A political philosophy based on this statement would be rather skimpy. Jesus says nothing about the roots of political power, its legitimacy, its competence. He takes political power as a fact of life and offers nothing except submission to the fact. He places no limitation on the exercise of political power except the sovereignty of God; this is a vital limitation, but he does not define it. One may say at least that if the Roman Empire usurped the sovereignty of God in any notable degree, we should expect Jesus to say something about it. The apostolic and postapostolic Church saw clear usurpations and refused submission. We may notice in passing that their only weapon against the usurpation was passive resistance; we shall have to return to this. But as long as Caesar is there he can ask and get his tribute. Jesus offers no reason for paying it and no reason for withholding it.

The saying of Jesus thus interpreted shows a certain indifference to the Empire, to say the least; and we shall have to see whether this impression is correct in the course of our discussion. If it is so interpreted, it is in harmony with the saying preserved in John about his kingship. The denial of any mutual concern between Jesus and the government is maintained consistently in both passages. Here we must remind ourselves that we may not extend the application of the New Testament beyond due limits. The Roman Empire is not the abstract state as such; and the attitude of the Christian toward the state is not necessarily the same if the character of the state changes. But it is important to get the attitude of the New Testament as clearly in our minds as we can; for it should not be assumed that the New Testament is irrelevant to the more recent state.

The Power in St. Paul

The second saying is found in Romans 13:1–7. I take this as the typical passage; the state is mentioned in a few other epistles, but no passage adds anything to what is found in Romans. Here Paul commands submission to authority, for all power is from God. To resist authority is to resist God, for authority is God's minister for good. Therefore, submission is a duty of conscience. This passage seems to offer a much broader base for a political philosophy; and much Christian political ethics appeals to Paul for support. The problem is that the easiest political philosophy to erect from this passage is the divine right of kings. No one in modern times thinks this is what Paul means; and when the passage is interpreted in some other way, there is a vague suspicion that the interpreters are not catching the mind of Paul.

Here, as so often, the mind of Paul is more surely apprehended if we look at the Old Testament background of his thought. In the Old Testament there are only two political societies: Israel and the nations. Israel is the people of God. It existed in a political society which God destroyed because of the sins of Israel. It was destroyed by the nations who were the agents of God's wrath. The nations, like Israel, are under judgment for sin, and they too will inevitably fall. The Old Testament recognizes no durable political society; it passes from the nations of the world to the Reign of God.

Power From God

Where does Paul put Rome in this scheme? It is not Israel, certainly; and it is even more certainly not the Reign of God. Has Paul without warning given the Roman Empire a dignity and a permanence which no other state possesses in biblical thought? Such a departure from biblical thought demands more and clearer evidence than this passage. If it is taken to mean the divine right of government, it says so much more than Jesus said about tribute that a genuine problem arises. The key may perhaps lie in the idea of power. In the Old Testament all power is from God; but power as such is morally neutral. No nation and no person can have any power which is not committed to it by God; but the exercise of the power is not thereby authenticated. Assyria was the rod of God's anger for Israel (Is 10:5); Assyria was still Assyria, an object of judgment no less because it was an instrument of judgment. God brought down the kingdom of Judah and the city of Jerusalem through Nebuchadnezzar of Babylon; and Jeremiah preached submission to Nebuchadnezzar because God had given him the rule of the earth (Jer 25:8–11; 27:1–15) and counseled the Jews who had been transported to Babylon to seek the welfare of the city (Jer 29:5–7). I think one recognizes in these passages the ideas in which Paul moves; and they permit one to say that Paul does not clearly give the Roman Empire any value which the Old Testament does not give to Assyria and Babylonia. If Rome has power, it must be because God has given it power. God gives it power as he gave power to the nations of the East, for the purpose of punishing evildoers; to resist this power is to resist God, and this is true both of Babylon and of Rome. No positive value is attributed to either state as such.

Cosmic Power

Paul like Jesus says that Caesar should receive what is his — taxes, respect, and honor. He should receive it because he has the power to exact it. Paul adds what Jesus did not, that the power is committed by God as a punishment of evildoers. And here an idea begins to emerge which it is difficult to translate into more modern language without the risk of going beyond the ideas of the New Testament. The effort, nevertheless, must be made; for it suggests an insight into the gospel. There is only one power in the universe and that is the power of God. This is a power to judge and to save. God exercises his power through agents. Nature is such an agent; the stories of the exodus from Egypt show God saving and judging through the phenomena of nature. Men and nations are likewise such agents; unlike nature, they are moral agents. But when they act as agents of God's power to save or to judge, they are morally neutral in so far as they are agents; it makes no difference whether they are good or bad, for God can use either. Samson as savior and the Assyrians as agents of judgment are not men of morally elevated stature. When God commits his power to them, they are on the moral level of the phenomena of nature. They will be judged on other factors than the commission of power.

Hence the power through which God executes his saving acts and his judgments can be considered a part of the cosmic structure; and it is not by mere coincidence that I return here to the phrase which I used earlier to describe the world state of Rome. It belongs to the cosmos as nature belongs to the cosmos; it is indeed created precisely for the evildoers. Man suffers the state because he is under judgment, and the state is a part of the curse which lies upon him for his sins. The Roman Empire is a component of the universe of Sin and Death; man must accept it as he accepts concupiscence and disease. It belongs to the fourfold plague which Jeremiah mentions several times: the sword, famine, pestilence, and captivity.

This view of the state, I believe, sets the state much more neatly in biblical thought than the view of it as a divine institution. It suits both the sayings of Jesus, who said that the power which Pilate had over him came from above (Jn 19:11), and the prophetic view of the state. No one has thought of using John 19:11 as evidence of the divine right of the state; yet Jesus is not saying anything different from Paul. The power is given from above in the sense described; the power can be used to punish evildoers and it can be used to crucify Jesus. It is the same power in either case, and it is not diminished by its misuse. If one nation falls, God establishes another as the agent of his judgment. Nothing suggests that Paul thought that Rome would endure forever; there is nothing likewise to suggest that he thought it would be succeeded by anything but another Rome. The New Testament, like the Old, puts nothing between the kingdoms of the nations and the Reign of God.

Legitimacy of Power

I have observed that the New Testament introduces no consideration of the legitimacy of government or of the just use of the powers of government. Tribute is to be rendered to Caesar; I think it is legitimate to extend this to all the Caesars, whether it be Tiberius, in whose reign the saying was uttered, Caligula, Claudius, Nero, Vespasian, Titus, or Domitian; and where shall we end the line? The New Testament knew Caligula, a madman, Nero, a psychopath, and Domitian, probably a paranoiac. Even the Apocalypse does not suggest that Caesar is no longer Caesar when he is a paranoiac. The legitimacy of Rome's claim to rule was in almost every instance based on conquest, which is not the most ethical of claims. The administration of the Empire was, as we have seen, generally superior to the administration of the kingdoms which Rome conquered; when we have said this, we have not said much. The American colonists rebelled over a tax on tea, and they have become national heroes. Had the subjects of Rome ever thought of rebelling over taxes, they would have had a much more urgent case than the merchants of Boston. When we mention these things we know they are unimportant. The New Testament examines neither the credentials of Rome nor its use of its power; it would make no more sense than the examination of the credentials of an earthquake. There is no concern with whether the government is just or not; it is to be obeyed because it exists. Would the answer of Jesus have been different in any other state? Would he have altered the saying if Nero had been Caesar? Would he have altered it if he had lived under George III or Abraham Lincoln? And if we alter it, we should be sure we have the right to do so. The impact of the New Testament sayings is that Caesar has no more claim to power because he is just and no less claim because he is unjust.

The Christian and the Modern State

The implications of this take us so far that one may properly ask whether the idea is there from which we draw the implications. It is not a question of whether the New Testament says something; it is a question of something which the New Testament does not say, and which we cannot read into it for the only state which it knows, the Roman Empire. The modern Christian may admit the implications but deny their validity for his own condition; for the modern Christian does not live in the Roman Empire. He will observe that there are many modern moral problems for which the New Testament gives no explicit solution; the Christian must think his own way to a solution, as we have said in the preceding chapter. If the New Testament gives very few directions for living in the Roman Empire, it does not follow that the Christian cannot derive from the New Testament a considerable body of doctrine on how to live in the modern state.

This position must be granted; but it should be noticed that the absence of any extended treatment of the relations of the individual person to the state in the New Testament may itself be revealing. This may suggest that in the New Testament the problem is of only secondary importance. If the problem were vital, we should expect the New Testament to say more than render to Caesar what is his, to obey civil authority, and to pay your taxes. One might expect some directions on how to Christianize the Roman Empire. Those who had a commission to proclaim the gospel to all nations might have expected that to occur which did occur; the population of the Empire became Christian by a tremendous majority. This permits us to ask another question: Is the Roman Empire considered an object of redemption? Can it be saved? Can it be brought under the Reign of God? We shall return to this question. At the moment let us turn to the problem of the modern Christian; does the New Testament tell him anything about his relations with the state in which he lives?

The Secular State

The modern Christian, it should be noticed, is not faced with the problem of the Christian state. A discussion conducted by historians and theologians on whether a Christian state has ever existed would be highly interesting; certainly a number of those present would maintain the thesis that a Christian state has never existed, and some would maintain that it is impossible to create one. We need not settle this nonbiblical question here. The modern Christian in most of the world encounters not the Christian state but the post-Christian secular state; and it is difficult to distinguish this state from the Roman Empire as far as its theological value is concerned. But a distinction should be made nevertheless. The post-Christian state is the heir of thousands of years of Christian tradition, some features of which have worked their way into the political structure, and this fact may affect the attitude of the Christian.

Here we have to consider the state in the abstract as far as such a consideration is possible; the abstraction which we make will designate no existing state exactly. I suggest that we measure the state viewed abstractly against the fundamental standards of Christian morality and see whether in this respect it can be given the designation of Christian or even of neutral. If it is anti-Christian there is no further problem. We can notice that the Christian state is an insertion into history for which the New Testament leaves no room. Like the Old Testament, the New Testament goes from the secular state to the eschatological Reign of God. This is not insignificant, and it fits what has been noticed above; the New Testament foresees no Christianization of the Roman Empire. It scarcely need be stated that a state is not Christian by the simple fact that its leadership and its citizens are all Christians. A state is not Christian even by the union of Church and state, unless the word "Christian" is deprived of almost all of its meaning.

The Common Good

It is a conventional statement of Christian political philosophy that the end of the state is the good of its membership, the common good being more than the sum of the good which can be procured by all the members as individuals. The common good is attainable only by an organized political society which has jurisdictional authority. It includes such things as peace and public order, the administration of law and justice, and in modern times a certain number of public services. Christian political philosophy insists that the competence of the state lies in the temporal order exclusively, otherwise the state would intrude into the competence of the Church. Temporal good is not synonymous with material goods; political freedom, for instance, is not a material good, but it is a temporal good. I think this abstraction fits all states in the sense that it is what they ought to be.

When one enumerates the elements of the common good, one cannot miss the fact that the state is concerned with just those values which we saw in the preceding chapter are overturned in the proclamation of the gospel. A state which in modern times would permit its citizens in the mass to live without sufficient food and clothing would be judged to fail in its essential end; and a state which fails to achieve its essential end loses its legitimacy. Yet unconcern with these basic matters is precisely what Jesus recommends to his disciples. Whatever the state is when it concerns itself with temporal good, it is not Christian. It is not anti-Christian either; it is simply irrelevant to the Christian way of life. When the state has achieved the common good, it has not enriched the Christian life of its citizens one bit. When it fails, it has not diminished the Christian life. It is of the essence of the Christian life that it can be lived independently of the temporal welfare of the Christian. Jesus did not intend to put those who live under misgovernment — and this is the vast majority of mankind — under a spiritual disadvantage in comparison to those who live under a wise and just government. If we take the Sermon on the Mount seriously, Jesus seems to have placed the spiritual advantage with the misgoverned.

Civil Law

The state is a society of law; and we have seen in the preceding chapter that the gospel frees the Christian from law. This is not an attempt to present the gospel as Christian anarchy; this thesis cannot be got off the ground, in spite of the superficial attractiveness of the philosophical thesis that no man is fit to govern another. Law is a part of the reign of Sin and Death; and this is the area in which the state reigns. The Church is a community of love; and it is obvious that a community of love tends to destroy the community of law. And now we return to a point raised above; it is for this reason that the New Testament sees no redemption of the state. It must disappear with the Sin and Death which make it possible for the state to exist. It is a part of the condition of fallen man which cannot endure in the eschatological Reign. The Bible knows no civil society which is not ephemeral; and nothing in existing societies leads one to think that they have achieved enduring reality. They too bear within themselves the principle of corruption which manifests itself in every historic state. Whatever the attitude of the Christian toward his state may be, it is directed to a perishing object. One man who is assured of no lasting achievement is the statesman.

Public Morality

When we look at the means by which the state achieves its end, certain dissonances between public morality and Christian morality appear. We have said that love is the moral structure of the Christian life; and we have referred to the classic impracticalities of the gospel, particularly in the Sermon on the Mount. The state does not resist evil; it does not turn the other cheek. It does not give the tunic when its mantle is taken, nor does it walk two miles when it is forced to walk one. It does not love its enemies. It does distinguish very sharply between Jew, Greek, Scythian, and other national and racial groups. Only Matthew has preserved the saying that they who take the sword shall perish by the sword (Mt 26:52). If one wants to press the point — and many want to press this one — Jesus did not say that the use of weapons is wrong. He did not even say it is foolish; he did say that it is fatal to the one who uses them. The state is not a Good Samaritan, although public generosity is not unknown; sometimes Christian morality breaks through public morality. Yet what looks like public generosity is often recommended to the citizens not as generosity but as a cheaper way of purchasing their own security.

Public morality is not Christian; and one would answer that a state whose morality is Christian could not survive. This I gladly concede; my point is not only that the state is not Christian, but that it cannot be Christian. In all fairness it must be admitted that the experiment of a Christian state has never really been attempted. Christians are convinced that a truly Christian state cannot survive, and this conviction effectively means that one will not arise. The ethical theory of the state is that the state is not a subject of moral obligation. Its members are subjects of moral obligation, but only as individual persons. When they assemble into a political society, they are not bound by any Christian principles. They may decide upon actions which if done by individuals would be murder, arson, theft, and mendacity. One looks for this exception in vain in the New Testament. Historically the ethics of war have always been determined by the party who was willing to gain an advantage by abandoning ethics. The same is true of the ethics of diplomacy and trade. The state can be above nothing unless every other state is above it. The Christian state is perhaps in worse condition than the secular state, because the self-righteousness of Christians moves them so quickly to identify their national security with the security of the Church. Thus we have such examples of Christian public morality as the Crusades, in which the cross of him who refused defense and the sword became a military banner under which the Christians invited the infidel to baptism — or else.

The Ethic of Survival

None of these things are thought immoral when the state does them except in unusually outrageous incidents; and these incidents are not thought outrageous by those who are responsible for them, because they are done for national security. What really determines the state to be un-Christian is the basis of its ethics. The ethics of the state are the ethics of survival. States live in a moral jungle. Retaliation justifies anything. The supreme good of the state is that it continues to exist; and no other good can be maintained if that good threatens survival. The question of whether the state has a right to survive in any hypothesis cannot be asked and has not been asked really since the Israelite prophets of the eighth and seventh centuries B.C. The individual Christian may and indeed must face the possibility that there are occasions in which there is no Christian way to survive. The state, which is entirely of this world, can admit no such occasion. Behind all the political ethics of defense and security one can see the cornered rat with fangs bared. This is Christian? Jesus died so that men could act like cornered rats with a good conscience?

If the ethics of survival could be confined to public morality, we would be no worse off morally than men were in the Roman Empire. Unfortunately the ethics of survival do creep into the personal life even of Christians. It is something of a puzzle how a morality which permits war should prohibit dueling. Recite the magic incantation "public authority" over dueling and it becomes man-ennobling war. There are other forms of private combat besides the duel, however; and when survival is in question, or thought to be in question, the ethics of the jungle come out. Christians, cleric and lay, have been willing to risk arson, bloodshed, and the danger of disease and starvation for their fellow men in order to maintain the value of their real estate or to keep the labor market in short supply. Compared to this the Roman conquests seem rather dignified; at least the Romans stole some art treasures. Perhaps we are unfair to the jungle. In a forest fire, I understand, the animals run for escape without regard to their natural enmities.

The Ethic of Allegiance

The ethics of survival do affect the citizens of the state more directly. The state claims the allegiance of its citizens; and the first duty of allegiance is the protection of national security. I am not speaking primarily of military service. The modern state controls the lives of its citizens to a degree which was not attained by the Caesars. The limitations of the moral freedom of the individual are more severe than we realize unless we sit down and count them. Since 1789 the United States government has presented its Christian citizens with no moral problem of critical magnitude. This may mean that the moral integrity of the United States is magnificent; it may also mean that Christian citizens do not recognize a public moral problem when they see it. In the morality of reason and nature the state can do no wrong, particularly when its survival is in question. Decisions made by public authority are not subject to the critical review of the individual citizen. The citizen may abdicate his personal responsibility to the state before he knows it. And if the state becomes the supreme judge of moral good and evil in public affairs, if it can demand unquestioning obedience in its service, what is the difference between the modern state and the Caesar cult except that the worship of Caesar was a merely symbolic act? It is the demonic quality of the state that it tends to become a god. Christians of the Roman Empire were faced with a simple moral problem of giving cult to Caesar. This they knew they must refuse. The cult which the modern state demands is far more subtle; and the citizens of the modern state are schooled to believe that the state can do no wrong.

The Enmity of Church and State

Martin Dibelius once wrote a perceptive article on the relations of Rome and the early Church. He proposed the intriguing view that some time elapsed before a few Christians and a few Roman administrators endowed with unusual acuteness saw that Rome and the Church were mortal enemies. To this insight he credits the persecution of Decius, the first serious effort to exterminate Christianity. Both Christians and Romans who knew what was going on could see that the Church and the Roman ethos could not live peacefully together. If the Church were allowed to grow, the Roman ethos would perish. The Christians who saw this knew that when the New Testament speaks of "the world," it is not speaking of some abstract entity. It means the concrete world of existing men; and the patronal genius of "the world" was the government of the Roman Empire. It could not be Christianized; it had to disappear. Dibelius' thesis is a splendid study of the development of an idea; can it be extended to other states than Rome?

I have drawn up a rather horrendous list of features of the state which do not seem to fit the Christian way of life. The Christian must, it appears, stop thinking and living like a Christian when the service of the state falls upon him. In a democratic society, however theoretical the popular sovereignty may be, he is a party to national decisions whose ethics are questionable at best. As far as the list goes, the irreducible and uncompromising hostility which Dibelius points out existed between Rome and the Church. still exists between the Church and modern states. Neither the Church nor the individual Christian can accept the modern state simply and without reservation. The Christian way of life tends to destroy the morality of the state. There are times when civil disobedience is a duty; and one wonders that its occurrence is so rare. When it does occur, the Christian is not denying his allegiance any more than Roman Christians denied their allegiance to Caesar. They were rendering to Caesar no more than what is his. Historically this has usually not been enough for Caesar. To give Caesar credit, it has not always been enough for the Church either. Many churchmen for nearly a thousand years have cherished the image of the Emperor Henry on his knees in the snow at Canossa. This, they think, is the proper position of the state before the Church. It is not; if any image represents the encounter of Church and state, it is the image of Jesus before Pilate. That the history of the Church is so largely a history of quarrels with the state is not entirely the fault of the state. Christians have no legitimate measure against an overbearing state except nonresistance, civil disobedience unto death. They die for the state by refusing to cooperate with its immorality. When they do anything else, they have parted company with Jesus.

Christian Engagement in the State

I have said above that the New Testament does not support a thesis of Christian anarchy. Neither does it support a thesis of Christian withdrawal. The Christian lives in the state whether he wishes to or not. The two statements we have on this both tell the Christian to do his duty. It should not be necessary to add that his Christian life is the best service he can render his community. The strongest assurance the state can have that the demonic quality in it will not break out is the Christian faith of its citizens, who will not support the state in its immoral endeavors. They cannot accept the survival of the state and the common temporal good as supreme values. Moral values are more important. What the state gains by immoral actions is to a Christian no gain but a loss; this is the position he must take. In the world of politics as in the world of individual conduct, the Christian is not free to postpone doing what is right until everyone else has done it before him. I hardly think that such conduct in the state can be called withdrawal. Engagement in political affairs need not mean the adoption of the ethics of the jungle.

The Concrete Reality of the State

It is time we bring the state back from the level of abstraction on which we have been keeping it. I have said that the abstract state describes no existing state. The state is a collection of persons. Strictly speaking "the state" does nothing. The state is men in action. Men who act for the state act not for themselves but for the body of men whom they represent. In a sense even absolute monarchies must reflect the popular will if they are to survive. We cannot blame "the state" as if it were a responsible person. Men do things in crowds which they will not do alone; we hope very few people in a lynching mob would murder on their own behalf. The Christian must look at the state as the pressure of other men. He cannot share their desires and yield to their pressures simply because they outnumber him. The capacity of the state to do evil makes it quite clear that the Christian is not free to let the state make his decisions for him. He knows that men hide behind a crowd and find there an outlet for desires which they usually mask or restrain. Whether he changes the popular will or not is unimportant; what is important for him is whether he acts according to the Spirit as a member of Christ. He needs no help from the crowd to do this.

Our problem has been complicated by the history of Church and state. So much of it is a history of the state attempting to do the work of the Church and of the Church attempting to do the work of the state that it is no wonder we are confused. The state is not an agent of the Reign; and the Church is not an agent of the temporal good. Whether they can cooperate in anything is a question; it seems that each loses something by using the other, and the one which is used loses even more. The Christian lives in the state as he lives in his house, as he eats his food and wears his clothing. These are the things of this world which man cannot escape; and most of his life is spent in procuring them. Somehow through his preoccupation with survival it is possible for him to live in Christ; but he expects a fulfillment which will not be of this world. The state, like the house, the food, and the clothing is essentially perishable and therefore essentially unimportant. To give it more attention than it deserves may be like the man in the parable who tore down his barns to build bigger ones (Lk 12:15–21). To him Jesus said, "You fool, this night they will look for your life; and whose will be the things you have accumulated?"

XIII *APPROACHES TO GOD*

A Lesson in Prayer

One of the sayings of Jesus which is always rationalized in practice and ignored in theory is found in Matthew 6:7–8: "When you pray, do not babble like the heathen; for they think that by talking much they will be heard. Do not be like them; for your Father knows what you need before you ask him." Matthew then inserts into his Gospel the Lord's Prayer as a model for the disciples. Luke (11:1–4) gives the Lord's Prayer as an answer to the request of the disciples that Jesus, whom they had seen at prayer, would teach them how to pray. The word I have translated "babble" is an extremely rare Greek word of uncertain meaning; lexicographers suggest babble, prate, speak without thinking. It certainly means the mechanical recitation of formulae with no attention to their meaning; and the following clause indicates that it also includes lengthy formulae. Whatever the Greek word means, the Lord's Prayer is not an example of long prayer; and here we can ask ourselves why Christians have so often been unable to take this saying of Jesus seriously. Of us also it can be said that because we talk much, we think we will be heard.

The prayers of Judaism of the New Testament period were lengthy; many of them have been preserved, and they are in obvious contrast to most of the Psalms, which can be recited in a minute or two. Jesus knew of these long prayers, and he spoke of them once; he pronounced a heavier judgment on those who devour the houses of widows while they pray long prayers (Mk 12:40; Lk 20:47). The prayer of Jesus himself is mentioned several times (Mk 1:35; Mt 26:36–46 = Mk 14:32–42 = Lk 22:40–46), and Luke (6:12) says that he passed the night in prayer before the naming of the Twelve. The conversation between Jesus and his Father, however, can scarcely be proposed as a model to be imitated by those whose relation with the Father is other than natural sonship. The Lord's Prayer does not furnish material for a night of prayer. Here the teaching of Jesus seems to be even more than usually clear; and we meet again the paradox that the clearer his words are, the more readily we take them as suggestions, counsels, recommendations which we are free to follow unless we can think of something better.

Prayer in the New Testament

Prayer is mentioned frequently in the New Testament; it was certainly a normal and an important part of the Christian life, as it was important in Judaism. But there is little or nothing specific in the allusions to prayer. It is either public or private, conducted in the place of worship or in any place. A saying of Jesus warns against making of prayer a display of piety (Mt 6:5–6). Where prayer is mentioned in specific terms, it is almost always the prayer of petition which is mentioned. The Christian cult groups used the Psalms in their common worship; and a number of New Testament passages have been very probably identified as liturgical selections. These show that the hymn, the song of praise, was prominent in the worship of the primitive Church. But these materials add up to little. One cannot construct from the New Testament a manual of prayer or of the methods of prayer. The sole positive direction remains the Lord's Prayer.

One sees, then, something less than perfect harmony between the only teaching of Jesus on how to pray which we have in the Gospels and the long-established practices of the Christian community. I say less than perfect because Christian practice is itself a guide to the interpretation of the words of Jesus; and one hesitates to say that Christian practice is completely out of line with the Gospels. But the practice, it seems, would be strengthened if it were better founded in the New Testament. That I do not see how it will be founded in the New Testament is no reason to think that no one else will see it; I think I can express a personal desire that this work be done. The contrast between the austere and simple prayer of the New Testament and the profusion of prayer formulae in Christian practice is too sharp to be casually dismissed with the remark that, after all, it is one and the same thing. It may not be important whether one prays briefly or at length, and one cannot say that the question is treated with emphasis in the New Testament. But we do have a saying of Jesus which the apostolic Church took the trouble to preserve.

Prayer in the Church

Let us be specific; but let us also be cautious. The Church approves any prayer which she offers for general use; it is within the scope of her office to determine whether a prayer formula is a proper way to address God or not. Prayer is a profession of faith. The practice of the Church in approving prayer certainly shows that prolixity in prayer is not unorthodox; and nothing that is said here should be taken as implying that it is. It is necessary to understand what the approval of the Church means in this instance. The approval of prayer, like the approval of religious orders, means not so much that the thing approved is good as that it is not bad. When one uses the thing approved, one will not by its use deviate from orthodox faith. The thing approved may be an imperfect expression of orthodox faith, and its use may be unsafe without proper precautions; the Church does not pretend that it can foresee all possible abuses. It can and does judge the thing as it is presented and in the context in which it is presented. Religious orders may be very well adapted to one period and culture and very poorly adapted to others. When the Church approves religious orders, I suppose she assumes that the members of the order will have sense enough to adapt themselves to history; it is not the fault of the Church if they fail to adapt. Forms of piety and devotion may be likewise well adapted to particular times, particular regions, particular needs, and ill adapted to others. One often hears Catholics say that they do not find the Psalms a sympathetic form of prayer. This candor, permissible when an inspired book is under discussion, can be quite dangerous if exhibited toward the Rosary or the devotion to the Sacred Heart. I merely note the freedom with which we treat the Bible and pass on.

Private Revelation

A review of the history of piety and asceticism would take us far beyond the limits of the book, and would exceed the task which I have set myself: the treatment of the New Testament. Such histories have been written; and it is unfortunate that the material which they contain is not more widely known. I limit myself to a few items which can be handled in general terms. The first of these items is the private revelation as a source of devotional practices. Very few prayer formulae have ever been widely accepted which were not authenticated by a private revelation. It is well known that the Church has never made any private revelation her own. A Catholic is entirely free to doubt or to deny that St. Dominic received the Rosary from our Blessed Mother or that Jesus Christ ever appeared or spoke to St. Margaret Mary Alacoque. A Catholic is equally free to abstain from the Rosary as a form of prayer and to take no part in devotional practices directed to the Sacred Heart. The Catholic is not free to say that either of these devotions is opposed to any element of Catholic faith and morality. The Catholic is not free to say that anyone who does not recite the Rosary or practice devotion of the Sacred Heart deprives himself of any of the fullness of Catholic faith and Catholic life. The position of the Church toward private revelations and private devotions is eminently safe and sane; if all the members of the Church accepted her position, we would have spared ourselves much trouble.

Misconceptions of Private Revelation

But all the members of the Church have not always accepted her position; and some attention given to the misconception of the private revelation and the private devotion will repay us. This attention must be given without looking at any private revelation or private devotion in particular; where sensibilities are so tender, discretion is the better part of valor. It is my personal opinion that a number of very popular devotions founded on private revelations have no foundation in fact at all; that the revelations are manifestly not revelations and can be recognized as the speech of man and not the speech of God by their very content. This can be proposed as no more than an opinion; I know that the opinion is shared by many of my colleagues in exegesis and theology, and this is not trivial. The question I ask is why there appears in the Church a recurring need for something which is met by private revelation, authentic or not. Some years ago an alleged vision occurred in an otherwise undistinguished community called Necedah, Wisconsin. When the vision was announced in the press, all rail and highway routes to Necedah were jammed. The affair was so patently fraudulent that ecclesiastical authorities moved with more than usual swiftness, and it is now forgotten. Was the incident, perhaps, a sign of a usually latent pathological condition in our spirituality? Is it a sign of good health that an alleged vision generates an excitement which is not generated by the daily wonder of the Eucharistic sacrifice — admitting that contemporary liturgical practices have not been calculated to show the wonder of the act in its full magnificence? Does God have to create a vulgar sensation to attract our attention?

Europeans have been heard to say that American Catholicism is doubtful to them because our people have never been gifted with visions and private revelations. For a few days at one time it looked as if Our Lady of Necedah might take her place with Our Lady of Lourdes, Our Lady of Walsingham, Our Lady of Fatima, and Our Lady of Guadalupe of our sister republic of Mexico; and thus she would take away the reproach of the United States, which has to invoke our Lady as national patron without the title of a local apparition. Our Lady of Necedah turned out to be something else than the Mother of God; and we still stand abashed before the world because our soil is not good enough for her blessed feet. This, of course, is sheer and arrant nonsense; but that such nonsense is seriously uttered may be cause for concern. We have to face the fact that nothing was needed except a few clergy who knew the meaning of promotion to make of Necedah another Lourdes or Fatima. I think we can afford to be proud of the fact that such clergy did not appear.

The Need of Assurance

So here we have at least one need which private revelations fulfill: they fulfill the need for assurance that we are right with God. They are no such assurance even if they are authentic; but they are taken as assurances, and when they are so taken they are harmful. The New Testament is clear that no one can reach a state of complete assurance concerning his relations with God, and the Church has declared it an article of faith that no one can be certain of his salvation. But this does not keep Christians from seeking the assurance which the gospel and the Church tell them they cannot have. They assume that an apparition is a sure token of God's good pleasure; it is not, of course, a personal token to each individual, so the individual hastens to identify himself with the group which has made the private revelation its own. Devotional practices arise which barely escape affirming what the Church says cannot be affirmed, that salvation is infallibly assured by persevering in devotional practices through a certain number of Fridays or Saturdays. I dare say that those who are faithful to these practices do not deny that salvation is primarily assured by the observance of the commandments and by the love of God and the neighbor. If the substantials are maintained, it makes no difference how many prayers one recites on any or every day of the week; if they are not observed, a perpetual novena is nowhere in the New Testament recommended as an adequate substitute. Nine Fridays are easier than ten commandments; and if they give greater assurance, one can scarcely blame people for putting their faith in the Fridays.

Dissatisfaction With the Gospel

The search for assurance, when analyzed, discloses an unspoken dissatisfaction with the gospel and the Church. We have a demand which the gospel and the Church do not meet, and we think they ought to meet it; they should remove from us the perpetual concern which we feel if there is doubt about the permanence of our good relations with God. We think that there should be some single decisive act which we can perform and get it over with; then we can go on to the normal and urgent business of living. We feel that the necessity of making a new decision each day is an unfair demand. We would not dream of seeking this assurance from any other than God. God has not given it through the only channels which are his authentic voice; but fortunately he has opened up unofficial channels. It is easy to see which of the two we esteem more highly. One often meets Catholics who are much more fluent on the revelations of Fatima than they are on the Gospels or the Epistles of Paul.

Gnosticism

In the history of the postapostolic Church one encounters the obscure heresies lumped under the name of Gnosticism. I call them obscure because the tedious literature of these sects is so confused that it is often nearly unintelligible. Tedious as the literature may be, the study of these texts has a morbid fascination; they are splendid examples of pathological spirituality. The word "Gnostic," from the Greek word for knowledge, is chosen to designate these sects because they have in common the element of knowledge; they proposed a new and a recondite knowledge gained by revelation which is not shared by the common run of Christians. Their beliefs were based on pseudo Gospels and pseudo Epistles attributed to apostles or to those closely associated with the apostolic college. In these documents one finds the secret teaching of Jesus. The secret knowledge may not be attributed to Jesus himself; it can be the revelation made to some prophet or prophetess after the close of the apostolic age. For Gnosticism the gospel and the Church were not enough; the Gnostics were dissatisfied with the revelation of God in Jesus Christ. This revelation was not intellectual enough, or it was not philosophical enough, or it was not ascetical enough, or it was not spiritual enough — there are a dozen ways in which it can be found lacking, if one looks for them. In any hypothesis, the gospel could be directed only to the general run of Christians and not to the spiritual elite which joined the Gnostic sects.

The Search for New Revelation

No parallel between the Gnostic sects and more recent private revelations is intended beyond the obvious parallel that both are manifestations of the desire for more revelation than we have in the gospel and the Church. The Gnostic sects were unhealthy exhibitions of this desire. The private revelations do not fall to this level; but it would not be difficult to point out instances where they have not been altogether healthy. There is a basic error in the desire for new revelation if it implies the assertion that the Christian revelation is insufficient for its purpose. Where this assertion is not explicit the Church does not repudiate private revelation; but she has not that control over the minds of her members which keeps them from an error in the understanding of the place of private revelation in the Christian scheme. She cannot restrain those of her members who seek the sensational and the exotic, or who look for an easier and simpler way to unite themselves with God than the way of faith, hope, and love.

The desire for new revelation usually arises from a failure to grasp the Christian revelation. That it is not grasped is not always the fault of those who pursue new revelations. We have had occasion more than once in this book to notice ways in which the proclamation of the gospel is obscured by the officers of the Church. Where they fail in the duty of their office, others will arise to do what they have left undone; but these others do it the wrong way. The only subtlety of the gospel lies in its simplicity; we find it very hard to believe that the will of God can be so easily stated and so easily understood. I would almost say so easily executed, and it is easily executed in the sense that its execution is uncomplicated. A total commitment is not complicated, whatever else it may be. In the ultimate analysis substitutes and supplements for the gospel often look like evasions of the total commitment; they are spiritual patent medicines.

We fail to reflect what a dreadful and blasphemous insult it is to imply that the work of Jesus Christ is not quite satisfactory enough for us; that there are spiritual needs which cannot be met by searching through the riches of the gospel and the Church.

We fail to reflect how arrogant it is for anyone to say that what Jesus Christ did, he or she can do better. Some risk is involved in attaching to the repetition of a set prayer formula or to the attendance at a novena an efficacy which we do not attribute to the Eucharistic sacrifice and to the other sacraments. That the Church does not instantly suppress certain practices does not prove that these practices are not excesses. Despite what many of her members think, the Church does not have and should not have this kind of efficiency. She cannot clean out all the tares; and we have observed more than once that she does not assume the personal responsibility of her members. Officers of the Church do her no service when they imply that the Church makes all the decisions. We can at least learn from this the vital importance of presenting the gospel in its fullness and in its purity. There is no assurance against deviations; but those who are responsible for the proclamation of the gospel are not thereby excused from unremitting effort to see that they furnish no occasion for deviations.

The Spiritual Man

Gnosticism suggests another phenomenon in the history of Christian spirituality which ought to be mentioned. The Gnostic sects inherited that type of Hellenistic philosophical thought which considered man as a spirit. This type originated with Plato. The highest activity of the spirit is knowledge; for Plato the highest knowledge was the contemplation of subsistent truth in its purity. The True and the Good he thought existed as separate realities, perceptible only to the mind which had been purified of matter and material interests. Knowledge which man obtains through his senses is not real knowledge, for sensible reality is not true reality. By a process of philosophical discipline it is possible for man to attain genuine spiritual knowledge; but the perfection of this knowledge is possible only after the soul has been released from the body by death. Plato stoutly affirmed the immortality of the soul; it must be noticed that he did not affirm the immortality of man.

Philosophical Contemplation

Philosophical contemplation was pursued by the Platonic schools; of these schools Neo-Platonism had no slight influence on the Fathers of the Church. It was rather easy to identify the type of philosophical contemplation practiced in Neo-Platonism with the knowledge of the revealed truth of God. For the intellectual who became Christian, or the Christian who became an intellectual, knowledge was the beatitude of man; and the highest knowledge was the knowledge of the supreme truth, God. Revelation had made a new knowledge of God possible; the techniques of philosophical contemplation applied to revealed truth should give new insights into revelation. So far so good; but the introduction of philosophical contemplation into Christianity opened the way for some deviations from the gospel.

The Gnostics are clear examples of these deviations. It is clear from what has been said above that salvation for them was identified with knowledge. This knowledge was not available to all Christians; it demanded the purification of the soul from matter which, they asserted, was possible only by Gnostic discipline. For them the fall of man consisted in the union of soul and body. Each Gnostic myth relates in its own obscure way how some spiritual being fell, and from this fall through complex emanations and evolutions there ultimately arose the material world, in which the divine soul of man is imprisoned. Creation could never be an act of God in the Gnostic systems; the creator was a demon, an enemy of God and the spiritual world. Redemption could consist in nothing else but the revelation of knowledge; and man was saved by a process of dematerialization. When he became once again a pure spirit, his salvation was accomplished.

Contemplative Perfection

The Gnostic sects are extreme examples of a tendency. Some of the Fathers of the Church are restrained examples, and their attraction to contemplation did not lead them into the bizarre heresies of Gnosticism. But the tradition which they established is open to misinterpretation. In many of its elements it is non-biblical at best; and conclusions can be drawn and have been drawn from their tradition which do not, it seems, entirely render the gospel. The tradition of the contemplative life is long and noble; it is well established in the Church, and it has enriched the Church. Like any particular mode of the Christian way of life, it fails to attain the totality of the life of Christ, which only the Church as a whole can attain; the Church is a body of many members, each of which performs a function which is not performed by the others. There should be no more contention about the relative dignity of one state over another than there should be contention as to who is first among the disciples.

One can ask, and one ought to ask whether the contemplative tradition has always shown due respect to other members of the Church. There are, as we have noticed, certain features of philosophical contemplation which appeared in Gnosticism and which do not easily incorporate themselves into the gospel and the Christian way of life. About these we can ask; and the first is the proposition not infrequently found in spiritual literature that the contemplative life is the highest form of the Christian way of life, the supreme achievement of the presence of Christ in the world. The first remark that occurs when this proposition is encountered is that it strangely lacks biblical foundation. Canon Jacques Leclercq once observed that the only biblical text which can be adduced in favor of the contemplative life is the episode of Martha and Mary (Lk 10:38–42). Any exegete knows that to identify Martha with the active life and Mary with the contemplative life, the better part, is ridiculous exegesis. The passage is both more complex and more simple than that. The saying certainly contrasts solicitude about food with the hearing of the word, and as such it is quite in harmony with Matthew's sermon on the mount and the whole thrust of the gospel, as we have already observed. We observed that the Christian community has historically not been excessively sympathetic to this thrust.

To say that something has no biblical foundation does not render it suspect by that very fact; the Church has had to live in many cultures and in many centuries, and it has had to go beyond biblical sources to assert its identity. It has always remained within a biblical framework. But to say that a thing lacks biblical foundation does not recommend it either; and in particular it does not recommend it as the highest form of the Christian life. Were this true, one might have expected a hint to this effect in the New Testament. We do not even have a hint, as I trust will appear shortly.

A Spiritual Elite

No reputable writer on the theology of the spiritual life has ever proposed the idea of a spiritual elite, a church within the Church. But not all writers on the theology of the spiritual life are equally reputable; and the readers of reputable writers have not always followed their restraint. It takes very little reading in the history of the Church and no more than superficial observation of the contemporary scene to recognize that spiritual snobbery not only exists in the Church, but is accepted. The effort to form select groups and find for them a way of life which will be at least a little above the "common" level never seems to end. I do not imply that the Church has no mediocrity within it; such an implication would be unreal. But I do mean that the "common" spiritual level will, if one lives on it faithfully, produce a full Christian life. It is not equally well guaranteed that elite groups with special dispensations will succeed as well. The effect of a spiritual elite is less a leaven in the Church than a loud implicit affirmation that the life of the ordinary faithful is mediocre by definition. It is not easy to distinguish such spiritual snobbery from Pharisaism.

Nor is the spiritual asceticism which aims at the dematerialization of man absent from the contemplative tradition. One of the most widely used and respected classics of the spiritual life invites the reader to contemplate man as a soul imprisoned in a corruptible body; this is sheer Neo-Platonism. Fortunately the rest of this classic does not continue to move in this direction; the author picked up a spiritual cliché current in his day without realizing its implications. Asceticism founded on this principle believes that perfection is achieved simply by abstaining as much as possible from the use of material goods; and this, in spite of the importance of this element in the gospel, is not the chief factor in the Christian life. This asceticism can lead also to disengagement and to withdrawal; and when this point is reached, the gospel has been seriously obscured. The Church is not a disengaged eschatological group; and there is no license for any of her members to form such a group.

Action and Inaction

The above should not be taken as an attack on the contemplative life; the contemplative life has often been under attack, and it has withstood the attacks rather well. Its best critics have come from within the contemplative state, and there is little one can add to what they have said. My concern here is with that attitude toward the contemplative life which leads to disdain of other states within the Church. The tendency of most Christians has not been toward the contemplative life, and one might think that other states need no defense. It is my perverse conviction that they do — or if they do not need defense, they at least need some assurance that they are not doomed by their state to mediocrity and imperfection. His Holiness the late Pius XII once spoke of "the heresy of action." In our restless age the view that the Christian life can be lived with no emphasis on its interior basis is congenial to our thinking; it is another way in which Christianity is secularized, and takes on the form of the world in which it exists. We have already noticed that external achievements are not a sign of genuine Christianity.

But there is a heresy of inaction too. Gnosticism was the earliest form of this heresy. And just as Pius XII did not mean to put the formal stigma of heresy on those who are too much concerned with external and measurable achievements, so the phrase "heresy of inaction" attaches no formal stigma to an overemphasis on dispositions to the point where deeds are treated as accessory to the Christian life. Both phrases are rhetorical. But it is not without interest that the heresy of action can adduce many more texts from the New Testament in its support than the heresy of inaction can. Those who refer to St. Paul's antithesis between faith and works have not always seen that the works he means are the works of the Law. Paul is as emphatic on the need for the works of love as any New Testament writer, as emphatic as the sayings of Jesus in the Gospels. We have already referred to these sayings, and we need not repeat ourselves. Jesus never speaks of the love of the neighbor without mentioning some positive external action by which love is exhibited. The Christian sentiment of love permits no withdrawal from the neighbor when he is in need; and in one of the extreme utterances of the sermon on the mount, Jesus tells his disciples to postpone worship until they have been reconciled with their brothers (Mt 5:23-24). This establishes a fairly clear priority between the external deed and prayer. The story of Martha and Mary should not be read independently of the conclusion of the sermon on the mount, where Jesus speaks of those who "hear" his words without "doing" them (Mt 7:24-27; Lk 6:47-49). The deed of love is the peak of the Christian life, the summit of the work of Jesus present in the Church and of the indwelling Spirit. The person who achieves this has reached the highest point of the new life which has been conferred upon him at baptism.

The Universal Gospel

It is an important part of the Christian revolution that Jesus has put the fullness of his gospel within the reach of anyone who accepts it. The idea of a spiritual or intellectual elite is not new; it is as old as the wisdom of the ancient Near East. It appears in the philosophical contemplation of Platonism, which is evidently possible for no more than a few. It appeared in Judaism, and Jesus rejected the spiritual snobbery of the Pharisees in vigorous language. One will not find in the New Testament that he intended to replace the Pharisees by a Christian spiritual elite. It even appeared in the mystery cults, which were addressed to all levels of the population of the Hellenistic world; the cults had degrees of perfection, and few were admitted to the higher degrees. We have already seen how this idea was carried into Christianity in Gnosticism and related sects. Origen and the whole theological tradition which stemmed from him proposed a kind of orthodox Christian gnosis offered to a few select candidates. In the New

Testament the whole Church is the only spiritual elite which we can find; all that the Church offers is offered to all her members.

Obviously a contemplative life is not within the reach of most members of the Church; but active love is within the reach of any one. That contemplation is necessary to sustain a high level of Christian love is not said in the New Testament; the answer of Jesus on how to pray is still the Lord's Prayer. If he thought this was enough, and if he expressly forbade a return of the disciples to the long prayers of Judaism or heathendom, it is difficult to see how anything he said can be taken as an express commendation of the contemplative life as the highest form of Christianity or as a necessary means to reach the highest form. A Christian can scarcely open himself to the charge of deviation if he places the emphasis just where the New Testament places it. Contemplation is a more recent development within the Church. No doubt it will always remain what it has always been, a state of life suitable for no more than a few. That it can produce splendid fruits for the Church from these few has been abundantly demonstrated; that fruits equally splendid cannot be produced from an active life is a proposition which cannot be reconciled with the New Testament.

The Body and the Vine

Let us return for a moment to the Pauline image of the body of Christ and to the Johannine image of the vine and the branches. Both of these images reveal the unity of all Christians with Christ and in Christ and with each other. Both speak of the one divine life which animates all the members of the Church. In the Pauline image the members have different functions; Paul did not mean that the function of the layman is the same as the function of a bishop, or that the bishop has no opportunities both to serve the Church and to harm the Church which the layman does not have. He did mean that it is one and the same divine life which animates both the bishop and the layman, and that the layman is no less a Christian because he is not a bishop. The states differ; but the Gospels themselves do not favor, as we have seen, any interpretation of the states which makes one better than the other. All are Christian, and all offer opportunities and resources for the love which is the supreme act of the Christian. All states need other states for their fulfillment. A consideration of different states and modes of the Christian life which does not conclude with a vision of the unity of the Church has somewhere missed the point. It is a deplorable fact of the history of the Church that differences of state and modes have been an occasion of division more frequently than they have been a means of fostering unity. This has come about from the desire to promote one's own state or mode to the point where other states or modes are called inferior. Of all the states within the Church perhaps only the laity have cheerfully accepted the tag of mediocre which has so often been hung on them. When the clergy and religious ask themselves who of all the members of the Church has been most faithful to the injunction to accept the position of lackey and child, I think they have their answer.

XIV

Rudolf Bultmann

In 1941 Rudolf Bultmann, professor of New Testament at the University of Marburg, published a short article on the New Testament and mythology. The article was not the usual *wissenschaftlich* production which we are accustomed to expect in German journals; it was an address to an audience of theological students and pastors. Probably no one was more surprised than Bultmann when the article became the most celebrated piece of New Testament theology in our generation. One brief article has now built up a library of its own. The responses, counterresponses, explanations, and further explanations run into at least hundreds of pages. The article has been discussed in more lectures and seminars than one can easily count; academic courses have been given on the problems it raises. Even now the question is still discussed. Among many conservative Protestants and Catholics the name of Bultmann has become a curse and a hissing; this is quite unfair to a man who through a long and full life of scholarship has demonstrated a rare degree of honesty and candor and dedication to his faith. His errors are honest; and he is willing to have his opinions discussed and criticized, which is more than I can say for many who have attacked him personally.

Every scholar dreams of producing such a piece of writing, but very few have their dreams fulfilled. To reach so many people and to move them so deeply requires a complex set of circumstances which rarely come together; and not all of the circumstances are under the control of the writer. The writer can control certain factors. Bultmann is one of the most massively learned scholars of this generation. He writes in a style which commands attention because of his manifest deep conviction, in spite of a tortuous and compressed German which gives his translators a feeling of despair at times. He has an insight into the mind of his contemporaries which few scholars have; Bultmann does not live in an ivory tower. The article appeared at a moment when Christianity in his own country was threatened by the most pernicious form of post-Christian paganism which Germany has ever known. He wrote in a crisis of which he was a part, and he struck off an idea of startling originality. Put these things together and you have *Neues Testament und Mythologie*, "The New Testament and Mythology," which brought a new word, "demythologizing" (German *Entmythologisierung*) into English speech.

Bultmann's Thesis

"Demythologizing" as a popular term for Bultmann's thesis is inadequate and misleading. It suggests a negative approach; and Bultmann meant to make a positive contribution. He wishes to meet the prevailing post-Christian agnosticism; and he believes that contemporary indifference to the gospel comes from the difference between modern thinking and New Testament thinking. Modern man is welded to the scientific method for better or for worse, and to a scientific view of the universe. Bultmann indeed seems to think that scientific thought alone is valid as thought; this does not strengthen his position, but we need not discuss it here. In contrast to scientific thought he designates the New Testament thought world as "mythological." This term is not felicitous; Bultmann had not at the time he wrote the article taken the trouble to familiarize himself with mythological thought, which is in itself a valid approach to reality. One so convinced of scientism as Bultmann would not readily accept the validity of mythology. What he means by mythology in the New Testament is not always mythology — in fact, one may ask whether any of the things he includes are mythology. He includes the three-decker universe of heaven, earth and hell, the incarnation and the resurrection, the virgin birth, the eschatology of the New Testament, and the miracles. The New Testament must be purged of this mythology before the modern man can be interested in the gospel.

This enumeration is enough to show why Bultmann's article was taken as a frontal attack on the essentials of Christian belief; and Bultmann's vigorous statement of his case did nothing to mollify the reaction. This writer finds it easy to be sympathetic to Bultmann's genius for overstating his case. If the reader can throttle his irritation at reading what he thinks is seven devils worse than Strauss and continues, he will learn that the last thing Bultmann wants to do is to rewrite the essentials of Christianity. He is inconsistent, but he has not joined the post-Christians. His inconsistency, as I see it, arises ultimately from his uncritical acceptance of the scientific method as the exclusively valid method of thought. But one cannot quarrel with his desire to make the gospel intelligible to post-Christian man; one may quarrel about whether it is the gospel that he presents, and whether his presentation is successful.

Existential Interpretation

How is one to reach the modern man? Bultmann believes that he can be touched only by the categories of existentialist philosophy. This means — and I here completely oversimplify a philosophical movement of some magnitude — that the New Testament must answer his question about the meaning of human existence. The New Testament does answer this question, of course, but it speaks in mythological language to which modern man will pay no attention. The meaning of existence, Bultmann says, is found in the proclamation of the decisive eschatological act of God in Christ. The life and death of Christ have made existence meaningful and shown what its fulfillment is. The proclamation confronts each man with this event and compels him to a personal decision. If he refuses to accept this meaning he can find no meaning; if he accepts, he gives his existence the only meaning it can have. It is, in existentialist language, an encounter which issues in a commitment. We learn that one man became obedient to death, even to death on a cross, and thus fulfilled the highest possibilities of existence.

Obscurities in the Thesis

I think no one will deny that this is a Christian interpretation of the gospel; it is certain that almost every theologian has said that it evacuates the content of the New Testament. To reduce the proclamation to "the decisive eschatological event" is nearly as much of a reduction as Harnack's compression of the gospel into the fatherhood of God and the brotherhood of man. Again, to be fair to Bultmann one should not derive his theology from one short article. Bultmann is a prolific scholar; his interpretation of the New Testament can be found in dozens of books and articles which have not been read even by all New Testament scholars. The reading of these books does not entirely remove uneasiness. Bultmann does not believe that much is known about Jesus as a historical figure. The contributions of Jesus to the thought of the New Testament he thinks are almost impossible to identify, and they are so few as to be negligible. Bultmann really never has got around to telling us who is responsible for Christianity. Furthermore, his insistence on the existentialist restatement of the New Testament leaves one wondering whether he is not about to make a philosophy of the New Testament. If he removes everything characteristic of the New Testament when he demythologizes, there is no reason why the philosophy should be related to the New Testament at all. This uneasiness is confirmed when one becomes acquainted with Bultmann's handling of the Old Testament. As he sees it, the Old Testament has contributed nothing to the gospel; it is really an encumbrance which is more embarrassing than helpful. And thus he seems to detach Jesus and the gospel from their situation in history and raise them to the level of abstract timeless essences. Yet this is clearly not his intention; the student of Bultmann must accustom himself to paradoxes — or to borrow the figure of John Macquarrie, reading Bultmann is something like riding in a New York or Chicago taxicab. One is constantly being carried at full speed up to a red light at which the vehicle always stops abruptly — or almost always stops; the Catholic interpreter finds that Bultmann has run a few intersections.

The Proclamation of the Event

For Bultmann affirms that the gospel is a proclamation and not a philosophy. It proclaims the act of God in Christ which is known by revelation. In his own way Bultmann is a supernaturalist; the saving event is not the product of the course of nature or of pure historical forces. In Christ man encounters God. The event which he calls "eschatological" is not purely historical; it is a perpetually present event, and the proclamation makes it present to each man. He believes that the Church has failed to fulfill its mission of proclaiming the gospel in modern times. It has not spoken the language of those to whom its message was addressed, and it has remained too much in the past, in the realm of pure history. What it has proclaimed has often not been the gospel; or it has been the gospel so overlaid with antiquated systems of human thought that the gospel was no longer clearly discernible. He is convinced that the gospel has the power to break through the incrustation of theology and appear in its luminous and compelling clarity.

The Gospel and Modern Man

It is unnecessary to enumerate all that Bultmann leaves out. His article is the most controversial theological statement of our generation not because he gives the right answers but because he asks the right questions. It is my purpose here not so much to answer these questions as to pursue some lines of thought which Bultmann's questions have opened. The failure of the gospel to reach modern man is a concern of everyone who calls himself a Christian; and when I say it fails to reach modern man, I am not thinking only of the post-Christian agnostic. I am thinking of many who are members in good standing of the Catholic Church in both the clerical and the lay states. To specify could be unkind, and I therefore do not; I count on the humility of every

Christian by which he will confess that he has not fully accepted the gospel or even understood it well enough to refuse it. If we do not like Bultmann's analysis that it is the refusal of modern scientific man to accept mythology, then we ought to find another analysis. More likely we shall find that there is no single cause; this does not absolve us from finding as many causes as we can. Some of these causes have been suggested in preceding chapters. Let us add here that each generation has its own reasons for refusing the gospel or for discounting it. It will not do to say in general terms that man is sinful, that he is demonic, that he is concupiscent, that he is rationalistic, that he is political, that he is avaricious, that he is just downright beastly; man is all these things. But the genius of the Church, which we call the Spirit, lies in finding the soft spot in the armored selfishness of each man in his concrete reality. The Spirit operates through the Church, which means through men; have the members of the Church looked for the soft spots? In the history of the Church there are many who are called apostles, some properly in the New Testament sense and others in an improper sense because they so eminently carried on the apostolic mission, with or without a prelacy. When we look at these men and then at ourselves, we suspect that our apostolic attitude would not be too harshly paraphrased by saying, "If you want what we have, come and get it."

The Gospel in Modern Language

The ghost of Modernism has been raised so many times that it seems to walk as often as the ghost of Hamlet's father; and one sure way to evoke it is to mention the proclamation of the gospel in language which will be more sympathetic to modern man. Because Modernism was an unsuccessful effort to do this, apparently we are not going to attempt another effort. One might say that the language of the gospel is good enough. This we can concede; and we can add that an effort to proclaim the gospel in its own language might be worth the trouble. We do not use the language of the gospel, which is biblical. We use other languages; in particular, we use philosophical language which is not spoken by modern man, and therefore he finds it unintelligible. He should not be blamed for this. To use philosophical language is to put oneself in a definite period of philosophical evolution. The philosophical language which we use was once "modernist," and it was offensive to many for that very reason. The principle by which this language was developed seems to have become invalid with the development of the language. Or are we to assume that evolution has reached a point of perfection beyond which no improvement is possible? In the latter hypothesis, the rest of the world has not yet caught up with us. This may be granted for the sake of the argument; I ask what we are doing to close the gap.

Theological Diversity

The problem of demythologizing and of proclaiming the gospel in existentialist language or in any language raises another and a deeper problem. What is the language of the proclamation? The unity of the New Testament cannot be seriously questioned; but it is unity, not homogeneity. The New Testament itself shows more flexibility than many of its interpreters. We write theologies of the New Testament with full awareness that the phrase "theology of the New Testament" is not entirely accurate. A correct designation would be "theologies of the New Testament"; and books on the subject usually are divided into the theology of the Synoptic Gospels (which has to be subdivided), of Paul, of John, etc. A single faith does not imply a single theology; and it is this diversity in unity which shows us the way out of Bultmann's problem. The way is not new — in fact, it is as old as the proclamation of the gospel; but it has not always been honored. Historians now generally agree that if the Roman Curia had permitted the gospel to be proclaimed in China in the eighteenth century with certain adaptations to Chinese culture, the country would have become substantially Catholic. This is hindsight and it could be wrong; but the permission was not granted, and the mission was a failure. Perhaps it was merely coincidental; it is clear that the mission was not a failure because the missionaries were allowed to make the adaptations.

What Is Theology?

Before we say any more about different theologies in the New Testament, it will be wise to state briefly what we mean by a theology. In Catholic thinking the theological synthesis of Thomas Aquinas has become the model after which all theology is named; and theology in this sense means a systematically structured exposition of belief. Theology need not, however, be so rigidly structured to deserve the name; for theology is more properly an exposition of belief in terms of a philosophy. Hence one can speak of an Augustinian theology, although Augustine wrote no massive synthesis like the synthesis of Thomas Aquinas. Augustine's philosophy, however, can be discerned, and the philosophical conceptions which he employs to set forth his beliefs can be isolated. Scholars prepare syntheses of Augustinian philosophy and theology which Augustine never prepared himself; they make it easier for the modern reader to comprehend what is often implicit in any particular work or passage.

Biblical Theology

In a wider sense, theology is not restricted to an exposition of belief in philosophical terms; and we mean theology in a wider sense when we speak of biblical theology, either of the Bible or of either Testament as a whole, or of particular books. The books of the Bible are not written in philosophical language and imply no philosophical ideas, systematic or unsystematic (Chapter II). We speak of biblical theology not as philosophical but as cultural and even as personal. Each biblical writer utters his belief in a language which he has not created and in a situation in life which is formed by history. He employs the language and ideas which he derives from his culture; and by his own original genius, which can be more or less original, he professes his belief in these forms. The modern interpreter who writes a biblical theology attempts to identify the master ideas and the forms in which the biblical books are written. From this he proceeds to a systematic exposition which is his own.

The construction of a system of biblical theology presents the major problem; for what is to determine the form which the system takes? When the modern writer employs philosophical categories, he introduces a foreign element which may distort the material rather than clarify it. If he adheres to those categories which can be deduced from the biblical material itself, he may produce a formless mass which adds nothing to the understanding of the original; he fails in the first duty of the interpreter, which is to interpret. For these reasons biblical theology is a science in a fluid condition — indeed some would refuse it the name of science, for it still lacks a rigorous method. Perhaps it can never have a rigorous method; and if a rigorous method is an essential component of science, then biblical theology cannot be a science. It may have to content itself with the more modest designation of art.

The absence of a rigorous method comes from the complexity of the material as much as from anything else. If there are theologies of the New Testament rather than a theology, and if there are as many theologies as there are writers, then the word "theology" becomes so flexible that it might be better to drop it and find another word to designate what we are doing. There are multiple theologies; and here is located the problem with which we are now concerned. There is, as we have quoted several times, one Lord, one faith, one baptism — and one gospel and one Church; how then can there be many theologies? And what value can we derive from them?

Theology and Mystery

Theology, we have said, is not the gospel and it is not faith; it is not compelled to that unity which faith and gospel imply. Truth is one in its totality; but no theology is an apprehension of truth in its totality. The truth which theology attempts to express is the mystery of God revealed in the gospel; this truth is beyond human comprehension and human expression. Whatever we may say about it, there is more to be said. In whatever categories we express it, it overflows our categories. The character of theology as a statement of belief is not altered by the fact that in the Bible we speak of the theology of inspired writers. Their theology is a part of the inspired work; it is the nature of theology to be diversified, and they are inspired to write diversified theologies. It is not so much a question of how multiple theologies are possible; it becomes obvious that nothing else but multiple theologies is possible.

At the risk of seeming to wander, I illustrate the diversity with a few examples from New Testament Christology. The title "Son of Man," we noticed, is an Aramaic title meaningful in that language against an Old Testament background. It is used in the Gospels but not in the epistles. Scarcely any interpreter doubts that the title was so meaningless to Gentiles that the apostolic Church simply dropped it rather than attempt to explain it. If "Son of Man" is taken as an absolute value the Church could not have abandoned it; it did abandon it, and we know it is not an absolute. What term then is an absolute? The word "Christ" (Greek *christos*) translates the Hebrew "Messiah," "anointed." The word is used nearly exclusively in the Gospels with full awareness of its significance in Judaism. In the epistles it has become nearly a personal name of Jesus with no reflection of the concept of Messiah in many uses; it begins to be used almost as it is used today by Christians. Jesus is not called God in the New Testament; we have seen why the language could not allow this use, for it would identify him personally with the Father. He can be called the son of God. All these are examples of theological development in the use of the Christological titles; and none of them is an absolute. The absolute is the reality, which is Jesus and the Father; and this reality is supremely mysterious. No title does more than suggest it, but some titles can suggest something other than the reality. All titles which express the relation of Jesus to the Father are open to misunderstanding.

When I say that these terms are not absolute, I do not imply theological relativism. The term "Son of God" is an absolute in the sense that I may not say that his sonship is of the same quality as the sonship which the Christian receives at baptism. I may say that my conception of sonship admits no enrichment only when I understand it as well as Jesus himself understands it. Enrichment is the fruit of theological reflection; and it is a form of change. A theology which admits no change is not a theology; it is not even a form of understanding.

Theology and Understanding

The theologies of the New Testament represent enrichment of understanding, and that in two ways; of the understanding of the Church as a whole, and of the understanding of the individual writers of the New Testament books. These two ways are not mutually independent; for the individual writers are members of the Church and they draw upon her for their material. They are, as we have seen, her spokesmen. We speak of the understanding of the Church where we meet features of the presentation which are not easily attributed to the individual writer; and when we speak of the individual writer, we must remember that his utterance may be less original than we think. The originality of Pauline theology is striking; but we have not the sources from which we can analyze just how much of this theology is strictly Pauline.

The Gospel and the Gentiles

In the course of the preceding chapters we have often had occasion to advert to differences in approach and expression in the various New Testament books. We have also had occasion to point out some of the factors which differentiated the approach and the expression. The most decisive factor of all, we have observed, was the controversy over Judaism (Chapter X). Behind the controversy was the problem of "demythologizing" which the primitive Church faced early in its career: the problem of how to proclaim the gospel to Gentiles. A Palestinian Jewish theology had to be translated into a Hellenistic theology. There is scarcely any New Testament book which does not show the effect of the translation; even Mark, the earliest of the Gospels, was obviously written primarily for Gentiles. It would be wrong to think of Mark as a theologically neutral source, even if the theological background is less obvious in Mark than it is in Matthew and Luke. Traditionally Matthew has been regarded as a Jewish Gospel and Luke as a Gentile Gospel. Neither designation is entirely accurate. Matthew has more anti-Jewish passages than the other Gospels; Luke, the Gentile Gospel, has the fewest such passages; and where Luke and Matthew are parallel one can see how Luke has softened some passages. All three Gospels witness the development of the understanding that the Church is one for both Jews and Gentiles. If the New Testament has any document of Jewish Christianity of the Jerusalem community it is the epistle of James. If James is a Jewish document, it is a paradox that it is written, in the words of Wikenhauser, ". . . in good Greek . . . the language is purer and more cultured than in any other New Testament book . . . it employs a rich vocabulary and shows a fondness for sophisticated language. . . ." The Judaizing "James" wrote better Greek than the Hellenizing Paul; and this illustrates theological development as well as anything else.

Theological Revision

I have mentioned that Luke softens some anti-Jewish passages. This Gospel affords a number of striking examples of what can be called theological revision — or adaptation, if the word "revision" is too strong. In some instances the revision is indeliberate; the Gentile Luke was never completely inside the Palestinian Jewish mind. In the story of the healing of the victim of the palsy (Mk 9: 1–8; Lk 5:17–26), Mark narrates that the bearers of the litter dug a hole in the roof through which they let down the man. Luke says that they went through the tiles — a feat scarcely less remarkable than the healing. The beaten earth roof of the Palestinian house was usual to Mark: apparently Luke had never seen one, did not understand what was being described, and assumed that the house had the only type of roof he knew, a tile roof. Luke was sometimes no more at home in Palestinian religious language than he was in Palestinian architecture. When he was not, he stated the gospel in the terms he knew, not hesitating to alter or omit phrases which were unintelligible to Gentiles — and possibly to himself. Yet his theological reflection is much more than negative. Luke has notable material which is peculiar to himself, and this includes some of the best known and most quoted parts of the Gospels such as the parables of the Prodigal Son and of the Good Samaritan. We have noticed that his conception of the Spirit is not paralleled in Mark and Matthew.

The originality of the theology of Paul needs no elaboration here. It is because he is so original that the New Testament interpreter finds that he recurs to Paul more than to any other New Testament writer. His treatment of the saving act of Jesus and of its sacramental reenactment is much fuller than the treatment given these themes in the other books. His Christology likewise is fuller. We attribute these developments to his engagement with the Gentiles of the Hellenistic world. But the sources of his development are not Hellenistic. Paul depends on the Old Testament for his own theology of the proclamation and the teaching. His interpretation and use of the Old Testament is rabbinical, even pharisaical; he turns the arms of Judaism against Judaism and uses them to proclaim the gospel for the Gentiles. He is steeped in the traditions of the scribes. The Gospels depend on the Old Testament also; the teaching, we have noticed, was an explanation of the mission of Jesus in Old Testament terms.

John's theology is also of an originality which is easily recognized — so easily that it presents problems. The interpreter ultimately realizes that the Church which accepted John as an exponent of its faith knew what it was doing, and that the unity of faith is not sundered by the peculiar theological approach of John. His themes, we have seen, must have been present in the teaching of Jesus; and we have observed that they must have been less prominent in the teaching of Jesus than they are in John. But the Johannine themes show that the Synoptic writers as well as John wrote theological interpretations of the proclamation of Jesus. What we have is not a static body of doctrine cast in immobile prose; we have a Church unceasingly reflecting on the experience of the Christ event and proposing the fruits of its reflections as they come.

The Growth of Understanding

The New Testament is the record of a community which began as a group of the disciples of an itinerant rabbi. The community became articulate with its realization that it had a mission to continue what he had begun. Its utterances take different forms as it realizes that it is more than another Jewish sect. The utterances are more deeply transformed as the group realizes that it must grow to dimensions which will admit anyone who in faith seeks baptism. The community is transformed again with the realization that it is the sole legitimate heir of the traditions of Judaism. Its awareness of who Jesus is and of its identity with him reveals its resources and its strength as well as the revolutionary movement which it must sustain. An acute eschatological sense is modified by its consciousness of its engagement with the world. With Paul it is a Jew to the Jews, a Greek to the Greeks, all things to all men — without ever losing its own identity. It can and must respond to history and to culture. The mysterious reality which is revealed in Jesus Christ cannot be encased in one single safe and immutable formula. Each generation and each man must experience it for himself; and this means that he must respond personally. Each man, when he responds to the gospel, proclaims it to himself.

Encounter and Response

And this is the lasting impact of Bultmann's thesis. He has recalled to our minds the New Testament theme that the proclamation is a personal encounter which demands a personal response. Perhaps we needed to be reminded that the response is more than submission to an organization. The existentialist terms of encounter, engagement, commitment are suitable to modern man; and they are excellent theological statements of what the New Testament demands. The Christian must decide to be a Christian; and this means more, we have said, than the absence of a decision to be something else.

To insist on carrying into the modern world intellectual patterns of earlier centuries may resemble carrying Judaism into the Gentile world in the primitive Church. The Church could not divorce herself from her origins in Israel and never attempted to do so. She could and did discern what belonged to her structure and what did not. She was not afraid to translate the gospel into another language and another culture; and she knew it could not be translated without change. Unity, we have said, was what she showed, not homogeneity. It cannot be theologically argued that the Church is unable to do now what she did in the first century; and when we say the Church, we do not mean exclusively her officers. We have already adverted to the part which all the members of the Church have in her mission. Historically the development of theology has been carried on within the Church but not by her officers.

"Demythologizing," then, is an inept term for an activity which the Church has carried on from her beginning. The apostolic Church in no way resembled a beleaguered fortress, the metaphor which has often been applied to the Church of the latter half of the nineteenth century. That day should be over; and it might be rewarding to study closely whether the Church ought ever to have adopted this position. It resembles somewhat the position of the Twelve in the upper room before the coming of the Spirit. Once the Church emerged from the upper chamber, she showed herself able to meet anyone on any terms. Nor does her subsequent history exhibit a habitual unwillingness to modify her proclamation. The Christological controversies of the fourth and fifth centuries are studied as models of the development of doctrine. It should not be forgotten that the councils of Nicaea, Constantinople, Ephesus, and Chalcedon defined the belief of the Church in language which was nonbiblical and at the time novel. The controversies could not be settled by a simple repetition of the formulae of the New Testament and the apostolic Fathers. Nor should it be forgotten that in these controversies, as in the controversies of the sixteenth century, there were many who feared that harm would be done by tampering with traditional formulae. They thought that theological terms were absolutes; the Church has always regarded any dogmatic definition as a point of departure for a further definition.

The Task of Theology

We shall not call our task "demythologizing," even if there are some elements which can loosely be called mythological and which we scarcely need in our theology. Nor shall we call it modernizing the gospel; the very word "modern" is something of a panic signal, and here it is inaccurate. The gospel is never out of date, and therefore cannot be modernized. We have spoken of diversified theology, by which we mean the presentation of the gospel in the language of a particular culture and a particular period of history. We do not seek another formula which might become an absolute. If we succeed in speaking to our own generation, we should not expect that our presentation will reach those who come after us. If growth is the law of life, we can expect that even we shall become antiquated. But it is better to become antiquated in the future than to plan to be antiquated in the present. We are entitled to our own theology as much as anyone else.

Challenge

Bultmann has said that Christianity does not present a challenge to the modern man; it calls for no decision. Passive acceptance is not a decision. The challenge which is the essence of the gospel can be obscured; this we have proved. Quite simply, the timid do not issue challenges. Those who prefer to speak the language of the past rather than the language of the present because it is safer furnish excellent reasons for inquiring whether they are timid. St. Paul, we have recalled, once made a bold effort to speak to the Athenians in their own language. We should be comforted by the fact that an apostle could fail to do well something which we are afraid to attempt. He renounced the effort and proclaimed Christ crucified; but to proclaim this gospel was scarcely to take refuge in safe traditional formulae. It is altogether evident that Paul was a venturesome soul who could not be recommended for a jurisdictional office in the modern Church. Paul wanted to present a challenge. His success in challenging is well attested in 2 Corinthians 11:23–28. We, I think, could have told him how to fulfill his commission without getting himself involved in such affairs as these. Yet Paul seemed to think that his floggings, imprisonments, stoning, and assorted perils from men were the surest attestation that he was a genuine apostle.

The particular form of challenge with which we are concerned here is the challenge of finding a language for the gospel which contemporary man cannot ignore or pretend he does not understand. The gospel is always new in the world; and modern man must see that it is something new before he will attend to it. To present its novelty to the post-Christian agnostic is a problem which the Church has never really had to face before. The infidel of earlier centuries did not know Christianity; the post-Christian agnostic thinks he does. He also thinks that it is an antiquated system; and it is unfortunate that one can count on some Christian spokesman to strengthen his opinion at almost regular intervals. The Church must now convince him that she is not what he thinks she is. Of how much of her past and present must she divest herself before she can do this? Can we afford to cling to some features of her organization and discipline, some of her cherished popular misconceptions, as the Judaizing Christians wished to cling to the Law? Obviously more than a theological development is involved here; yet one cannot expect the Church to move in any direction except as the result of a theological development.

It would be quite unfair to leave the impression that the Church is making no effort to be articulate to modern man. The number of men — and of women — who are proclaiming the gospel in the language of their contemporaries is impressive. But it is not large enough; and there are other factors which limit their range. Not infrequently one hears it asked of some Catholic writer: "He speaks in quite contemporary language; but does he speak for the Church?" One senses the fear both among Catholics and among others that the private individual cannot be trusted; and this in spite of the fact that the greatest spokesmen of the Church have with few exceptions spoken as private individuals in the sense that they were not members of the hierarchy. There is a basic fallacy here which if carried to its full conclusion would deny to anyone outside the hierarchy any part in the apostolic mission of the Church. One senses another fear which has been in the air for the past fifty years: the fear that a Catholic who speaks on theology in any other than conventional language will be suppressed. This, again, in spite of the fact that the greatest spokesmen of the Church spoke in unconventional language; it is not their fault that it has become conventional since, and I doubt that it was their intention to become monuments.

The task of issuing the challenge of the gospel to modern man does not mean that the Catholic will abandon Thomism and set existentialism in its place. Existentialism as a system of thought promises to be no more durable than Thomism, to say the least; and nothing is gained if we replace one false absolute with another. And here we can return to the New Testament, from which we may seem to have wandered, and answer the question we put about the value of different theologies in the New Testament. Their chief value, of course, is that they multiply our insights into the ineffable reality revealed in Christ. They have also the value that they show us how diversity of theology deepens our understanding, and furnish the greatest example we have of diversified theology within a single faith. The New Testament shows clearly that a monolithic immutable theology is foreign to the genius of the Church. We ought to have confidence that we can proclaim the gospel in the language of modern man, and we should approach the task with the boldness with which St. Paul proclaimed the gospel to the Gentiles. I trust that no one will say that St. Paul had the guidance of the Spirit which we lack.

The Center of the Proclamation

To return to Bultmann once more: I said that his compression of the gospel to "the decisive eschatological event" was too radically simple. But he has erred in the right direction. He consciously echoes the words of Paul, who compressed his own gospel into one phrase, Christ and him crucified. Paul implied in this phrase much more than Bultmann implies. But Bultmann has pointed out the central elements of the proclamation; and he is absolutely right, I am convinced, in thinking that this is the element which will challenge modern man to a decision. For this is the base of everything in Christianity which is novel and unconventional, which makes a man question the meaning of his existence. It is the supreme paradox, the supreme affirmation and denial. Without this centrality the Church can become a form of Pharisaism. I am not aware that we have yet learned to proclaim the supreme paradox in language which will challenge modern man — or should I say jolt him. I think modern man has shown that he will not accept the Church as an anchor of spiritual security, as a source of infallible doctrine, as a mutual benevolent society, as the defender of a rigid moral code. The Pharisees were all these things. He does not think the Church can create a brave new world; he thinks she had her chance at this when Europe was Christendom, and he does not see why she should have another chance. In fact he often cannot distinguish between the Church and Pharisaism; and so he feels no challenge.

The Needs of Modern Man

But he does feel need; and we have not yet spoken to his need. Our drill in apologetics has moved us to try to beat him into intellectual submission, and we cannot do it; we lack the talent for that. He has the feeling that the Church is not concerned with his need; he thinks she wants to win him, to subdue him, not to help him. Actually she wants none of these; she wants Christ to be born in him. How is he to learn that this fulfills his needs? The first step, no doubt, is to hear this from Christians who are convinced that it is true; and not all of us are convinced. The second is to speak of his needs in terms which will show that we understand what they are and what he thinks they are. The third is to unwrap the novelty of the gospel and use whatever words we must to disclose it. It is rather terrible, on reflection, to make safety of doctrine the end of the Church. Her end is salvation — and safety is derived from the same Latin word as salvation. Her end is achieved in safety of persons, not of doctrine. One gathers from the New Testament that if she never fails in her concern for the safety of persons, which is synonymous with her mission of love, that safety of doctrine will follow. Theology is a means, not an end. A means which is not adapted to the end ceases, in good Thomistic metaphysics, to have any reality.

I do not know how many of those who write books on the New Testament conclude their writing with regret that they ever undertook the work and hesitation about presenting it to the public. I know these are my sentiments. To write a book on the New Testament means reading the books of the New Testament many times, reflecting on them at length and consulting a good deal of the vast literature on the New Testament. The literature makes one painfully aware how difficult it is to be even slightly original, but this is not the major psychological block. The major block is the New Testament itself. When one reads and reflects long enough and often enough, the New Testament seems to become so clear that it appears sheer futility to attempt to state its contents in any other words than its own.

There is another obscurity in one's mind more difficult to express and not without some dangers. Reflection on the New Testament gives one a keener sense of the differences between the Church which wrote the New Testament and the contemporary Church. If one wanders down this path far enough, one will find oneself at its end in the company of the Reformers; and a Roman Catholic cannot join this company. Nothing in the preceding pages, I trust, suggests a lack of identity between the primitive Church and the contemporary Church; I am assured that nothing does because I am well aware of another effect of prolonged reading and reflection. This other effect is a perception of the identity of the Church which I am sure is not gained except through reflective reading of the New Testament. A deeper knowledge of what the Church is makes it easier for one to see the enduring Church of Christ.

But the problem arises from something which is more superficial and more quickly seen: the differences between the Church of the first century and the Church of the twentieth. One learns this from the New Testament, that the Church by no modification at all in twenty centuries would clearly prove herself a fossil. It has become clear to me at least that growth and development are as much a part of the Church as her hierarchical structure. She must move with history and she has moved with it. To move with history involves the risk of identifying herself with it. Substantial identification with history is contrary to her nature; if this happened, she would perish. But partial identification, while contrary to her nature, is not totally corruptive; and it is partial identification which raises uneasiness about the differences mentioned above.

However the question is to be answered, the answer is not to be sought outside the Church. The gospel lives in the Church or it does not live anywhere. If it does not live anywhere, it has never lived at all. Only if this truth is grasped can one then deal with the question why the gospel does not always live in the Church in all its force and vigor. The obvious answer to this question, of course, is that any one person should be primarily interested in that part of the Church where he can surely make the gospel live; and that is in himself.

But this answer with nothing added suggests a kind of spiritual solipsism which is foreign to the New Testament. We are the Church, all of us, and we share its one life. No one of us can afford to say that anything which happens in the Church is none of our business. Even from the somewhat selfish viewpoint of one's personal spiritual welfare one must admit that one suffers harm if the Church suffers harm. And who is to say that it is the concern of this one and not of that one if the Church suffers harm? If the Church is one body, then no one of her members knows how much one's personal contribution or omission means to the whole. All one gathers from the New Testament is that it may mean everything.

In this book I have attempted to present the New Testament emphasis on personal responsibility and personal decision. A lengthy demonstration that this emphasis is no less suitable now then it ever has been scarcely seems necessary. The basic and perpetual danger which the Church always faces is that she will be secularized — not entirely, for her inner strength does not permit this; but she can take on too much of the character of the world in which she finds herself. I do not believe I have to prove that an abdication of personal responsibility is a besetting vice of our own age. Mr. Orwell's hideous vision of Big Brother was a caricature too close to life to be comfortable. Big Brother cannot establish control over the minds and wills of a community unless the community surrenders control to him. And why does a community surrender control? If we knew the answer to that, we should resolve most of our problems. The New Testament teaches us that personal responsibility is maintained by a daily decision to maintain it.

The secularization of the Church, when it has happened, has happened from a variety of reasons; it can take as many forms as there are forms of worldliness, and these are beyond counting. If the danger of secularization in our own age seems to lie primarily in the conversion of the Church into a power structure, it is no more than a faithful reflection of the world in which we live. Stalin's famous question about the number of divisions at the disposal of the Pope was a candid expression of secularism, and Catholics were wounded by the contempt implied. They are happy when spiritual power shows itself equal or superior to secular power, and when the Pope attains a position of world leadership higher than the position of the chairman of the Central Committee of the Communist Party. Is their joy at the vindication of the influence of the Pope also a reflection of their acceptance of the power struggle as a normal part of life, in which the Church must engage to fulfill her mission? Once again we are awaiting the coming of the emperor to Canossa. If he comes, what will have been proved?

But even if the Church now were engaged in such a power struggle, it would not be the first time in its history that it has done so. The judgment of the results of involvement in the struggle I leave to historians and theologians; what their judgment has been is fairly well known. But the establishment of a power structure within the Church is much more difficult to explain. If the Church needs power to defend herself against her enemies — an assumption which obviously I do not accept — she certainly needs no power to defend herself against her members. To them, at least, power should be the power of love and nothing else. Where the Church exhibits any other power as characteristic, both her members and others find it difficult to recognize her identity with the Church of the New Testament.

To ask which comes first, the establishment of a power structure or the acquisition of material goods, may be something like asking whether the hen or the egg is prior. One so obviously supports the other that the progress of secularization can begin at either end. Yet there are abundant examples of men whose lust for power rendered them as indifferent to material goods as any Trappist monk could hope to be. There are also abundant examples of men who care not for power as long as they have wealth; these are perhaps more numerous. But the ambitious man must have the disposal of material goods, whether he spends them on himself or not; and the avaricious man must have that security rooted in power which removes any threat to his enjoyment of wealth. But in the popular mind the lust for power is a more spiritual vice than the lust for wealth, and hence more easily disguised as something else. For this reason popular Christian tradition has associated this vice with Satan — except when the power is sought for the Church. This exposition has been directed to show that both lusts are in direct and violent opposition to the gospel; that Jesus renounced both power and wealth as means of accomplishing his mission, and that his Church is unfaithful to him when she stoops to the use of either.

The reflective reading of the New Testament makes the Church emerge in all her purity as a community of love. This theme, the dominant theme of the New Testament, must dominate every treatment of the New Testament. And it is this theme which is the most discouraging to the New Testament interpreter. He knows that here surely he cannot say more or say it better than the New Testament says it, but this is again a minor block. The New Testament speaks of love because it rises from an uncreated love. The modern interpreter learns first of all from the New Testament how far he himself is from the love which the New Testament so simply and so gently imposes upon him as his habitual state. And he wonders whether anyone is entitled to talk about Christian love except one who is filled with it.

Yet the interpreter stumbles ahead. The reason he goes ahead is an awareness of his duty to use the professional skill which he has acquired at some trouble to himself and to others. Possibly learning may enable him to say something of value; and since he is a biblical scholar, he will remember that Samson slew a thousand Philistines with the jawbone of an ass. If he is faithful to his sources, he will at least avoid distorting them; and acquaintance with biblical literature is a quick way to learn how easy it is to distort them. But interpreters are not the only Christians who distort the gospel; and, considering that interpreters have a limited circle of readers, their influence is much less than the influence of those who are able to distort the image of the Church into something else than a community of love.

These are hints about some differences between the modern Church and the Church of the New Testament which the modern Church can do better without. The substantial unity of the Church reposes on the love which makes it a community; and it is this central principle of life which keeps the differences from becoming alarming. The individual Christian can find the reality of the Church if he really wishes it, and most do find it. For it is impossible to suppress or conceal a reality which is not the work of man. The true life and reality of the Church is the life of Christ and the indwelling Spirit. Is not the life of the Church a perpetual death in Christ? And is it not likewise a perpetual resurrection? When she is weak, then she is strong; and her strength is proof even against her members. The love which unites and sustains the Church is uncreated and indestructible.

I had thought of giving this book some such title as "The Christian Revolution" or "The Permanent Revolution." Both titles lack originality and are somewhat misleading. A revolution is always an excessive response. A revolution does not occur until a situation has become intolerable, and it destroys the entire situation, even the elements which ought to be preserved. Revolution does not exhibit man at the height of his rationality, but rather elicits all his ugly passions. The revolution does not replace what it destroys with a stable structure; this is left to postrevolutionary activity, which presumably can be carried on with more calmness and deliberation.

Yet the gospel is in some ways revolutionary, and no other word seems to do it justice. Efforts to conventionalize the gospel and to curb its dynamism take away much of its effect. In the preceding exposition we have by choice dwelt upon just those elements of the gospel which are in direct contradiction to accepted beliefs and ideas. The world, we said, both of men at large and of the individual person, is irreparably altered by the Christian event. This suggests revolution. The old man of sin dies, and his world dies; this also suggests revolution. Even the element of violence is not lacking from the Christian event, although the violence comes from the death struggles of the dying world and not from the Christian event. The Christian event occurs when the situation has become intolerable, with the difference that the situation never has been tolerable.

But the Christian event is not itself violent; and its effects are not felt through vulgar power. Jesus himself spoke of its power in the parables of the leaven and the mustard. It arouses no hot passions, and it does not divide except when it is rejected; Jesus said he came to bring not peace but a sword. Man's resistance to the inbreak of God creates a situation compared to which most revolutions are playful. Man resists it because he cannot grasp the direction of the Christian revolution. It moves to give man something, not to take anything away; and man is so incredulous in the presence of such a paradoxical event that he resists it with all his strength. Man is not yet ready for love. He never has been.

The essential note of the Christian revolution is that it is perpetually new. It is no less a challenge to the old world of sin and death now than it was at the beginning of the Christian era. Its demands are no less, and the total commitment which the Christian must make has not been diminished. The reflective reader of the New Testament comes to sense that what he reads is thoroughly contemporary, and that the tension between history and eschatology is resolved in him. And when it is resolved in him, he knows that it is resolved in the Church. Jesus lives — yesterday, today, and the same forever. History has not changed him at all, nor has it changed his meaning for human existence. By union with him the Christian is released from the prison of history; and this is eschatology by definition. We end where we began, with an event which is more than historical. It is the one enduring reality in the created world, and in it man achieves enduring reality and value.

Lightning Source UK Ltd.
Milton Keynes UK
UKHW021619031122
411585UK00026B/547